Grammar 5 Teacher's Book

Teaching grammar, spelling and punctuation with the
Grammar 5 Pupil Book

Written by

Sara Wernham and Sue Lloyd

Edited by Philippa Neville

Contents

PART 1: THE GRAMMAR PROGRAMME

    Introduction   3

    Teaching Ideas for Grammar   5

    Teaching Ideas for Spelling   23

    Spelling and Grammar Lessons   30

PART 2: LESSON PLANS

    Teaching with the Grammar 5 Pupil Book   35

PART 1

Introduction

For ease of use, this *Teacher's Book* has been divided into two distinct parts. The first part gives a comprehensive introduction, which explains the teaching method in detail. It is a good idea to read this part of the *Teacher's Book* before using the *Grammar 5 Pupil and Teacher's Books* in the classroom. The second part of the *Teacher's Book* provides a thorough and structured lesson plan for each day of teaching. The lesson plans in this part of the book are designed specifically for use with the corresponding pages in the *Grammar 5 Pupil Book*.

The *Grammar 5 Pupil and Teacher's Books* are designed to follow on from the *Grammar 1, 2, 3* and *4 Pupil and Teacher's Books*. They are intended to:

- extend and refine the children's understanding of the grammar already taught,
- introduce new elements of grammar,
- teach new spelling patterns systematically,
- develop dictionary and thesaurus skills,
- improve vocabulary and comprehension, and
- reinforce the teaching in the *Grammar 1* to *4 Pupil and Teacher's Books*.

Like the activities in the previous *Pupil Books*, the teaching in the *Grammar 5 Pupil Book* is multisensory and active. In the *Grammar 5 Pupil Book*, particular emphasis is placed on consolidating the children's learning and helping them to apply their new skills. As before in the *Grammar 1* to *4 Pupil Books*, each part of speech is taught with an accompanying action and colour. The actions not only enliven the teaching, but also make the parts of speech easier for the children to remember. The colours, which are useful when identifying and labelling parts of speech in sentences, are the same as those used in Montessori Schools. As in previous *Teacher's Books*, the *Grammar 5 Teacher's Book* explains all the essential teaching ideas.

Children's Achievement

The most dramatic improvements to result from using the *Grammar 5 Pupil and Teacher's Books* will be found in the children's writing. After completing the *Grammar 5 Pupil Book*, the children will spell and punctuate more accurately, use a wider vocabulary and have a clearer understanding of how language works.

In their first year at school, the *Phonics Pupil Books* taught the children to write independently by listening for the sounds in words and choosing letters to represent those sounds. This enables the children to write pages of news and stories. It is a joy to read their work and to see the great pride and confidence they derive from their newly acquired skills. It is important to build on this foundation in the following years.

The *Grammar Pupil and Teacher's Books* provide teaching ideas designed to develop the children's writing skills. The children become more aware that they are writing for a purpose: that their words are intended to be read and understood. They learn that their writing is easier to understand if it is grammatically correct, accurately spelt, well punctuated and neatly written. The children also learn that, if they use interesting words, their writing can give real pleasure. Even in the early stages, it is valuable for the children to have a simple understanding of this long-term goal.

INTRODUCTION

The Format of the Pupil and Teacher's Books

The programme for *Grammar 5* consists of a *Teacher's Book*, offering detailed lesson plans, and a corresponding *Pupil Book*, with activities for each lesson. Enough material is provided in these books for 36 weeks' teaching, with two lessons for each week. The *Grammar 5 Pupil Book* is designed so that there is one activity page for each lesson. Each lesson is intended to take up about one hour's teaching time.

Although it is referred to as the *Jolly Phonics Grammar Programme*, there are in fact two elements, namely spelling and grammar. The material in the *Pupil and Teacher's Books* is organised so that the first of the week's lessons concentrates on spelling and the second on grammar. However, the terms are used loosely and there is some overlap: punctuation and vocabulary development are among the areas covered in both spelling and grammar lessons. This is deliberate, as the two elements complement each other when combined. The overlap is particularly noticeable in the *Grammar 5 Pupil Book*, where there are now two spelling activity pages per lesson. The second of these usually features one activity based on a related, or recently introduced, grammar point and another that looks at sentence structure within a grammar context.

The *Grammar 5* programme covers the more structured aspects of literacy, and is intended to take up only part of the teaching time set aside for literacy work. If two days' literacy lessons are devoted to grammar and spelling each week, this leaves three lessons that can be devoted to the areas not covered by *Grammar 5*, such as comprehension, group and individual reading, formal and creative writing and handwriting practice. The children should be shown how spelling and grammar relate to their other literacy work. For instance, if the children have recently covered the perfect tenses or phrasal verbs and there are examples in the text they are studying, the children should be encouraged to look, for example, at how the past participles have been formed, or discuss whether the phrasal verbs are separable or inseparable.

For each activity page in the *Pupil Book* there is a corresponding page in the *Teacher's Book*, offering a detailed lesson plan and useful teaching guidance. More detailed explanations and advice are provided in the two following sections: 'Teaching Ideas for Grammar' and 'Teaching Ideas for Spelling'. Relevant material from the *Grammar 1* to *4 Teacher's Books* has also been included for easy reference.

To avoid confusion, the *Jolly Phonics* grammar materials follow the convention of using different parentheses to distinguish between letter names and letter sounds. Letter names are shown between these parentheses: ‹ ›. For example, the word *ship* begins with the letter ‹s›. By contrast, letter sounds are shown between these parentheses: / /. For example, the word *ship* begins with the /sh/ sound.

Teaching Ideas for Grammar

The benefits of learning grammar are cumulative. In the early stages, the children's grammar knowledge will help them to improve the clarity and quality of their writing. Later on, their grammar knowledge will help them to understand more complicated texts, learn foreign languages with greater ease, and use Standard English in their speech and writing.

The accents and dialects in spoken English vary from region to region. The grammar we learn first is picked up through our speech and varies accordingly. However, at times, there is a need for uniformity. If we all follow the same linguistic conventions, communication throughout the English-speaking world is greatly improved. An awareness of this fact helps those children who do not speak Standard English to understand that the way they speak is not wrong, but that it has not been chosen as the standard for the whole country. All children need to learn the standard form of English, as well as appreciating their own dialect.

In their first four years of *Grammar*, the children were introduced to the concepts of sentences, punctuation and parts of speech. In the *Grammar 1 Pupil Book*, they learnt about proper and common nouns, pronouns, verbs, adjectives and adverbs, and they learnt to use verbs to indicate whether something happened in the past, present or future. In the *Grammar 2 Pupil Book*, the children's knowledge was extended and their understanding deepened. Their knowledge of sentences was refined and they learnt to punctuate with greater variety and precision. They were also introduced to irregular verbs and to new parts of speech, namely possessive adjectives, conjunctions, prepositions and comparative and superlative adjectives. In the *Grammar 3 Pupil Book*, the children's understanding is further refined. They learnt how to distinguish between a phrase and a sentence, how to identify the subject and object of a sentence and how to organise sentences into paragraphs. In dictation, they received regular practice in writing direct speech with the proper punctuation. The children also learnt how to form the continuous tenses and were introduced to new parts of speech, namely collective nouns, irregular plurals, possessive pronouns and object pronouns. They also had regular dictionary and parsing practice with the aim of building their dictionary skills, improving their vocabulary and reinforcing their grammar knowledge.

The *Grammar 4 Pupil Book* continued to build on the previous years' teaching. The children learnt the difference between simple and compound sentences, about how statements can be turned into questions and how to distinguish between a phrase, a clause and an independent clause. They had regular parsing practice, both at sentence and verb level, to secure their understanding of parts of speech and of grammatical person and tense. The children were also introduced to the idea of simple subject-verb agreement, seeing what happens to the words in a sentence when a singular subject is made plural or, for example, when a sentence in the first person singular is rewritten in the third person. They were also taught new parts of speech, namely infinitives, noun phrases and concrete, abstract and possessive nouns.

The *Grammar 5 Pupil Book* extends, consolidates and refines the teaching of previous years. The children learn about transitive and intransitive verbs, phrasal verbs, past participles and how to form the perfect tenses. They learn that verbs can be modified by prepositional phrases as well as adverbs, and that adverbs can modify other adverbs and adjectives. They look indepth at how adverbs fall into the categories of manner, degree, place, time and frequency and how adjectives tend to be written in a certain order. They are shown how to use parentheses correctly and how to punctuate vertical lists using colons and bullet points. They also have regular practice working with 'sentence walls' – a simplified form of sentence diagramming – with the aim of refining their knowledge of sentence structure and deepening their understanding of how different parts of a sentence relate to one another.

Both *Grammar 4* and *5* work on improving the children's vocabulary and writing, with a focus on developing their knowledge of antonyms and synonyms, prefixes and suffixes, and commonly confused homophones. They are also encouraged to use onomatopoeia and different forms of comparatives and superlatives (*Grammar 4*), and are introduced to homographs, homonyms and heteronyms (*Grammar 5*).

The *Grammar 5 Pupil Book* builds upon the teaching in the *Grammar 1 to 4 Pupil Books*, so the children's understanding of this teaching must be secure before moving on. For this reason, it is important to go over anything the children are unsure of before introducing new concepts. The *Grammar Pupil*

TEACHING IDEAS FOR GRAMMAR

Books provide a systematic approach to revision. This enables even the slowest learners to keep up, while ensuring that more able children master their skills thoroughly and develop good grammatical habits. Every lesson should include some revision. Suggestions are provided in the lesson plans, but teachers should feel free to use their own judgment when deciding which areas their children need to revisit.

The term *grammar* is used broadly with children of this age. Definitions of the parts of speech, and of what constitutes a sentence, phrase and clause, have necessarily been simplified to age-appropriate working definitions. As the children grow older, these definitions can be expanded and refined.

Nouns

A noun denotes a person, place or thing. On the most basic level, nouns can be divided into proper nouns and common nouns.

Proper Nouns

Proper nouns were introduced in the *Grammar 1 Pupil Book* and revised in the subsequent levels. A proper noun starts with a capital letter, and is the particular name given to the following:

Action: The action for a **proper noun** is to touch one's forehead with the index and middle fingers. This is the same action as that used for *name* in British Sign Language.
Colour: The colour for all types of noun is black.

- a person, including that person's surname and title,
- a place, for example a river, mountain, park, street, town, country, continent or planet,
- a building, for example a school, house, library, swimming pool or cinema,
- a date, for example a day of the week, a month or a religious holiday.

In the early years, the focus was on people's names and then on the names of the months, including their correct spelling and sequence. In the *Grammar 3 Pupil Book* the focus moved to place names. The children learnt that in longer place names, such as the *Tower of London*, only the important words need a capital letter, not the short joining words.

Common Nouns

All nouns that are not specific names or titles are called common nouns. Common nouns can be further divided into concrete nouns (e.g. *table* or *child*), abstract nouns (e.g. *warmth* or *kindness*) and collective nouns (e.g. *the **group*** or *a **flock*** *of birds*). As abstract nouns and collective nouns are more difficult for young children to grasp, only concrete nouns are taught in the early years. However, the term *concrete nouns* is not introduced until *Grammar 4*.

Action: The action for a **common noun** is to touch one's forehead with all the fingers of one hand.
Colour: The colour for all types of noun is black.

Everything we can see has a name by which we can refer to it: for example, *table*, *chair* and *pencil*. As these names are not specific to any one object, but refer to tables, chairs and so on in general, they are called common nouns and not proper nouns. At this stage the children find it useful to think of nouns as the names for things they can see and touch. A good way to help the children decide if a word is a noun is to encourage them to say *a*, *an* or *the* before the word and see whether it makes sense. For example, *a chair*, *an elephant* and *the table* make sense, whereas *a fell*, *an unhappy* and *the ran* do not. (The words *a*, *an* and *the* are the three articles, and are explained later.)

In general, children understand the concept of nouns easily and have no trouble when asked to think of examples. Despite this, it can still be difficult for them to identify nouns in written sentences. This becomes easier with regular parsing practice, which is provided in the *Grammar 3* and *4 Pupil Books*.

Collective Nouns

Collective nouns were introduced in the *Grammar 3 Pupil Book*; they are words used to describe groups of people, animals or things: for example, *a **crowd** of people, a **herd** of cows* or *a **fleet** of ships*. Collective nouns can also describe groups of abstract nouns: for example, *a **host** of ideas* or *a **wash** of emotions*. Abstract nouns are explained below.

Collective nouns are usually singular (e.g. *a bunch, a band, a flock*) because they describe the group as a whole; whereas the nouns that make up the group are plural (e.g. *a bunch of **flowers**, a band of **robbers**, a flock of **birds***) because there are many of them. Collective nouns are a type of common noun, so they do not need a capital letter. Often, the same collective noun can be used to describe a number of different things; for example, *bunch* can be used to describe, among other things, flowers, keys and bananas. Sometimes more than one collective noun can be used to describe the same item; for example, a group of whales can be described as *a pod* or *a school*. Many collective nouns are used to describe groups of animals and birds. Some are very common (e.g. *herd, flock, pride*), while others, particularly those used for birds, are quite obscure (e.g. *a **murder** of crows*). Many new collective nouns, like *a **bounce** of kangaroos*, are not officially recognised, but are nevertheless entertaining for the children.

It is important not to confuse collective nouns with uncountable nouns. Uncountable nouns, such as *furniture, water* and *meat*, are almost always singular. Collective nouns, on the other hand, can be referred to in the plural when they describe more than one group of a particular type of object (e.g. *two **colonies** of ants*).

Concrete Nouns

In the *Grammar 4 Pupil Book*, the children learnt that the things they can see, hear, smell, taste or touch – that is, things that exist in a physical form – are called concrete nouns. The children are encouraged to think about different types of concrete noun and to categorise them according to the five senses.

Action: The action for a **concrete noun** is to gently tap one's forehead twice with one hand.
Colour: The colour for all types of noun is black.

Abstract Nouns

Once the children have learnt about concrete nouns, they can be introduced to the concept of abstract nouns. In the *Grammar 4 Pupil Book*, the children learnt that abstract nouns are things that cannot be experienced through the five senses. They are typically the names for things like ideas (e.g. *justice*

Action: The action for an **abstract noun** is to move one's hand away from the forehead in a spiral action.
Colour: The colour for all types of noun is black.

or *peace*), feelings (e.g. *anger* or *love*), qualities (e.g. *bravery* or *wisdom*), and actions and events (e.g. *a walk* or *a meeting*). Children should be at the stage now where they are able to understand the concept of abstract nouns, at least in principle. With regular parsing practice they will find it easier to identify abstract nouns in their reading and writing.

TEACHING IDEAS FOR GRAMMAR

Possessive Nouns

In the *Grammar 2 Pupil Book*, the children were taught that adding ‹'s› to a person's name shows possession, so that *Tiffany's bike* means *the bike belonging to Tiffany*. The apostrophe is there to show that the ‹s› is not there to make the proper noun plural. In the *Grammar 4 Pupil Book*, the children went on to learn that this is called a possessive noun. They learnt that common nouns, as well as proper nouns, can be possessive, as in *the **girl's** coat* and *the **kangaroo's** pouch*. The children were also taught that possessive nouns can be plural. Most plurals already end in ‹s›, in which case only the apostrophe is required, as in *the **girls'** coats* and *the **kangaroos'** pouches*. However, if the plural is irregular and does not end in ‹s›, both the apostrophe and the ‹s› are added, as in *the **men's** watches* or *some **mice's** tails*.

It is important the children do not confuse *it's*, which is a contraction of *it is*, with the possessive adjective *its*. Possessive adjectives (covered in more detail on page 13) are used in place of possessive nouns, so that *the **girl's** coat* becomes ***her** coat* and *the **kangaroo's** pouch* becomes ***its** pouch*. Possessive adjectives already indicate possession, so they do not need ‹-s› at the end. With regular practice, the children will learn to distinguish between the homophones *it's* and *its* and use them correctly in their writing.

Despite its name, a possessive noun acts as an adjective in a sentence because it describes another noun. The children are already familiar with the idea that nouns can function as adjectives; in the *Grammar 3 Pupil Book* they learnt that nouns act as adjectives in compound words such as ***apple** pie* and ***rabbit** hutch*.

Plurals

Most nouns change in the plural, that is, when they describe more than one. In the early *Grammar Pupil Books,* the two main ways of forming the plural were introduced: adding ‹-s› to the noun (as in *dogs* and *boys*), and adding ‹-es› to those nouns that end with ‹sh›, ‹ch›, ‹s›, ‹z› or ‹x› (as in *brushes, dresses* and *foxes*). These endings often sound like /z/ and /iz/, respectively, as in *girls* and *boxes*. Learning that these words are plurals will help the children remember to spell the /z/ sound correctly. In the *Grammar 3 Pupil Book*, the children learnt that nouns ending in ‹o› also take the ‹-es› suffix, as in *tomatoes, potatoes* and *tornadoes*, unless the word is foreign, abbreviated, or has a vowel before the ‹o›, as in *pianos, kilos* and *studios*.

In the *Grammar 2 Pupil Book*, the children also learnt the two ways of forming the plural of nouns that end with a ‹y›. If the letter immediately before the ‹y› is a vowel, then the plural is simply made in the usual way by adding ‹-s› (as in *days, boys* and *monkeys*). However, if the letter immediately before the ‹y› is a consonant, then ‹y› is replaced by a 'shy ‹i›' before adding ‹-es› (as in *flies, babies* and *puppies*). The children should already know that 'shy ‹i›' does not like to be at the end of a word and is often replaced by 'toughy ‹y›'. This helps them understand that while we would be unlikely to find 'shy ‹i›' at the end of a word like *puppy*, we will find it in the plural, *puppies*, when 'shy ‹i›' is no longer at the end of the word.

The *Grammar 2 Pupil Book* also introduced some common irregular, or 'tricky', plurals in the weekly spelling lists (e.g. *children* from *child, women* from *woman,* and *mice* from *mouse*). Tricky plurals can be formed by modifying the root word, altering its pronunciation, adding an unusual ending, or a combination of the three. Sometimes, the pronunciation of the root word alters even when the spelling does not; for instance, the letter ‹i› makes a long /ie/ sound in *child*, but a short /i/ sound in *children*. Some plurals, such as *sheep, fish* and *deer*, are tricky because they have the same form for both singular and plural; these are introduced in the *Grammar 3 Pupil Book*.

In the *Grammar 4 Pupil Book*, the children learnt that other plurals are tricky because their singular forms end in ‹f› or ‹fe›, whereas their plurals are made by removing the ending and adding ‹-ves›, as in *shelves* and *knives*. Not all singular nouns ending in ‹f› or ‹fe› make their plurals in this way, so the spellings have to be learnt. The children also learnt that, when using a plural in a sentence, the other words connected to it must agree. While most children will be making these adjustments automatically, the teaching was made more explicit in the *Grammar 4 Pupil Book* (see pages 19–20, Grammatical Agreement).

The *Grammar 5 Pupil Book* introduces the irregular plural ‹-i›, which is added to some words that have a Latin origin, as in *nucleus* and *alumnus*. It is irregular because not all words that derive from Latin and which end in ‹us› take this plural; in fact most are formed in the regular way by adding ‹-es›, as in *viruses* and *choruses*. However, a small number of scientific or academic words like *nuclei* and *alumni* do use this plural. Even more can take either plural, such as *hippopotamus*, *cactus*, *crocus* and *fungus*. In order to be sure, the children need to look up words that end in ‹us› in the dictionary.

Pronouns

Pronouns are the little words used to replace nouns. Without them, language would become boring and repetitive. They can be divided into personal pronouns (e.g. *I* and *me*), possessive pronouns (e.g. *mine*), relative pronouns (e.g. *who*) and reflexive pronouns (e.g. *myself*). Only personal pronouns were taught in the early *Grammar Pupil Books*. Possessive pronouns were introduced in the *Grammar 3 Pupil Book*. The relative pronouns and reflexive pronouns can be taught when the children are older.

Singular Pronoun Actions:

I (**me**): point to oneself
you (**you**): point to someone else
he (**him**): point to a boy
she (**her**): point to a girl
it (**it**): point to the floor

Plural Pronoun Actions:

we (**us**): point in a circle including oneself and others
you (**you**): point to two other people
they (**them**): point to the next-door class

Colour: The colour for pronouns is pink.

Personal Pronouns

In the *Grammar 1 Pupil Book*, the children were taught the eight personal pronouns: *I, you, he, she, it, we, you* and *they*. In modern English, we use the same word, *you*, for both the second person singular pronoun and the second person plural pronoun, but this is not the case in many foreign languages. In order to make learning such languages easier later on, the *Grammar Pupil Books* introduce the children to the distinction between *you* used in the singular and *you* used in the plural.

In the *Grammar 3 Pupil Book*, the children learnt how to identify the subject and the object of a sentence. They also learnt that the personal pronouns can change, depending on whether they are the subject or the object of the sentence. In the *Grammar 4 Pupil Book*, the children learnt that personal pronouns are called 'personal' because they mostly relate to people: when talking about ourselves, we use *I* and *we*; when talking directly to one or more people, we say *you*; and when talking about someone or something else, we use *he, she* and *it* for the singular and *they* for the plural. These three groups are known as first, second and third person and they can be singular or plural (see below). Once the children were introduced to grammatical person, they were given regular practice parsing the verb in the spelling lessons. They also learnt that when the person in a sentence is changed, the verb and the rest of the sentence must agree.

Subject Pronouns	I	you	he	she	it	we	you	they
Object Pronouns	me	you	him	her	it	us	you	them

The children practise using the subject pronouns whenever they conjugate verbs. They do the actions and say, for example, *I swim, you swim, he swims, she swims, it swims, we swim, you swim, they swim*. These same actions can also be used to revise the object pronouns.

Possessive Pronouns

There are eight possessive pronouns: *mine, yours, his, hers, its, ours, yours* and *theirs*. These pronouns correspond to the personal pronouns: *I/me, you/you, he/him, she/her, it/it, we/us, you/you, they/them*,

TEACHING IDEAS FOR GRAMMAR

and the possessive adjectives: *my, your, his, her, its, our, your, their*. A possessive pronoun replaces a noun and its possessive adjective, so that *my hat* becomes *mine*, and *their house* becomes *theirs*. These pronouns are possessive because they indicate who the noun (which they are also replacing) belongs to. Possessive pronouns can be practised using the same colour and actions as for the personal pronouns.

Verbs

A verb denotes what a person or thing does or is. It can describe an action, an event, a state or a change. It is easiest for children to think of verbs as 'doing words' at first. The infinitive form of a verb is made by putting the word *to* before the verb root, as in *to run, to hop, to sing* and *to play*. Early on the children learn that an infinitive is the 'name' of the verb,

Action: The action for **verbs** in general is to clench fists and move arms backwards and forwards at one's sides, as if running.
Colour: The colour for all types of verb is red.

but gradually the term *infinitive* should be introduced. In the *Grammar 4 Pupil Book* the children learnt that infinitives can be used in a sentence, although they are never the main verb and do not have a subject.

Verb Tenses and Conjugation

The children were introduced to verbs in the *Grammar 1 Pupil Book*, where they learnt to conjugate regular verbs in the present, past and future (because verbs in English are very complicated, only the simple tenses were introduced initially). Conjugating means choosing a particular verb and saying the pronouns in order with the correct form of the verb after each one. Conjugating verbs aloud with the pronoun actions is very good practice for children. It promotes a strong understanding of how verbs work, which helps them make sense of their own language, and is invaluable when they come to learn foreign languages later on. Revise the conjugations regularly, using the pronoun actions.

Past	*I jumped*	*you jumped*	*he jumped*	*she jumped*	*it jumped*
	we jumped	*you jumped*		*they jumped*	
Present	*I jump*	*you jump*	*he jumps*	*she jumps*	*it jumps*
	we jump	*you jump*		*they jump*	
Future	*I shall/will jump*	*you will jump*	*he will jump*	*she will jump*	*it will jump*
	we shall/will jump	*you will jump*		*they will jump*	

The children need to remember the following points:
- In the simple present tense, the verb changes after the third person singular pronouns: *he, she* and *it*. For regular verbs, ‹-s› is added to the root (except when the word ends in ‹sh›, ‹ch›, ‹s›, ‹z› or ‹x›, when ‹-es› is added). This is called the third person singular marker.
- The simple past tense of regular verbs is formed by adding the suffix ‹-ed› to the root. If the root ends in ‹e› (as in *bake*), the final ‹e› must be removed before ‹-ed› is added. The ‹-ed› can be pronounced in one of three ways: /t/ (as in *slipped*), /d/ (as in *smiled*) or /id/ (as in *waited*).
- With simple verbs, we add the auxiliary verbs *shall* or *will* to the verb root to denote the future. The auxiliary verb *will* can be used with all of the pronouns, but *shall* should only be used with *I* or *we*.

The children learnt these regular conjugations in the *Grammar 1* and *Grammar 2 Pupil Books*, and continued to revise them in the *Grammar 3 Pupil Book*. In the *Grammar 2 Pupil Book*, the children were also introduced to some of the most common irregular, or 'tricky', verbs and their past forms: for example, *sat* (from *to sit*), and *ran* (from *to run*). In addition, they learnt to conjugate and identify the irregular verb

Teaching Ideas for Grammar

to be in both the present and past tenses. This is especially useful for those children who are not in the habit of using standard forms in their speech: children who say, for example, *we was* instead of *we were*. Chanting the conjugations regularly will help these children avoid making mistakes in their written work.

The irregularity of the verb *to be* often makes it difficult for the children to identify in sentences. It is important to overcome this problem, as the verb *to be* is used frequently. In the *Grammar 2 Pupil Book*, the children learnt that every sentence must contain a verb and they were taught to identify sentences by looking for the verb. For this reason, it is crucial that the children are able to identify all verbs with confidence.

A familiarity with the verb *to be* also helped the children when they came to learn the continuous tenses in the *Grammar 3 Pupil Book*. The continuous tenses (e.g. *I am walking, I was walking, I shall be walking*) are formed by adding the present participle (e.g. *walking*) to the auxiliary verb *to be*. In order to form the continuous future, the children must first learn the future of the verb *to be*, which was introduced early on in the *Grammar 3 Pupil Book*. Later, in the *Grammar 5 Pupil Book*, the children learnt the perfect tenses, which are formed by adding the past participle (the same form as the simple past in regular verbs) to the auxiliary verb *to have* (as in *I had walked, I have walked, I shall have walked*).

Once the children have learnt how to form the continuous tenses, it is important to give them plenty of practice in identifying all of the verb tenses taught so far. In this way, they will be able to distinguish between the simple and continuous forms more easily and this in turn will help them understand how the different tenses are used. For now it is enough that the children understand that the simple tenses describe actions that start and finish within a specific time (although the simple present also describes repeated or usual actions, as in *I swim in the pool every day*); the continuous tenses describe actions that have started and are still happening (either at that very moment or as a longer action in progress, as in *I am learning to swim*); and the perfect tenses are used to describe actions that have already been completed (especially general experiences, events that happen at unspecified times, as in *I have swum in that pool several times*, or actions that, although complete, still have some connection to the present, as in *I had just finished swimming in the pool*). For reference, the table below shows all three forms in past, present and future.

	Past	Present	Future
Simple	*looked*	*look*	*will look*
Continuous	*was looking*	*is looking*	*will be looking*
Perfect	*had looked*	*have looked*	*will have looked*

Technically there is no future tense in English since, unlike the past tense, the future is not formed by modifying the verb root itself. However, at this stage it is helpful for the children to think of verbs as taking place in the past, present or future. The complexities can be taught when the children are older.

Past Tense Action: The **past tense** action is pointing backwards over one's shoulder with a thumb.

Present Tense Action: The **present tense** action is pointing towards the floor with the palm of the hand.

Future Action: The action for verbs that describe the **future** is pointing towards the front.

Participles

The ‹-ing› suffix, which is added to root verbs, is introduced in the *Grammar 2 Pupil Book*. In the *Grammar 3 Pupil Book* the children learnt that this form of the verb is called the present participle. In the *Grammar 4 Pupil Book* they learnt that the present participle can be used as an adjective, as in *There is no running water*, and later they learnt that it takes the same form as the gerund (the noun form of a verb), as in *I like running*. The past participle is introduced in the *Grammar 5 Pupil Book* in preparation for the perfect tenses. Unlike present participles, past participles of irregular verbs are 'tricky', as they

Teaching Ideas for Grammar

can be formed in a variety of ways and have to be learnt. *Grammar 5* introduces two of the most common spelling patterns: verbs which change their vowel sound to indicate tense, for example *swim* (simple present), *swam* (simple past) and *swum* (past participle) and those where the past participle is formed by adding either ‹-n› or ‹-en› to the present tense form, as in *write, wrote, written* and *fall, fell, fallen*. A good dictionary will always list the irregular past tense and past participle of a verb, so if the children are not sure which form to use in their writing, encourage them to look it up.

Phrasal Verbs

The *Grammar 5 Pupil Book* introduces phrasal verbs. These consist of a verb plus one or more other words, which are usually prepositions or adverbs. Put together, these words make a new verb with a new meaning, such as *to break down* (meaning *to stop working*) and *to break out* (meaning *to escape*). Like other verbs, phrasal verbs can often have more than one meaning. For example, you can *blow up* (destroy) something with dynamite, or *blow up* (inflate) a balloon, or *blow up* (enlarge) a photograph. The parts of a phrasal verb can often be separated by the object (including any modifiers). For example, we can say either *I **brought** your book **back*** or *I **brought back** your book*. In fact, when a pronoun is the object of a sentence it always separates a separable phrasal verb: *I **brought** it **back*** can never be written *I brought back it*, for example. However, some phrasal verbs are always inseparable. We cannot say, for example, that *I looked your book for* or *I looked it for*: the correct form is *I **looked for** your book* and *I **looked for** it*.

Adjectives

An adjective is a word that describes a noun or pronoun. It can be used either directly before the noun or pronoun, as in *the **big** dog*, or elsewhere in the sentence, as in *the dog was **big***. The children are encouraged to use adjectives imaginatively in their writing.

Action: The action for all types of **adjective**, including **possessive adjectives**, and **comparatives** and **superlatives**, is to touch the side of the temple with one's fist.
Colour: The colour for all types of adjective is blue.

Adjectives were introduced in the *Grammar 1 Pupil Book*, where the children learnt how to use them before a noun. In the *Grammar 2 Pupil Book*, adjectives were revised, and the children practised identifying them wherever they were placed in the sentence. In the *Grammar 3* and *4 Pupil Books*, the children learnt that adjectives can sometimes be formed by adding certain suffixes to other words: for example, by adding the suffixes ‹-y› or ‹-al› to a noun, as in *windy* and *logical*, or by adding suffixes like ‹-less›, ‹-ful› and ‹-able›, as in *helpless, helpful* and *enjoyable*. The children also learnt that other parts of speech can sometimes act as adjectives: for example, in the compound word *apple pie*, the first noun *apple* is describing the main noun *pie*; in the phrase *the running water*, the present participle *running*, which is a verb form, is describing the water; and possessive nouns always act as adjectives to describe another noun, as in *the peacock's tail*.

The *Grammar 5 Pupil Book* further refines the children's understanding of adjectives by introducing them to adjective order. In English, we tend to write adjectives in a certain order, depending on which category they belong to. The children learn that there are seven general categories, which are often written in the following sequence:

- Determiners (a, an, one, two, some, many, any, this, that, etc)
- Opinion (lazy, good, nasty, expensive, bad, etc)
- Size and shape (fat, thin, small, broad, rectangular, oval, etc)
- Condition and age (broken, battered, hungry, full, ancient, recent, etc)
- Colour and pattern (black, brown, white, tartan, zigzag, etc)
- Origin (Welsh, Polish, African, Japanese, Australian, etc)
- Material, including nouns acting as adjectives (leather, iron, diamond, etc)

12

This is only a general rule and sometimes the order changes. For example, when shape and age are both included in a description, shape tends to come before age, as in *the old square box*. However as a general guide it can be useful, especially for non-native English speakers.

Possessive Adjectives

The children's understanding of adjectives was extended in the *Grammar 2 Pupil Book* to include the eight possessive adjectives: *my, your, his, her, its, our, your* and *their*. These correspond to the personal pronouns: *I/me, you/you, he/him, she/her, it/it, we/us, you/you, they/them*, and the possessive pronouns: *mine, yours, his, hers, its, ours, yours, theirs*. A possessive adjective replaces one noun and describes another, by saying whose it is. For example, in the sentence *Lucy fed her cat*, the possessive adjective *her* is used in place of *Lucy's* and describes *cat*, by saying whose cat it is. (As the possessive adjectives also function as pronouns, they are sometimes known as the weak set of possessive pronouns. However, to avoid any confusion with the strong set of possessive pronouns, like *mine*, the *Grammar Pupil and Teacher's Books* do not use this terminology.)

Comparatives and Superlatives

The adjectives introduced in the *Grammar 1 Pupil Book* are called positive adjectives; they describe a noun or a pronoun without comparing it to anything else (as in *the girl is **young***). In the *Grammar 2 Pupil Book*, comparative and superlative adjectives were introduced. These adjectives describe a noun or a pronoun by comparing it to other items. A comparative is used when comparing a noun to one or more other items (as in *this boy is **younger** than Jim and Ted*). A superlative is used when comparing a noun to the other items in a group to which that noun also belongs (as in *he is the **youngest** boy on the team*).

Short positive adjectives usually form their comparatives and superlatives with the suffixes ‹-er› and ‹-est›: for example, *hard, harder, hardest*. In the *Grammar 4 Pupil Book*, the children learnt that with longer adjectives, we often use the words *more* and *most*: for example, *difficult, more difficult, most difficult*. However, some two-syllable adjectives also make their comparative and superlative by adding *more* and *most*, especially those which have a suffix, as in *most careful, more helpless, most daring, more shaded* and *most famous*. The children need to listen and decide which sounds right in the sentence. The children also learn about other comparative and superlative forms, such as *less* and *least*, *better* and *best*, *worse* and *worst*.

Adverbs

An adverb is similar to an adjective, in that they are both describing words. However, an adverb describes a verb rather than a noun. Usually, adverbs describe how, where, when or how often something happens. In the *Grammar 5 Pupil Book*, the children learn that these types of adverb are called adverbs of manner, place, time, degree and frequency.

Action: The action for an **adverb** is to bang one fist on top of the other.
Colour: The colour for adverbs is orange.

The children were introduced to adverbs in the *Grammar 1 Pupil Book*. Initially, they were taught to think of an adverb as a word often ending with the suffix ‹-ly›. In the *Grammar 2 Pupil Book*, adverbs were revised and the children were encouraged to identify less obvious adverbs by looking at the verb and deciding which word describes it. For example, in the sentence, *We arrived late last night*, the adverb *late* tells us something about the past tense verb *arrived*. Point out examples of adverbs in text whenever possible to help the children develop this understanding. In the *Grammar 3 Pupil Book*, the children learnt that adjectives can sometimes be turned into adverbs by adding the suffix ‹-ly›, as in *quickly, slowly* and *softly*. In the *Grammar 4 Pupil Book*, the children learnt that adjectives can be turned into adverbs by adding ‹-ly› or ‹-ally› when the adjective ends in ‹-ical› or ‹-ic›, as in *musically* and *basically*. In *Grammar 5*, the children look at how adverbs do not always go next to the verb. They also learn that adverbs do not always describe verbs: they can describe other adverbs (as in *really quickly*), as well as adjectives (as in *quite surprising*).

TEACHING IDEAS FOR GRAMMAR

Prepositions

A preposition is a word that relates one noun or pronoun to another. In the sentence, *He climbed over the gate*, for example, the preposition *over* relates *he* to *gate*. The 'pre' of preposition means *before* and 'position' means *place*, so together 'preposition' means *placed before*, because it is placed before a noun or pronoun. A preposition is also placed before any describing words that may already come before the noun or pronoun (words such as adjectives, possessive adjectives or the articles *a*, *an* and *the*), as in the phrases **after** a long pause, **by** her favourite author, **in** my purse, **under** the bridge.

Action: The action for **prepositions** is to point from one noun to another.
Colour: The colour for prepositions is green.

Prepositions, as introduced in the *Grammar 2 Pupil Book*, often describe where something is or what it is moving towards. Practise prepositions by calling out examples and asking for nouns to go with them. For example, for *in*, the children might suggest *the box* or *the classroom*, and for *under* they might suggest *the mat* or *the table*. Many common prepositions are short words like *at, by, for, of, in, on, to* and *up*. Other common examples include: *above, after, around, behind, beside, between, down, from, into, past, through, towards, under* and *with*. However, many of these words can also function as adverbs if they do not come before a noun or pronoun. For example, in the sentence, *I fell down*, the word *down* is an adverb that describes *fell*, whereas in *I fell down the stairs*, the word *down* is a preposition that relates *I* to *stairs*.

In the *Grammar 5 Pupil Book*, the children learn that not all prepositions are prepositions of place. Sometimes, a preposition relates something to a time or event, as in *Owls sleep during the day*, or *The seasons change throughout the year*. They also learn that phrases like *during the day* and *throughout the year* are called prepositional phrases, which start with a preposition and are usually followed by a simple noun phrase or pronoun. A prepositional phrase usually has one of two roles: it can either act as an adjective, as in *the girl with red hair*; or, as the children learn in *Grammar 5*, it can act as an adverb describing how, where or when something happened, as in *I played with my friends*, *They ran down the street*, or *They arrived in the afternoon*. When prepositional phrases fulfil the adverb function they can also be called adverbial phrases, but to avoid confusion *Grammar 5* describes them simply as prepositional phrases acting as adverbs.

Conjunctions

A conjunction is a word used to join parts of a sentence that usually, but not always, contain their own verbs. Conjunctions allow the children to write longer, less repetitive sentences. Instead of writing, for example, *I eat fish. I eat peas. I like the taste*, the children could use the conjunctions *and* and *because* to write: *I eat fish and peas because I like the taste*. Where the shorter sentences were stilted and repetitive, the new one is flowing and concise.

Action: The action for **conjunctions** is to hold one's hands apart with palms facing up. Move both hands so one is on top of the other.
Colour: The colour for conjunctions is purple.

The *Grammar 2 Pupil Book* introduced conjunctions, focusing on six of the most useful ones: *and, but, because, or, so,* and *while*. In the *Grammar 4 Pupil Book*, the children learnt that the conjunctions *for, and, nor, but, or, yet* and *so* can be used to join two simple sentences to make a compound sentence. When the children are older they will learn that these are called the co-ordinating conjunctions and can be remembered by the acronym FANBOYS.

The ability to vary the length of their sentences will greatly improve the quality of the children's writing. Display a list of common conjunctions in the classroom to encourage the children to use other words besides *and*: examples include *although, if, now, once, since, unless, until, when* and *whether*.

Teaching Ideas for Grammar

Definite and Indefinite Articles: the, a, an

The words *a, an* and *the* are known as articles. *A* and *an* are used before singular nouns and are called the indefinite articles, as in *a man* and *an egg. The* is used before singular and plural nouns and is called the definite article, as in *the dog* and *the boys*. The articles are a special sort of adjective, although the term *determiner* is often used as well. Determiners are words used in front of nouns to show, or determine, which things or people are being referred to.

In the *Grammar 1 Pupil Book*, the children learnt when to use *an* instead of *a*. They were taught to choose the correct article by looking at the noun that follows it. When the noun begins with a vowel sound, the correct article is *an*, as in *an ant, an eagle, an igloo, an octopus, an umpire*. Otherwise, the correct article is *a*. Note that it is the first sound that is important, not necessarily the first letter. If, for example, a word starts with a silent consonant and the first sound is actually a vowel, the correct article is *an*, as in *an hour*. If, on the other hand, the word starts with the long vowel /ue/, pronounced /y-oo/, then the correct article is *a*, as in *a unicorn*.

Simple and Compound Sentences

The full definition of a sentence is complicated and so, in the *Grammar Pupil Books*, a simple working definition is gradually expanded and refined: in the *Grammar 1 Pupil Book*, the children learnt that a sentence must start with a capital letter, end with a full stop and make sense. In the *Grammar 2 Pupil Book*, the children learnt that a sentence must always have a verb and end with a full stop, question mark or exclamation mark. In the *Grammar 3 Pupil Book*, this definition was further refined when the children learnt that a sentence always has a subject and may have an object; the subject is the noun or pronoun that 'does' the verb action, as in **Sam** hit the ball and the object is the noun or pronoun that 'receives' the verb action, as in *The ball hit* **Sam**. In the *Grammar 4 Pupil Book*, the children learnt that when two or more sentences are joined together with one of the co-ordinating conjunctions (*for*, *and*, *nor*, *but*, *or*, *yet* and *so*), it is called a compound sentence, and the two original sentences are called simple sentences.

Later, in the *Grammar 5 Pupil Book*, the children are introduced to the idea that subjects and objects can also have simple and compound forms. The children are encouraged to identify the simple subject or object when parsing or writing on the sentence walls (see pages 20–21). The simple subject or object consists of the head noun only rather than the whole noun phrase. A compound subject or object consists of two or more subjects or objects in the one simple sentence, as in **Jack** *and* **Jill** *went up the hill*, or *He bought two* **shirts** *and a* **tie**.

The children are also introduced to the idea that at its most basic level, a sentence has two parts: the subject, including any words that modify it, and everything else, including the verb, which is known as the predicate. Lastly, they learn that verbs that have an object are called transitive and those that do not are called intransitive.

Statements, Questions and Exclamations

In the *Grammar 1* and *2 Pupil Books*, the children learnt to recognise a question as a sentence that asks for further information and ends in a question mark. They were also taught the ‹wh› question words (*what, why, when, where, who, which, whose*). In the *Grammar 2 Pupil Book*, the children's knowledge was extended as they were introduced to exclamation marks, which are used at the end of exclamations to show that the writer or speaker feels strongly about something. Later, in the *Grammar 3 Pupil Book*, they learnt how to write questions and exclamations in direct speech.

In the *Grammar 4 Pupil Book*, the children learnt that sentences ending in a full stop are called statements, and they looked at some simple ways to turn statements into questions. If the main verb in a statement is *to be*, as in *This* **is** *the way to the park*, it can be made into a question simply by moving the verb to the beginning of the sentence and replacing the full stop with a question mark: **Is** *this the way to the park?* If the sentence has a main verb and an auxiliary, as in *I* **can** *go to the park*, only the auxiliary verb is moved to the front: **Can I go** to the park? Later, the children can learn that statements written in the simple past and simple present cannot be turned into questions in this way because they have no auxiliary verb. Instead the auxiliary *do/does* (simple present) and *did* (simple past) is added at the beginning of the sentence, so that *You went to the park* becomes **Did** *you go to the park?* using the infinitive form for the main verb.

Phrases

A phrase is a group of words that makes sense but has no verb and subject. In the *Grammar 3 Pupil Book*, the children learnt to distinguish between a sentence and a phrase. In the *Grammar 4 Pupil Book*, the children learnt that a noun, together with the words that describe (or modify) it, is called a noun phrase. There can be more than one noun phrase in a sentence and each noun phrase can be replaced with a pronoun. For example, in the sentence *I took three juicy apples from the big wooden bowl*, there are two noun phrases: *three juicy apples* and *the big wooden bowl*. These can be replaced by the pronouns *them* and *it* and still make grammatical sense: *I took them from it*. Not all words in a noun phrase come before the noun, as in *a girl with blonde hair*. This kind of noun phrase generally has a main noun (*girl*) and another noun helping to describe it (*hair*).

In the *Grammar 5 Pupil Book*, the children are introduced to prepositional phrases. These are phrases that start with a preposition followed by a simple noun phrase or pronoun, as in **down** *the steep hill*, or **between** *them*. They also learn that prepositional phrases can act as adverbs of manner, place or time (also known as adverbial phrases). Prepositional phrases often act as adjectives as well, as in *the room* **at the top of the stairs**, but the children can learn about this later.

Clauses

The *Grammar 4 Pupil Book* introduced clauses. A clause is a group of words that contains a subject and verb and makes sense. This is much like the working definition of a sentence; indeed, some clauses, called independent clauses, can stand alone as sentences, such as those found in a compound sentence. However, not all clauses are independent. For example, in the sentence *While he waited, he read his book*, the clause *he read his book* could stand alone as a simple sentence. However, *While he waited* could not, as it is not a complete thought; although it has a subject, a verb and makes sense, it leaves us to ask what else the subject did during that time. This type of clause is called a dependent or subordinate clause. Later, the children can learn that a sentence with both an independent clause and a dependent clause is called a complex sentence.

Paragraphs

In the *Grammar 3 Pupil Book*, the children began to learn about paragraphs. Paragraphs are used to organise information in a piece of writing so that it is easy to read and understand. Instead of one large block of text, writing is broken down into smaller groups of sentences called paragraphs. Each paragraph starts on a new line and is made up of sentences that describe one idea or topic. By putting paragraphs in a particular order, a piece of writing can move from one idea to another in a way that makes sense.

The children are encouraged to think about what they want to say and organise their thoughts before they start writing. They learn how to break down the topic they want to write about into subtopics and place their different ideas under subheadings. This helps them to make their writing flow and be more interesting. The children should be encouraged to write in paragraphs from now on.

Punctuation

The *Grammar Pupil Books* emphasise the importance of punctuation. The children are taught that their writing will be easier to read if it is accurately punctuated. In the *Grammar 2 Pupil Book*, the children revised full stops, question marks and speech marks, and were introduced to exclamation marks, commas and apostrophes. In the *Grammar 3* and *4 Pupil Books*, the focus was on using the correct punctuation when writing direct speech. In direct speech, the words are written exactly as they are said: for example, *'I'm tired,' said Tim.* (This is different from reported speech: for example, *Tim said he was tired.*) The children also revised speech marks, full stops, commas and contractions, and learnt how to use question marks and exclamation marks in direct speech. They were also introduced to some of the more straightforward uses of hyphens. In the *Grammar 5 Pupil Book*, the children learn how to punctuate vertical lists using a colon and bullet points and are shown how to use parentheses correctly.

Question Marks ‹?›

The children need to understand what a question is and how to form a question mark correctly. If a sentence is worded in such a way that it expects an answer, then it is a question and needs a question mark instead of a full stop. If the question is being written as direct speech, the question mark is kept at the end and not replaced with a comma.

Exclamation Marks ‹!›

An exclamation mark is used at the end of a sentence, instead of a full stop, to show that the speaker or writer feels strongly about something. When someone exclaims, they cry out suddenly, especially in anger, surprise or pain. What they say is called an exclamation. If the exclamation is being written as direct speech, the exclamation mark is kept at the end and not replaced with a comma.

Commas ‹,›

Sometimes it is necessary to indicate a short pause in the middle of a sentence, where it would be wrong to use a full stop. This helps the reader separate one idea from another. For this sort of pause we use a comma. The children will be used to being told to pause when they see a comma in their reading. However, learning when to use commas in writing is more difficult. The *Grammar 2 Pupil Book* introduced two of the most straightforward ways commas are used:
1. We use commas to separate items in a list of more than two items: *red, white and blue,* or *Grandma, Grandpa, Aunt and Uncle.* Note that a comma is not used before the last item in a list, but is replaced by the word *and* or *or*.
2. We also use commas in sentences that include direct speech. Here, the comma indicates a pause between the words spoken and the rest of the sentence. If the speech comes before the rest of the sentence, the comma belongs after the last word spoken but inside the speech marks: *'I am hungry,' complained Matt.* (If the words spoken are a question or an exclamation, then a question mark or exclamation mark is used instead of a comma in the same position.) If the speech comes after the rest of the sentence, the comma belongs after the last word that is not spoken but before the speech marks: *Matt complained, 'I am hungry.'*

Apostrophes ‹'›

The *Grammar 2 Pupil Book* introduced both of the main ways that an apostrophe is used. Apostrophes are very often incorrectly used. There are clear rules for using apostrophes and it is important to teach them early on before any children develop bad habits in their writing.
- An apostrophe followed by the letter ‹s› is used after a noun to indicate possession, as in *Ben's new toy* or *the girl's father*. The apostrophe is needed to show that the ‹s› is not being used to make a plural. Understanding this distinction will help the children use apostrophe ‹s› correctly. Encourage the children to think about the meaning of what they write and decide whether each ‹s› is being used to make a plural or the possessive case. In the *Grammar 4 Pupil Book*, the children learnt how to use apostrophe ‹s› with plurals that end in ‹s›

Teaching Ideas for Grammar

(e.g. *the boys' room*). These are called possessive nouns. Later, the children can learn how to use apostrophe ‹s› with names that end in ‹es› (e.g. *James' cat*).

Although the possessive adjectives (e.g. *my, your, his*) indicate possession, there is no risk of confusion with the plural, so they do not need an apostrophe. However, it is important to help the children avoid the common mistake of writing the possessive adjective *its* as *it's*.

- An apostrophe is also used to show that a letter (or more than one letter) is missing. Sometimes, we shorten a pair of words by joining them together and leaving out some of their letters. We use an apostrophe to show where the missing letter (or letters) used to be. This is called a contraction. There are many common contractions, such as *I'm (I am)*, *didn't (did not)* and *you'll (you will)*.

Encourage the children to listen to each contraction and identify which sound or sounds are missing. This will help them to leave out the appropriate letters and put the apostrophe in the right place, thereby avoiding some common mistakes. In *haven't*, for example, the /o/ of *not* is missing, so the apostrophe goes between ‹n› and ‹t›, to show where ‹o› used to be. It does not go between ‹e› and ‹n›, as in 'have'nt'. When *it is* is contracted to *it's*, as in *it's late*, an apostrophe is needed to show that the second ‹i› is missing. The children need to think about the meaning of what they are writing, so as to avoid confusion with the possessive adjective *its*. It is important that the children learn how to spell and punctuate contractions correctly. However, they should only use contractions when writing direct speech or informal notes. Contractions are not traditionally used in formal writing.

Hyphens ‹-›

Sometimes it is necessary to show that two or more words, or parts of words, are linked closely together, either in use or meaning. This helps the reader understand the text properly and avoids ambiguity. To do this we use a hyphen. Hyphens are found mostly in compound words and some words with a prefix, especially when it makes a word easier to read, as in *brother-in-law*, or avoids confusion with another word, as in *re-cover*.

However, not all compound words or words with a prefix need a hyphen, and hyphens are not used so commonly now as they once were; whether a hyphen is used or not often changes over time, and varies between dictionaries. Also, the rules for when to use hyphens are quite complex for children of this age, and so they should be encouraged to check such words in a dictionary and then make sure they use the spelling consistently in their writing.

Nevertheless, there are some instances in which a hyphen is nearly always used and these, along with the term *hyphen*, were introduced in the *Grammar 4 Pupil Book*. The children learnt to use a hyphen when the numbers between 21 and 99 are written as words, as in *twenty-one* or *thirty-three*, and when the first part of a compound word is a capital letter, as in *X-ray* and *T-shirt*. Later, children can learn about other common uses of the hyphen. These include joining fractions, as in *three-quarters* and *two-thirds*, and when a compound adjective comes directly before the noun it is describing, as in *the well-known phrase*. For now it is enough that the children understand what a hyphen is and how it can be used to make meaning clearer.

Colons and Bullet Points ‹:› ‹•›

In the *Grammar 5 Pupil Book*, the children learn how to write lists vertically down a page. Vertical lists are often used in presentations and reports or for practical reasons, like making a shopping list, as the layout makes the list easier to read at a glance.

However it is written, a list always needs an introduction. In normal writing, a list should be able to stand alone as a simple sentence, but in vertical lists this is not so important. The children learn that a vertical list's introduction has a colon (:) at the end. Like full stops and commas, a colon marks the place where we should pause in speaking: it is a longer pause than a comma, but not as long as a full stop. In the list itself, rather than using commas, each item starts on a new, slightly indented, line with a special symbol at the front. This symbol can vary in design, but is most commonly represented as a large dot or circle, and is known as a bullet. The bulleted items in a vertical list are called bullet points, although not all vertical lists use them; instead, the items could be numbered *1, 2, 3,* or *A, B, C,* for example. Unlike a traditional list, the *and* or *or* before the final item does not usually appear.

A vertical list item can be a word, phrase or clause and it can either have an open punctuation style (a lower-case letter at the start, except when writing proper nouns, with no full stop at the end) or be more formally punctuated; either way is acceptable as long as the style is consistent, although it is more common for clauses to be punctuated as sentences. The wording itself also has to be consistent, so that the list makes sense. For example, if a vertical list begins *At school I:* and the first two bullet points are *study hard* and *play sports*, the other items should follow the same format, starting with a verb in the simple present tense; it would not make sense to change style by changing the tense, using a participle, or writing a whole sentence, for example.

Parentheses «( )»

In a piece of writing, we sometimes provide further information which is interesting, but not essential. In the *Grammar 5 Pupil Book*, the children learn that the main way to do this is to put the information in parentheses, which is another name for round brackets that come in pairs, rather like speech marks; an opening bracket is placed at the beginning and a closing bracket is put at the end. When something is written in parentheses, the reader knows that the sentence would still be complete even if the extra information were removed. The extra information provided can be varied, but often includes such things as dates, prices, page numbers, explanations and alternative names; it can even be a sentence, and if it is written as such, with a capital letter at the beginning and a full stop at the end, the full stop goes inside the parentheses. Parentheses can also be used in a list of options: for example, *These shirts are available in (a) small, (b) medium or (c) large.* The children should be encouraged to read their writing through and make sure that if the words in parentheses were removed, the writing would still make sense.

Grammatical Agreement

From the beginning, the children are encouraged to think about the relationship between words in a sentence and to use their grammar knowledge to make their writing as clear and as accurate as possible. They learn that the indefinite articles *a* and *an* are only used with a singular noun, whereas the definite article *the* can be used for both singular and plural. They learn how to form a plural correctly and how to conjugate a verb. They also learn the personal pronouns and possessive adjectives and understand how they differ.

This knowledge helps children when they come to learn about grammatical agreement, which was introduced in the *Grammar 4 Pupil Book*. In most languages, certain word relationships have to match or agree. In English this agreement centres on person, number and sometimes gender. The form of a verb can change, for example, depending on which person is used for the subject: we say *I **am*** for the verb *to be* in the first person singular but *he **is*** for the third person singular. Whether the subject is singular or plural (grammatical number) can also affect the verb: we say *The rabbit **eats*** in the singular, but *The rabbit**s** **eat*** in the plural. When it comes to pronouns and possessive adjectives, gender can affect which word is used: in the singular, we say *he, him* or *his* for the masculine, *she, her* or *hers* for the feminine and *it* and *its* for the neuter.

While most children use simple grammatical agreement quite naturally in their spoken and written language, it is important that they understand the principles; this will help them as they start to produce longer, more complicated writing. The idea is introduced gradually. First, the children look at what happens when certain words in a sentence are changed, starting first with object nouns and the words that describe them and then with subjects and their verbs. Then, when the children have learnt about grammatical person, they look at how changing this can affect the verb and the rest of the sentence. Encourage the children to proofread their work and to make sure that all the relevant words in the sentence agree.

TEACHING IDEAS FOR GRAMMAR

Parsing: identifying parts of speech in sentences

Parsing means identifying the function, or part of speech, of each word in a sentence. The children must look at each word in context to decide what part of speech it is. This skill is worth promoting, as it reinforces the grammar teaching and helps the children to develop an analytical understanding of how our language works. Many words can function as more than one part of speech. For example, the word *light* can be a noun (*the light*), a verb (*to light*), or an adjective (*a light colour*). It is only by analysing a word's use within a sentence that its function can be identified.

The best way to introduce parsing is by writing extremely simple sentences on the board. A good example is: *I pat the dog*. This can be parsed as: pronoun, verb, (article), noun. Ask the children to identify the parts of speech they know (in this case: pronoun, verb, noun). They enjoy taking turns to underline the parts of speech in the appropriate colours. Gradually, when most of the children have mastered this, move on to more complicated sentences that use more parts of speech: for example, *She cheerfully wrote a long letter to her friend*. This can be parsed as: pronoun, adverb, verb (the infinitive of which is *to write*), (article,) adjective, noun, preposition, possessive adjective, noun. Remind the children that every sentence must contain at least one verb. They should begin parsing a sentence by identifying the verb (or verbs), and should supply each verb in the infinitive form. If there is time, the children should identify as many of the other parts of speech as possible, underlining them in the appropriate colours (as shown in the parsing colour key below).

Nouns	Verbs	Pronouns	Adjectives	Adverbs	Prepositions	Conjunctions
(Black)	(Red)	(Pink)	(Blue)	(Orange)	(Green)	(Purple)

In the *Grammar 3* and *4 Pupil Books*, the regular parsing practice in the spelling lessons will help the children become quick and competent at this task. If any children are unfamiliar with parsing, or find it difficult, they need to work on simpler sentences and build up their confidence.

Sentence Walls

Parsing a sentence can reveal a lot about the role of the individual words. It can also help the children identify the subject and object, which in turn allows them to decide whether a verb is transitive or intransitive. However, it does not really reveal the relationship between the words themselves or tell us much about the structure of a sentence.

The *Grammar 5 Pupil Book* introduces the idea of sentence walls, which is a simplified form of sentence diagramming, a useful method of teaching sentence structure to older students.* Sentence walls are an accessible and visual way to represent the building blocks of a sentence, as they allow the children to see at a glance the subject and predicate, the verb and object, the role of prepositional phrases acting as adverbs, and the words that are essential to the meaning of the sentence and those that provide extra information.

The sentence walls on the worksheets are portrayed as old stone walls to give some visual interest, but they basically consist of six boxes that can be drawn on the board and discussed with the children.

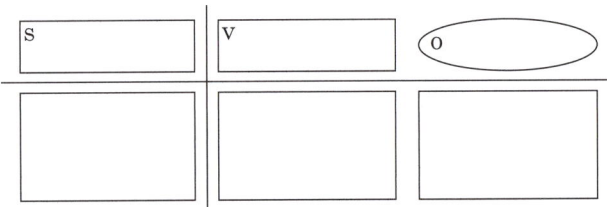

* Modern diagramming is based on Alonzo Reed and Brainerd Kellogg's work in *Higher Lessons in English: A Work on English Grammar and Composition*, first published in 1877. However, sentence walls are closer in format to Francis A. March's diagrams in *A Parser and Analyzer for Beginners* (1869), which were influenced by W. S. Clark, and his 'balloon' system (*A Practical Grammar*, 1847).

20

Teaching Ideas for Grammar

A short vertical line separates the two basic parts of a sentence: the subject and predicate. A long horizontal line separates the essential information from the extra information. Everything above the line – the simple subject, verb and simple object (if there is one) is necessary to the sentence and reads rather like a short newspaper headline. Everything below (such as articles, determiners, adjectives, adverbs and phrases) is additional information which modifies the words above.

A simple sentence like *The young girl has decorated her picture beautifully* can be parsed as normal and then it can be transferred to the boxes in the following way:

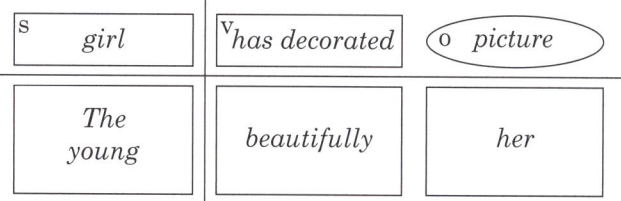

If the sentence contains a compound subject and object it would look like this:

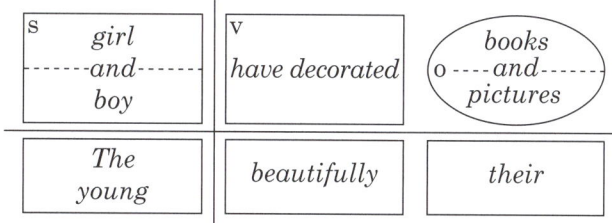

Similarly, if the main adverb is modified by another adverb or there is a prepositional phrase acting as an adverb, the boxes would be completed like this:

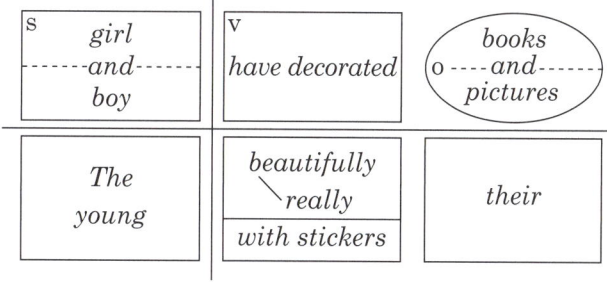

A sentence with an adverb describing an adjective would be written in a similar way to that above, but it would appear in the box below either the subject or object.

Alphabetical Order, Dictionary and Thesaurus Work

Many reference materials, including dictionaries, thesauruses and encyclopedias, organise their material alphabetically. The more familiar the children are with the order of the alphabet, the better they will be at using these resources independently. In the *Grammar 1 Pupil Book*, the children were introduced to alphabetical order and to using a dictionary. To help them find words, the children were encouraged to think of the dictionary as being divided into the following four approximately equal parts:

1. A a B b C c D d E e
2. F f G g H h I i J j K k L l M m
3. N n O o P p Q q R r S s
4. T t U u V v W w X x Y y Z z

Teaching Ideas for Grammar

It is a good idea to have a copy of the alphabet, divided into the four groups, available for the children to see. A different colour can be used for each group to help the children remember them. In the *Grammar Pupil Books*, red is used for group 1, yellow for group 2, green for group 3 and blue for group 4. These four colour-coded groups are incorporated into the *Jolly Phonics Alphabet Poster* and the *Jolly Dictionary*.

Knowing these letter groups saves the children time when using the dictionary. Before looking up a word, they decide which group its initial letter falls into, and then narrow their search to that section of the dictionary. For easy reference there is a copy of the alphabet, divided up into the four colour-coded groups, on the first page of the *Grammar 5 Pupil Book*.

The *Grammar 2 Pupil Book* improved the children's dictionary skills by teaching them to look beyond the initial letter of each word. The children practised putting into alphabetical order words that share the first two letters: for example, *sheep, shoe, ship,* and then words that share the first three letters: for example, *penny, pencil, penguin.* This skill is reinforced in the *Grammar 3* and *4 Pupil Books*, where a common activity in the spelling lessons involves putting the words from the spelling list into alphabetical order.

Most children can become quite proficient at using a dictionary designed for schools. When they finish a piece of writing, the children should proofread their work, identify any words that look incorrectly spelt and look them up in the dictionary. The children should also be encouraged to use a dictionary to look up meanings, particularly for homophones and homographs. Homophones are words that sound similar to one another but have different spellings and meanings (as in *hear* and *here*). Homographs are words that share the same spelling, but have different meanings. There are different types of homographs. Those that look and sound the same (as in *fly,* the noun – *The fly landed on my sandwich* – and verb – *I will fly to Australia*) are called homonyms. Those that look the same but sound different (as in *The two rocky paths wind among the trees* and *The wind blew the leaves off the tree*) are called heteronyms. There is a strong focus on homophones throughout the *Grammar Pupil Books*, particularly in the *Grammar 4 Pupil Book*, while homographs are introduced in the *Grammar 5 Pupil Book*.

In the *Grammar 3* and *4 Pupil Books*, looking up words for spelling and meaning is a regular activity in the spelling lessons. It helps the children understand how useful dictionaries can be and aims to develop the skills they need to become regular and proficient dictionary users.

The children were also introduced to thesauruses in the *Grammar 2 Pupil Book*. (These books list words by meaning, collating words with similar meanings to one another.) The children should be encouraged to make their work more interesting by finding alternatives to words that are commonly overused, such as *nice*.

In the *Grammar 4 Pupil Book*, the children learnt that words with a similar meaning, which are listed in a thesaurus, are called synonyms. They also develop their knowledge of antonyms, learning that many prefixes and some suffixes can be used to create them: ‹un-›, ‹im-› and ‹non-› mean *not*; ‹de-› and ‹dis-› mean *undo* or *remove*; ‹mis-› means *wrongly* or *not*; ‹ex-› means *out* or *away from*; and ‹-less› and ‹-ful› make adjectives with the opposite meaning, indicating that the word it is describing is either *without* something or *full* of it.

It can be helpful to give each child a 'Spelling Word Book' for listing words with a particular spelling pattern and keeping a note of any homophones or unusual words they come across. These books can then be used to help the children in their independent writing. The following extension ideas are also useful for improving alphabet and dictionary skills, or for those children who finish their work ahead of time:
- The children take the words from a page of their Spelling Word Book and rewrite them in alphabetical order.
- The children use the dictionary to choose the correct spelling of a word. For this activity, write out a word three or four times on the board. Spell it slightly differently each time, but ensure that one of the spellings is correct. It is a good idea to choose a word that contains a sound with alternative spellings: for example, *disturb*, which contains the /er/ sound. This word could be spelt 'disterb', 'distirb' or 'disturb'. The children write the correct spelling in their Spelling Word Book.
- In pairs, the children race one another to find a given word in the dictionary.

Teaching Ideas for Spelling

Most children need to be taught to spell correctly. In the *Grammar Pupil Books*, spelling is the main focus for one lesson each week. The spelling activities in the *Grammar 5 Pupil Book* are designed to consolidate the children's existing knowledge and introduce new spelling patterns. Its main focus is on 'word families', which are words which share a common root, and words with common prefixes and suffixes, especially those with similar spellings, like ‹-ance› and ‹-ence›, ‹-ancy› and ‹-ency›, and ‹-tion› and ‹-sion›.

The children first learnt to spell by listening for the sounds in a word and writing the letters that represent those sounds, and by systematically learning the spellings of key irregular, or 'tricky', words. After completing the *Phonics* and *Grammar 1 Pupil Books*, most children have a reading age of at least seven years and are starting to spell with far greater accuracy. As research has shown, children with a reading age of seven years or more are able to use analogy in their reasoning. This is a useful strategy for spelling. Children who want to write *should*, for example, might notice that the end of this word sounds like that of a word they already know, such as *would*. They could then use the spelling of *would* to write *should*, replacing the ‹w› with ‹sh›. If the children are unsure of a spelling, they may be able to find it by writing the word in several ways (e.g. *should* and 'shood'), and choosing the version that looks correct. If they have already encountered the word several times in their reading, they will probably be able to choose the right spelling. By introducing groups of spelling words that each feature a particular spelling pattern, the *Grammar Pupil Books* encourage the children to think analogically.

A focus on revising alternative spellings of vowel sounds and learning new ones helps the children consolidate and extend their learning. The alternative vowel spellings are what makes English spelling difficult and, by this stage, the children need not only to be revising the main ways of spelling the vowel sounds, but also improving their ability to remember which words take which spelling.

The *Grammar 5 Pupil Book* builds on the teaching of the previous *Pupil Books* and assumes that the children have some knowledge of the following spelling features, which are outlined in greater detail below:

1. Vowel Digraphs
2. Alternative Spellings of the Vowel Sounds
3. New Spelling Patterns
4. The Schwa
5. Syllables
6. Silent Letters
7. Identifying the Short Vowels
8. Spelling Rules

1. Vowel Digraphs

The vowel digraphs were introduced in *Phonics* and the *Grammar 1 Pupil Book*. The focus in the *Grammar 2* and *Grammar 3 Pupil Books* is on consolidating this learning. *Vowel digraph* is the term for two letters that make a single vowel sound. At least one of these letters is always a vowel. Often, the two letters are placed next to each other in a word: for example, the ‹ay› in *hay* and the ‹ew› in *few*. Two vowel letters are usually needed to make a long vowel sound. The long vowel sounds are the same as the names of the vowel letters: /ai/, /ee/, /ie/, /oa/, /ue/. Generally, the sound made by the digraph is that of the first vowel's name. Hence the well-known rule of thumb: 'When two vowels go walking, the first does the talking'.

Sometimes, the long vowel sound is made by two vowels separated by one or more consonants. In monosyllabic words, the second vowel is usually an ‹e›, known as a 'magic ‹e›' because it modifies the sound of the first vowel letter. Digraphs with a magic ‹e› can be thought of as 'hop-over ‹e›' digraphs: ‹a_e›, ‹e_e›, ‹i_e›, ‹o_e› and ‹u_e›. Once again, the sound they make is that of the first vowel's name; the 'magic ‹e›' is silent. Children like to show with their hands how the 'magic' from the ‹e› hops over the preceding consonant and changes the short vowel sound to a long one.

TEACHING IDEAS FOR SPELLING

The hop-over ‹e› digraphs are an alternative way of making the long vowel sounds, and are found in such words as *bake, these, fine, hope* and *cube*. The children need to be shown many examples of hop-over ‹e› digraphs, which are available in the *Jolly Phonics Word Book*. It is possible to illustrate the function of the magic ‹e› in such words by using a piece of paper to cover the ‹e›, and reading the word first with the magic ‹e›, and then without it. For example, *pipe* becomes *pip* without the magic ‹e›; *hate* becomes *hat*; *hope* becomes *hop*; and *late* becomes *lat*. The children may like to do this themselves. It does not matter if, as in the *late/lat* example, they find themselves producing nonsense words; the exercise will still help them to understand the spelling rule. When looking at text on the board or in other texts, the children can be encouraged to look for and identify words with a magic ‹e›.

Although hop-over ‹e› words are generally quite common, there are only a few words with the ‹e_e› spelling pattern. Examples include: *these, scheme* and *complete*. Words with an ‹e_e› spelling are not only rather rare, but often quite advanced. For this reason, the ‹e_e› spelling is not given quite as much emphasis as the other long vowel spellings, and is not made the focus of a whole lesson until the *Grammar 3 Pupil Book*.

2. Alternative Spellings of the Vowel Sounds

Children who have learnt to read with *Jolly Phonics* are used to spelling new words by listening for the sounds and writing the letters that represent those sounds. This skill enables the children to spell accurately the many regular words that do not contain sounds with more than one spelling, words like *hot, plan, brush, drench* and *sting*.

However, words like *train, play* and *make* present a problem for spelling. All three words feature the same vowel sound: /ai/, but in each case it is spelt differently. The table opposite shows the first spelling taught for each sound and the main alternatives introduced.

The alternative spellings of vowel sounds were introduced in the *Grammar 1 Pupil Book*

First spelling taught	Alternative spellings for sound	Examples of all spellings in words
‹ai›	‹ay›, ‹a_e›	*rain, day, came*
‹ee›	‹ea›, ‹e_e›	*street, dream, these*
‹ie›	‹y›, ‹i_e›, ‹igh›	*pie, by, time, light*
‹oa›	‹ow›, ‹o_e›	*boat, snow, home*
‹ue›	‹ew›, ‹u_e›	*cue, few, cube*
‹er›	‹ir›, ‹ur›	*her, first, turn*
‹oi›	‹oy›	*boil, toy*
‹ou›	‹ow›	*out, cow*
‹or›	‹al›, ‹au›, ‹aw›	*corn, talk, haunt, saw*

and then revised in the *Grammar 2* and *3 Pupil Books*, and should be familiar to the children. The alternative vowel spellings are what make English spelling difficult and it is very important to further consolidate this teaching. This can be achieved by revising the spelling patterns regularly with flash cards, and by asking the children to list the alternative spellings for a particular sound. The children should be able to do this automatically and apply their knowledge when writing unfamiliar words. For example, with a word like *frame*, they should be able to write 'fraim, fraym, frame' on a scrap of paper, before deciding which version looks correct.

3. New Spelling Patterns

Many of the less common spellings of familiar sounds are introduced in the *Grammar 2, 3* and *4 Pupil Books*. The tables opposite show the spellings first taught, and the new spelling patterns introduced. The children need to memorise which words use each of these new spelling patterns. It is helpful to make up silly sentences for each spelling, using as many of the words as possible. For example, for the ‹ie› spelling of the /ee/ sound, the children could chant the following: *I bel**ie**ve my n**ie**ce was the ch**ie**f th**ie**f who came to gr**ie**f over the p**ie**ce of sh**ie**ld she hid in the f**ie**ld.*

In the *Grammar 2* and *Grammar 3 Pupil Books*, the children learnt some new sounds that were not included in the *Phonics* and *Grammar 1 Pupil Books*. For example, the *Grammar 2 Pupil Book* introduced the sound /zh/, as in *vision*, when it taught the children the ‹sion› spelling pattern. Also in the *Grammar 2 Pupil Book*, the /ear/ sound was introduced initially as ‹ear›, as in *hear* and *earrings*. In the *Grammar 3 Pupil Book*, the children learnt the alternative spellings, ‹eer› and ‹ere›, as in *deer* and *cheer*, and *here* and *mere*. Similarly, the /air/ sound was introduced initially as ‹air›, ‹are› and ‹ear›, as in *hair, care* and *bear*. The *Grammar 3 Pupil Book* taught the ‹ere› spelling, as in *there, ere* and *where*. The children's knowledge of ‹ure› was also revised and extended in the *Grammar 3 Pupil Book*. The children revise the /cher/ sound made by ‹ture› in a word like *picture*, and learn that ‹ure› often follows ‹s› to make words like *pleasure* and *treasure*, where the ‹s› makes a /zh/ sound, or words like *pressure* where the ‹ss› says /sh/. The ‹ure› spelling pattern can also follow other letters to make words like *figure, failure* and *conjure*.

4. The Schwa

In the *Grammar 4 Pupil Book*, the children were introduced to the schwa, which is the most common vowel sound in English. It is used when the vowel in an unstressed syllable is swallowed and loses its purity, becoming more like an /uh/ sound. Although it is the most common vowel sound, the schwa is not taught earlier because it can be made by any unstressed vowel. This means that there is no helpful spelling rule for the children to use and so the spellings have to be learnt. Instead, encourage the children to 'say it as it sounds', stressing the pure form of the schwa and saying, for example, 'doct-or' rather than 'doct-uh'. This is a useful strategy for any word that is difficult to spell.

5. Syllables

An understanding of syllables will help to improve the children's spelling. A number of spelling rules depend on the children's ability to identify the number of syllables in a given word. Knowing about syllables will also help the children later on when they begin to learn about where the stress is placed in words. Although the rules of English sometimes let us down, they are worth acquiring. The more the children know, the more skilful they become, and the better equipped they are to deal with any irregularities.

In the *Grammar 2 Pupil Book* the children were encouraged to count the syllables in words using 'chin bumps'. Chin bumps are a fun, multisensory way of teaching syllables. The children place one hand

TEACHING IDEAS FOR SPELLING

First spelling taught for sound(s)	New spelling(s) for sound(s)	Examples of new spellings in words
Spellings taught in the *Grammar 1/2 Pupil Books*		
‹ai›	‹ei›, ‹eigh›	*veil, eighteen*
cher*	‹ture›	*capture, nature*
‹e›	‹ea›	*breakfast, ready*
‹ee›	‹ey›, ‹ie›, ‹y›**	*key, field, fairy***
‹f›	‹ph›	*graph, photo*
‹j›	soft ‹g›	*gem, giant*
‹k›	‹ch›, ‹ck›	*chord, cricket*
‹ngk›	nk**	*ink, bank, truck*
‹ool›*	‹le›	*handle, little*
‹or›	‹ore›	*more, snore, wore*
‹s›	soft ‹c›	*cell, city, cycle*
‹shun›*	‹sion›, ‹tion›	*tension, station*
‹u›	‹o›, ‹ou›	*month, touch*
‹w›	‹wh›**	*whale, whistle*
‹(w)o›	‹(w)a›	*swan, watch, was*
Spellings taught in the *Grammar 3 Pupil Book*		
‹ai›	‹a›	*able, taste, haste*
‹air›, ‹are›, ‹ear›*	‹ere›	*where, there*
‹ar›	‹a›	*koala, vase, lava*
‹ch›	‹tch›	*match, itch, fetch*
‹ear›*	‹eer›, ‹ere›	*cheer, deer, here*
‹ee›	‹e›, ‹e_e›	*athlete, secret*
‹f›	‹gh›	*enough, cough*
‹i›	‹y›	*myth, pyramid*
‹ie›	‹i›	*child, microwave*
‹j›	‹dge›	*edge, bridge, judge*
‹n›	‹gn›	*gnome, resign*
‹ng›	‹n›	*trunk, finger*
‹oa›	‹o›	*only, ogre, ago*
‹o› (after ‹qu›)	‹a› (after ‹qu›)	*squad, quantity*
‹ue›	‹u›	*menu, emu*
‹z›	‹s›, ‹se›, ‹ze›	*easy, pause, bronze*
Spellings taught in the *Grammar 4 Pupil Book*		
‹er›	‹ear›	*earth, pearl*
‹g›	‹gh›	*ghost, aghast*
‹oo›	‹u›	*truth, flu*
‹or›	‹ough›, ‹augh›	*ought, caught*
‹s›	‹se›, ‹st›	*goose, listen*
‹v›	‹ve›	*solve, curve*
‹(w)er›	‹(w)or›	*worm, worker*

TEACHING IDEAS FOR SPELLING

under their chin (with the hand flattened as though they are about to pat something). Then they slowly say a word, and count the number of times they feel their chin go down and bump on their hand. For *cat*, for example, they will feel one bump, which means it has one syllable. *Table* has two bumps, so two syllables; *any* has two bumps and two syllables; *screeched* has one bump and one syllable; and *idea* has three bumps and three syllables.

In the *Grammar 3* and *4 Pupil Books*, the teaching of syllables is extended and refined. In the *Grammar 3 Pupil Book*, the children learn that a syllable is a unit of sound organised around a vowel sound. If a word has three vowel sounds, for example, it will have three syllables. Words with three or more syllables are referred to as multisyllabic, or polysyllabic. If a word only has one vowel sound, and therefore one syllable, it is called a monosyllabic word. The *Grammar 4 Pupil Book* introduced the idea that, in English, stress is placed on at least one of the syllables in a multisyllabic word. The children also learn that a vowel in an unstressed syllable can lose its pure sound and become a schwa.

Spellings taught in the *Grammar 5 Pupil Book*		
‹iez›	‹ize›, ‹ise›	*capsize, surprise*
‹ij›	‹age›, ‹ege›	*privilege, advantage*
‹sh›	‹ch›, ‹che›, ‹sch›	*chef, moustache, schwa*
‹shor›*	‹sure›	*sure, assure*
‹shul›*	‹cial›, ‹sial›, ‹tial›	*controversial, initial, special*
‹shun›*	‹ssion›, ‹cian›	*mission, musician*
‹shus›*	‹cious›, ‹xious›, ‹tious›	*delicious, anxious, cautious*
‹us›*	‹ous›	*famous, dangerous*
‹sk›	‹sch›	*school, scherzo*

* *As the relevant lesson plans explain, this is only an approximation of the sound made by the new spelling.*
** *‹y› as /ee/, ‹wh› and ‹nk› are introduced in the* Grammar 1 Pupil Book.

The children are given regular practice identifying the syllables in words. They will find doing this aurally (using chin bumps or by clapping the syllables) quite easy with practice. The children are also encouraged to identify syllables on paper, by underlining the letters making the vowel sounds and then drawing a vertical line between the syllables. There are some simple rules the children can learn that will help them split words with double consonants, or with ‹ck› and ‹le› spellings:

- **Double consonants**: when a consonant is doubled, the line goes between them, as in *kit/ten*. However, the children should take care with words like *hopped*, *stopped* and *nipped*, where the ‹e› in ‹-ed› is silent. These may look like two-syllable words but they are, in fact, monosyllabic.
- **‹ck› words**: although ‹c› and ‹k› make the same sound and so act like double consonants, the line goes after the ‹k›, as in *pock/et*.
- **‹le› words**: the sounds represented by the ‹le› spelling are the same as those for ‹el› and ‹il› and consist of a small schwa before the /l/. This swallowed vowel sound can clearly be seen in *label* and *pencil* but not in *candle*: in ‹le› words there is no written vowel to underline in the last syllable. Instead, when the children see a word like this, they must listen for the schwa and draw a line before the consonant preceding it, as in *can/dle* and *sad/dle*. Again, ‹ck› words are an exception; the line goes after the ‹k›, as in *pick/le*, *cack/le* and *buck/le*.

Exactly how a word is split into syllables often depends on whether the syllable is 'open' or 'closed'. Open syllables are syllables ending in a long vowel sound, and closed syllables are syllables with a short vowel that end in a consonant. A word like *paper*, for example, tends to be split into *pa/per* rather than *pap/er*. The type of syllable is not always easy to determine, as many long vowels become swallowed and are pronounced as schwas in English. The guidance given in the lesson plans aims to follow these rules, but in practice there is no definitive way to split the syllables and different dictionaries will often do it in different ways. For now, the focus should be on improving the children's ability to identify the vowel sounds in a word and hear how many syllables there are.

6. Silent Letters

A number of English words contain letters that are not pronounced at all. These are known as silent letters. Some silent letters, such as the ‹k› in *knee*, show us how the word was pronounced in the past.

TEACHING IDEAS FOR SPELLING

Other silent letters, like the ‹h› in *rhyme*, indicate the word's foreign origins. The *Grammar Pupil Books* introduce the following silent letters:

- silent ‹b›, as in *lamb*
- silent ‹c›, as in *scissors*
- silent ‹h›, as in *rhubarb*
- silent ‹k›, as in *knife*
- silent ‹w›, as in *wrong*
- silent ‹g›, as in *gnome*
- silent ‹t›, as in *castle*.

The *Grammar 2 Pupil Book* introduced the first five silent letters. The *Grammar 3 Pupil Book* introduced silent ‹g› as part of the spelling pattern ‹gn›, which says the /n/ sound. The *Grammar 4 Pupil Book* introduces silent ‹t› as part of the spelling pattern ‹st›. Practising with the 'say it as it sounds' technique helps children remember these spellings. For the word *lamb*, for example, say the word to the class, pronouncing it correctly as /lam/. The children respond by saying /lamb/, emphasising the /b/.

The *Grammar 4 Pupil Book* taught the children that some silent letters often go with a particular letter, as in ‹mb›, ‹wr›, ‹kn›, ‹wh›, ‹rh›, ‹wh›, ‹sc›, ‹gh›, ‹st› and ‹gn›. The children are encouraged to think of these as silent letter digraphs.

7. Identifying the Short Vowels

One of the most reliable spelling rules in English is the consonant doubling rule. Consonant doubling is governed by the short vowels, so the children need to be able to identify short vowel sounds confidently. In the *Grammar 1* and *Grammar 2 Pupil Books*, a puppet was used to encourage the children to listen for the short vowels.

- For /a/, put the puppet **at** the side of the box.
- For /e/, make the puppet wobble on the **e**dge of the box.
- For /i/, put the puppet **i**n the box.
- For /o/, put the puppet **o**n the box.
- For /u/, put the puppet **u**nder the box.

The children pretended that their fist was the box and their hand was the puppet. Initially, the children were encouraged to do the appropriate action when the short vowel sounds were called out. Then, they learnt to do the actions when they heard short words with a short vowel sound (e.g. *hat, red, dig, pot, bun*). Once the children had learnt to distinguish between short vowels and long vowels (and the other vowel sounds) they were able to do the appropriate short vowel action when short words with a variety of vowel sounds were called out. For those that did not have a short vowel sound, the children kept their hands still.

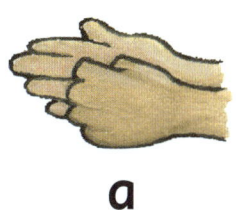
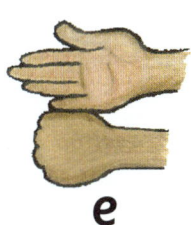

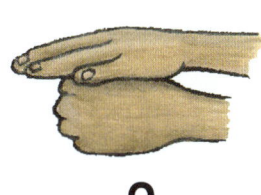
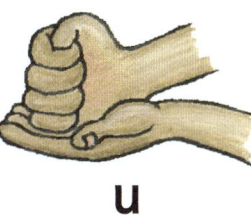

TEACHING IDEAS FOR SPELLING

The children are encouraged to revise the short vowel sounds regularly using the vowel hand. They hold up one hand so their palm is facing them; then, using the index finger of the other hand, they point to the tip of each finger, saying the vowel sounds in turn. First they point to the tip of the thumb for /a/, then to the first finger for /e/, and so on. Then, as they revise the long vowel sounds, they can point to the base of each finger as they say /ai/, /ee/, /ie/, /oa/ and /ue/. Activities like these help to keep the children tuned in to identifying the sounds in words and, in turn, help to prepare them for the consonant doubling rules.

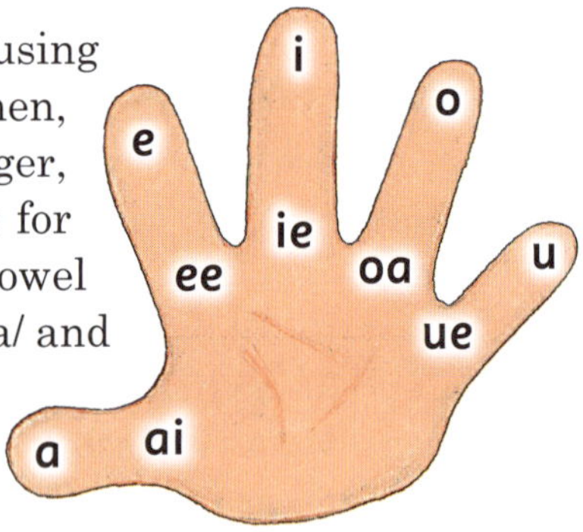

8. Spelling Rules

An ability to identify syllables and short vowels will help the children apply the following rules for consonant doubling and adding suffixes.

Spelling Rules for Consonant Doubling

a. In a monosyllabic word with a short vowel sound, ending in ‹f›, ‹l›, ‹s› or ‹z›, the final consonant letter is doubled, as in the words *cliff, bell, miss* and *buzz*. (The only exceptions to this rule include the tricky two-letter words: *as, if, is, of* and *us*.)
b. In a monosyllabic word with a short vowel sound, if the last consonant sound is /k/, this is spelt ‹ck›, as in the words: *back, neck, lick, clock* and *duck*.
c. If there is only one consonant after a short, stressed vowel sound, this consonant is doubled before any suffix starting with a vowel is added. For example, when the suffixes ‹-ed›, ‹-er›, ‹-est›, ‹-ing›, ‹-y› and ‹-able› are added to the words *hop, wet, big, clap, fun* and *hug*, the final consonants are doubled so that we get *hopped, wetter, biggest, clapping, funny* and *huggable*.
    Note that when ‹y› is a suffix, it counts as a vowel because it has a vowel sound. (This rule does not apply to those words where the final consonant is ‹x›, because ‹x› is really the two consonant sounds /k/ and /s/. This means that ‹x› is never doubled, even in words like *faxed, boxing* and *mixer*.) It can help if the children think of the two consonants as forming a 'wall'. If there were only one consonant, the wall would not be thick enough to prevent 'magic' hopping over from the vowel in the suffix and changing the short vowel sound to a long one. With two consonants, the wall becomes so thick that the 'magic' cannot get over (see Spelling Rules for Adding Suffixes, rule e).
d. When a word ends with the letters ‹le› and the preceding syllable contains a short, stressed vowel sound, there must be two consonants between the short vowel and the ‹le›. This means that the consonant before the ‹le› is doubled in words like *paddle, kettle, nibble, topple* and *snuggle*. No doubling is necessary in words like *handle, twinkle* and *jungle* because they already have two consonants between the short vowel and the ‹le›.

Spelling Rules for Adding Suffixes

a. If the root word ends with a consonant that is not immediately preceded by a short vowel sound, simply add the suffix. So, *walk* + ‹-ed› = *walked*, *quick* + ‹-est› = *quickest*, *look* + ‹-ing› = *looking* and *avoid* + ‹-able› = *avoidable*.
b. If the root word ends with the letter ‹e› and the suffix starts with a vowel, remove the ‹e› before adding

the suffix. So, *love* + ⟨-ed⟩ = *loved*, *brave* + ⟨-er⟩ = *braver*, *like* + ⟨-ing⟩ = *liking* and *value* + ⟨-able⟩ = *valuable*, but *care* + ⟨-less⟩ = *careless*.

The main exception to this rule is when the suffix ⟨-ing⟩ is added to a root word that has an ⟨i⟩ before the ⟨e⟩, as in *tie*. To avoid having two ⟨i⟩s next to each other (e.g. 'tiing'), both the ⟨i⟩ and the ⟨e⟩ are replaced with a ⟨y⟩. So *tie* + ⟨-ing⟩ = *tying* and *lie* + ⟨-ing⟩ = *lying*, even though these same words become *tied* and *lied* when adding ⟨-ed⟩. Another exception is when the ⟨e⟩ is part of the soft ⟨c⟩ or soft ⟨g⟩ spelling and the suffix ⟨-able⟩ is added. In this instance, the ⟨e⟩ is kept so that ⟨c⟩ is pronounced /s/ and ⟨g⟩ is pronounced /j/, as in *noticeable* and *changeable*. (Some words can be spelt either with or without the ⟨e⟩, so both *lovable* and *loveable* are correct; however, in these cases it is better for the children to be consistent and drop the ⟨e⟩ in their writing.)

c. If the root word ends in ⟨ce⟩ or ⟨ge⟩ and the suffix is ⟨-able⟩, do not remove the ⟨e⟩. This is because the ⟨e⟩ is part of the soft ⟨c⟩ and ⟨g⟩ spellings, making the ⟨c⟩ say /s/ and the ⟨g⟩ say /j/, as in *noticeable* and *changeable*.

d. If the root word ends in ⟨ce⟩ and the suffix is ⟨-al⟩, replace ⟨e⟩ with ⟨i⟩ before adding the suffix. So *commerce* + ⟨-al⟩ = *commercial*.

e. If the root word ends with a consonant that is immediately preceded by a short, stressed vowel sound and the suffix begins with a vowel, double the final consonant before adding the suffix. So, *stop* + ⟨-ed⟩ = *stopped*, *sad* + ⟨-er⟩ = *sadder*, *run* + ⟨-ing⟩ = *running* and *control* + ⟨-able⟩ = *controllable*, but *sad* + ⟨-ness⟩ = *sadness*.

Remind the children that two consonants are needed to make a 'wall', to prevent 'magic' from the vowel in the suffix from jumping over to change the short vowel sound (see Spelling Rules for Consonant Doubling, rule c.)

f. If the root word ends with the letter ⟨y⟩, which is immediately preceded by a consonant, replace the ⟨y⟩ with an ⟨i⟩ before adding the suffix. So, *hurry* + ⟨-ed⟩ = *hurried*, *dirty* + ⟨-est⟩ = *dirtiest*, *beauty* + ⟨-ful⟩ = *beautiful*, *vary* + ⟨-able⟩ = *variable* and *pity* + ⟨-ful⟩ = *pitiful*. However, if the suffix starts with the letter ⟨i⟩, the rule does not apply, so *worry* + ⟨-ing⟩ = *worrying*.

The letter ⟨y⟩ is unique in being able to function as either a vowel or a consonant. As a vowel, ⟨y⟩ replaces ⟨i⟩. In the *Phonics Pupil Books*, the children learnt that 'shy ⟨i⟩' does not like to go at the end of a word, so 'toughy ⟨y⟩' takes its place. As the last syllable of a multisyllabic word, the sound ⟨y⟩ makes is somewhere between the short /i/ in *tin* and the long /ee/ in *bee*. (This is also true of the rare instances when the letter ⟨i⟩ is the final syllable of a polysyllabic word, as in *taxi*.) Despite this confusing pronunciation, it is important for the children to think of ⟨y⟩ as replacing 'shy ⟨i⟩'. This will help them remember that the ⟨i⟩ returns when such words are extended (except in words like *worrying*, where it would look odd to have two ⟨i⟩s next to each other).

In the *Grammar Pupil Books*, suffixes and prefixes are taught with prefix and suffix fish. Prefixes are shown on the fish's head; the root (or *base*) word is shown on the fish's body and suffixes are shown on fish tails (see illustration opposite).

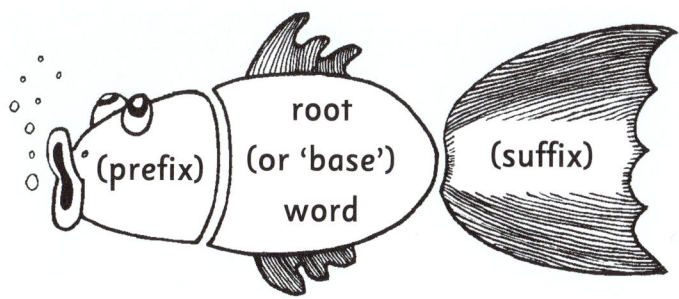

Spelling and Grammar Lessons

For each lesson, there is an activity page in the *Pupil Book* for the children to complete and an accompanying lesson plan in the *Teacher's Book*. The recommendations in the teacher's lesson plans are intended to be followed systematically. However, if a suggestion seems inappropriate for a particular class situation, it can of course be adapted to suit.

Each lesson plan also features a reduced copy of the relevant activity page/s in the *Pupil Book*. It can be helpful to refer to this prior to, or during, the lesson.

Grammar Lessons

Each grammar lesson has its own particular focus and the lesson plans vary accordingly. However, the grammar lessons all follow the same standard format, which helps to give them a recognisable shape. The format of the grammar lessons is as follows.

<blockquote>
a. Aim
b. Introduction
c. Main Point
d. Activity Page
e. Extension Activity
f. Rounding Off
</blockquote>

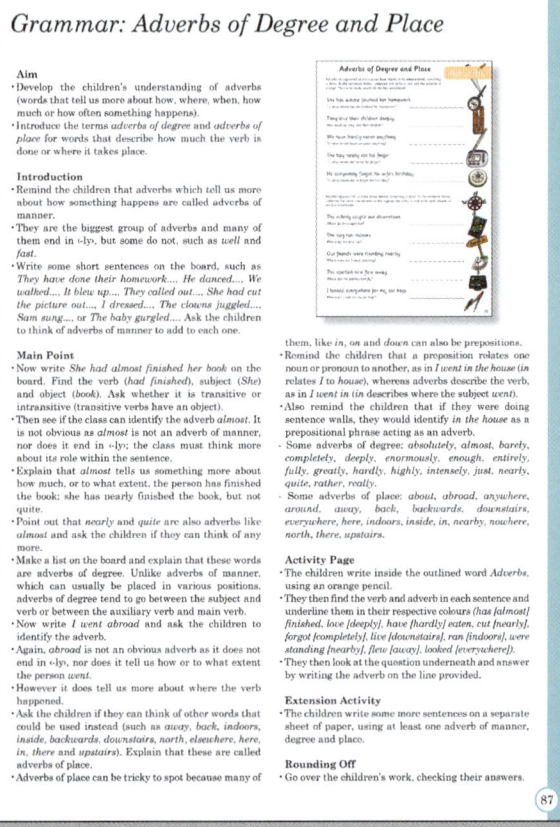

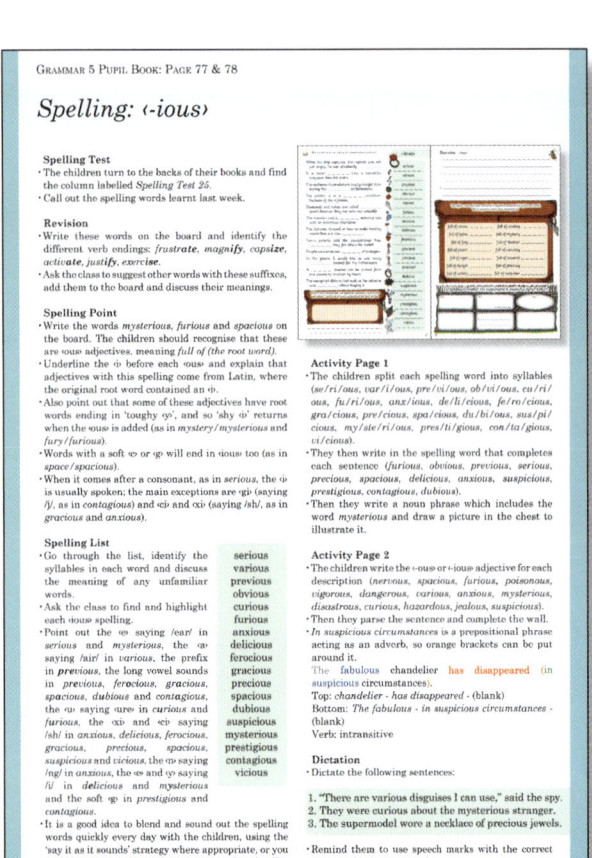

Spelling Lessons

The spelling lessons all follow the same basic format.

<blockquote>
a. Spelling Test
b. Revision
c. Spelling Point
d. Spelling List
e. Activity Pages 1 and 2
f. Dictation
</blockquote>

Many teaching points are common to all of the spelling lessons, so these are explained in further detail on the following pages.

30

SPELLING AND GRAMMAR LESSONS

a. Spelling Test

Six pages have been provided at the back of the *Grammar 5 Pupil Book* for the children's spelling tests (pages 110 to 115).
    Start by telling the children to turn to the back of their books and find the space for that particular week's spelling test. Call out the words one at a time for the children to write on the lines. Repeat each word twice, giving the children just enough time to write each word before moving on to the next one. The words can be called out in the same order as they appear in the list, but it is best if they are called out in a random order. Those children who are finding it difficult can be given fewer words to learn.

b. Revision

Each lesson should start with a short burst of revision. Early lessons use flashcards and sound dictation to revise the five long vowel sounds and their alternative spellings (in dictation, ask the children how they would write the /ee/ in *monkey*, for example). They go on to revise the common prefixes taught in earlier years and, as the year progresses, they focus on the prefixes, suffixes and other spelling patterns introduced in recent lessons. The teacher's notes provide suitable words to write on the board and discuss with the class.

c. Spelling Point

In the *Grammar 5 Pupil Book*, the focus of many spelling lessons is on commonly used prefixes and suffixes and on 'word families' that share a common root. Analysing different parts of a word and understanding how they convey meaning, or recognising when they form a certain part of speech, can help the children enormously with their comprehension, particularly when reading unfamiliar words for the first time.

Pupil Book page	Word bank
2. ‹age›, ‹ege›	*bandage, breakage, image, salvage, storage; allege, privilege, sacrilege*
5. ‹nge›	*binge, disarrange, hinge, lozenge, range, rearrange, shortchange, whinge*
8. Suffix ‹-ance›	*abundance, dance, elegance, finance, glance, ignorance, prance, stance*
11. Suffix ‹-ancy›	*discrepancy, fancy, inconstancy, reluctancy, tenancy, truancy, vacancy*
14. Suffix ‹-ence›	*benevolence, conscience, consequence, defence, hence, influence, offence*
17. Suffix ‹-ency›	*absorbency, infrequency, indecency, tendency, transparency*
20. Prefix ‹multi-›	*multibillionaire, multichannel, multidiscipline, multifrequency, multilingual*
23. Prefix ‹auto-›	*autograph, automate, autonomously, autonomies, autopsies, autoworker*
26. ‹mega-›, ‹micro-›	*megacorporation, megadeal, megapod; microanalysis, microclimate, microcosm*
29. Prefix ‹super-›	*supercharged, superfan, superfluous, supernatural, supernova, supervising*
32. ‹cent-›, ‹kilo-›, ‹milli-›	*centilitre; kilobyte, kilolitre, kilowatt; millionaire, millionth*
35. Prefix ‹post-›	*postal, postman, postbag, postdated, postmark, postponing*
38. Suffix ‹-tion›	*connection, deception, eruption, function, injection, motion, petition*

SPELLING AND GRAMMAR LESSONS

Pupil Book page	Word bank
41. Suffix ‹-sion›	*abrasion, allusion, conclusion, confusion, decision, envision, fusion, vision*
44. ‹ssion›	*commission, compassion, compression, recession, remission*
47. ‹cian›	*academician, cybernetician, diagnostician, dialectician, logician, theoretician*
50. Suffix ‹-ation›	*abbreviation, calculation, decoration, depravation, elation, fixation, pronunciation*
53. ‹ch›, ‹che› for /sh/	*brochures, chagrin, chalets, champagne; barouche, cliched, echelon, gauche*
56. ‹sure›	*counterpressure, erasure, exposure, pleasure, surely, treasure, underexposure*
59. ‹ture›	*adventure, capture, creature, feature, lecture, mature, puncture, vulture*
62. Suffix ‹-ible›	*accessible, collectible, inaudible, invisible, legible, plausible, suggestible*
65. Suffix ‹-ate›	*calculate, fumigate, humiliate, locate, migrate, operate, update, vacate*
68. Suffixes ‹-ise›, ‹-ize›	*agonise, customise, demise, organise, supervise, realise, wise; capsize*
71. Suffix ‹-ify›	*dehumidify, fortify, modify, purify, rectify, unify, vilify*
74. Suffix ‹-ous›	*ambiguous, hideous, marvellous, meticulous, ominous, raucous, wondrous*
77. Suffix ‹-ious›	*devious, envious, luxurious, melodius, oblivious, religious, tedious*
80. ‹tious›	*expeditious, flirtatious, rambunctious, unpretentious*
83. ‹cial›	*multiracial, noncommercial, ultracommercial, spacial, special*
86. ‹tial›	*celestial, essential, existential, nonsequential, prudential, torrential*
89. Words ending in ‹-i›	*alumni, antipasti, chilli, confetti, corgi, fungi, hi, porcini, rabbi, saki, sari*
92. ‹graph›	*cinematography, monograph, radiograph, seismograph, typography*
95. Suffix ‹-ology›	*apology, astrology, cardiology, criminology, microbiology, psychology, theology*
98. Suffix ‹-ment›	*abandonment, basement, cement, compliment, embodiment, judgement, lament*
101. Suffix ‹-ship›	*authorship, courtship, hardship, internship, ladyship, readership, worship*
104. Suffix ‹-ward›	*northward, eastward, southward, westward, rightward, leftward*
107. ‹sch›	*schmaltzy, schmoozing, scholarly, schoolbag, schoolbook*

d. Spelling List

Each week, the children are given eighteen words with a particular spelling pattern to learn for a test. It is a good idea to give the spelling homework at the beginning of the week and to test at the end of the week, or on the following Monday.

The spelling words have been carefully selected to enable every child to have some success. The eighteen words can be divided into three groups of six. The words in the first group are usually short, regular and fairly common; those in the second group are a bit longer and may have more alternative spellings in them; and the third group has longer, often less common words, with more varied spellings.

For those children who find spelling difficult, it may be appropriate to give them only the first six spelling words; the number can be increased when the children are ready. The number of spelling words given to the children is at the teacher's discretion, based on his or her knowledge of the children in the class.

Spelling and Grammar Lessons

It is important to go over the words during the spelling lesson. Look carefully at each spelling list with the class; discuss the meanings of any unfamiliar words; and look to see which parts of a word are regular and identify those parts that are not. The lesson plans in the *Teacher's Book* point out the words that need particular attention and suggest suitable learning strategies. The spelling activity pages will also help the children become more familiar with the words and their spellings. Go over the spelling words as often as possible during the week, ideally, blending and sounding out the words with the children every day.

Each child takes the list of spellings home to learn. If the children usually leave their *Pupil Books* at school, the words can be copied out into a small homework book for the children to take home. If the children do the writing, check that they have copied the words clearly and accurately before the books go home.

Test and mark the spellings each week. The results should be written in the children's *Pupil Books* for the parents to see. The marks can be shown either as a mark out of eighteen, or with a coded system if preferred. For example, a coloured star system might be used, with a gold star for 18/18, a silver star for 17/18 and a coloured star for 16/18. Most parents like to be involved in their children's homework, and are interested to see how many words their child spelt correctly and which words were misspelt.

Children need to be aware that accurate spelling is important for their future. Unfortunately, there is no magic wand that can be waved to make them good at spelling. In addition to knowing the letter sounds and alternative spellings thoroughly, a certain amount of dedication and practice is needed.

e. Activity Pages 1 and 2

Now that the children are older, there are two spelling activity pages per lesson. As in previous *Pupil Books*, the focus of each spelling page reflects the main teaching point. Every week, there are two activities on Activity Page 1 that use the words from the spelling list. In the first activity, the children have to write out the spelling words, splitting them into syllables. In the first twelve lessons, the spelling words are already split into syllables for the children to copy out on the lines below; in the middle twelve lessons, the children have to decide for themselves how to split the word, though the lines below the word indicate how many syllables there are; in the final twelve lessons, the children are not given any clues and have to work out the number of syllables for themselves. (For more information on syllables, see pages 25–26.) The second activity is more varied: it could be matching words to their descriptions, using words to complete sentences, solving anagrams, creating prefix and suffix fish, matching words to their root words, making word families, writing the meanings of words or using words in a noun phrase or sentence. These activities allow the children to engage actively with the spelling words, which makes learning the words more meaningful.

Activity Page 2 has three activities. The top and bottom activities are the same every week. At the top of the page, lines are provided for the weekly dictation. At the bottom of the page there is a parsing activity. Parsing involves identifying each part of speech in a sentence and underlining it in the appropriate colour. The children then identify the subject and (if there is one) the object of the sentence. From page 12 of the *Pupil Book* onwards, they then transfer the words to a 'sentence wall'. (Sentence walls are explained in more detail on pages 20–21.) Until page 36 of the *Pupil Book*, lines indicate the parts of the wall that need to be completed. However, this extra support is phased out, except when a new sentence wall feature is introduced. The middle activity on Activity Page 2 sometimes focuses on the main spelling point but, more often than not, it provides cross over with recent grammar lessons. This consolidates the grammar the children are learning and to puts grammar into a spelling context.

f. Dictation

As a weekly exercise, dictation is useful in a number of ways. It gives the children regular practice listening for the sounds in the words they write, and is a good way of monitoring their progress. Dictation

Spelling and Grammar Lessons

helps the children to develop their independent writing and encourages the slower writers to increase their speed. It also provides a good opportunity for the children to practise their punctuation, such as commas, speech marks and question and exclamation marks. The dictation sections in each lesson plan suggest the important things to point out to the children.

There are three sentences each week for dictation. All of the sentences revise the spelling focus for that week, and may also feature spelling patterns and grammar points from previous lessons. For example, when the spelling focus is the prefixes ‹mega-› and ‹micro-›, the dictation sentences feature words like *megaphone* and *microphone*, but they also feature previous spelling words like *multitalented* and *autobiography*. Furthermore, the perfect tenses appear regularly in the dictation sentences once they have been taught.

The children can write the dictation sentences on the lines provided at the top of Activity Page 2. Begin by calling out the first sentence for the children to write down. Give the children a reasonable amount of time to finish writing, but not too long, and then move on to the next sentence. The few children who have not yet finished should leave the sentence incomplete and move on. This encourages them to get up to speed. Afterwards, it is important to go over the sentences with the children and discuss the spellings, grammar and punctuation points.

PART 2

Teaching with the Grammar 5 Pupil Book

The following pages provide detailed lesson plans and teaching guidance for use alongside the activity pages in the *Grammar 5 Pupil Book*. It is a good idea to read through the relevant teaching guidance prior to each lesson, and to prepare any additional materials that might be required.

For a typical spelling lesson, the teacher will need to prepare flash cards for the revision session, as well as coloured pens or pencils, highlighters and dictionaries for the children's use. The teacher may also find it helpful to prepare a list of words featuring the spelling pattern(s) of the week prior to the lesson. (The word banks on pages 31 and 32 can be used as a starting point for this list.) The requirements for the grammar lessons are more varied. As for the spelling lessons, every grammar lesson requires the children to have access to dictionaries, thesauruses, and coloured pens or pencils. A number of the extension activities also require lined paper for extended writing.

GRAMMAR 5 PUPIL BOOK: PAGES 2 & 3

Spelling: ‹age›, ‹ege›

Spelling Test
- As the children have not been given any spelling words to learn yet, there is no spelling test in this lesson.

Revision
- Revise these spellings of the long vowel sounds and ask the children to suggest words for each one: /ai/ ‹ai›, ‹ay›, ‹a_e›, ‹ei›, ‹eigh›, ‹a›; /ee/ ‹ee›, ‹ea›, ‹e_e›, ‹y›, ‹ey›, ‹ie›, ‹e›; /ie/ ‹ie›, ‹y›, ‹igh›, ‹i_e›, ‹i›; /oa/ ‹oa›, ‹ow›, ‹o_e›, ‹o›; /ue/ ‹ue›, ‹ew›, ‹u_e›, ‹u›. Flash cards can be used for reading and sound dictation for spelling.
- Time should be set aside during the week for anyone who is unsure of these spellings or needs blending and segmenting practice.

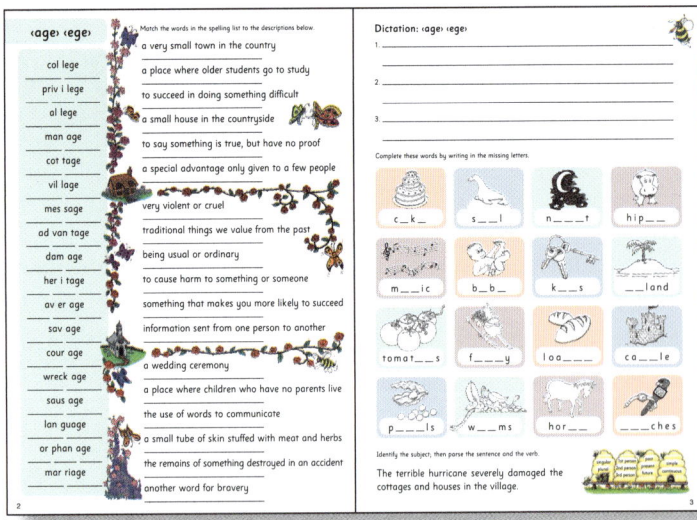

Spelling Point
- An understanding of syllables and stress in words can help with spelling (see Introduction, pages 25–26).
- Revise how to identify the vowel sound(s) and how to split a written word into syllables with a line, especially words with double consonants, ‹ck› and ‹le›.
- Write the words *college* and *wreckage* on the board and split them into syllables. Ask which syllable has the stress (the first one, as it is said slightly louder to give it more emphasis).
- Often the vowel in an unstressed syllable loses its pure sound and becomes a neutral schwa (sounding something like /uh/).
- However, sometimes something else happens. Ask the children what sound ‹a› and ‹e› are making in ‹age› and ‹ege›, and explain that in some instances the vowel does not become neutral, but changes to an /i/ sound.

Spelling List
- Read the words with the class and discuss the meaning of any unfamiliar words. Ask the children to find and highlight each ‹age› or ‹ege› saying /ij/.
- Point out that *allege* is different because ‹ege› is stressed and the ending is /ej/. Three of the most common ‹ege› words are in the spelling list (a fourth is *sacrilege*) and the more common spelling pattern is ‹age›.
- If the children know the ‹ege› words, they can be reasonably sure any other words will be spelt ‹age›. Making up a sentence like *It is alleged that you get privileges at college* will help them remember, especially if you 'say it as it sounds' and stress the /e/ in the words.
- Point out other spelling features, including schwas (*privilege* and *allege*, for example), the ‹ou› in *courage*, ‹ck› after the short /e/ in *wreckage*, the ‹au› in *sausage*,

college
privilege
allege
manage
cottage
village
message
advantage
damage
heritage
average
savage
courage
wreckage
sausage
language
orphanage
marriage

the ‹ph› saying /f/ in *orphanage* and the silent letters in *marriage* and *wreckage*.
- It is a good idea to blend and sound out the spelling words quickly every day with the class.

Activity Page 1
- The children copy out the syllables of each spelling word to help them remember the spelling.
- They then read the phrases and decide which spelling words they describe (*village, college, manage, cottage, allege, privilege, savage, heritage, average, damage, advantage, message, marriage, orphanage, language, sausage, wreckage, courage*).
- Encourage the children to use a dictionary if they are unsure of any words.

Activity Page 2
- The children write in the missing letters to complete the words (*cake, seal, night, hippo, music, baby, keys, island, tomatoes, fairy, loaves, castle, pearls, worms, horse, watches*).
- They then parse the sentence, underlining each part of speech in the correct colour, identify the subject (*hurricane*) and parse the verb (3rd person singular, simple past). *Severely* is an adverb made by adding ‹-ly› to the adjective *severe*.

The terrible hurricane severely damaged the cottages and houses in the village.

Dictation
- The children turn to the lines at the top of Activity Page 2. Dictate the following sentences for the children to write down on the lines:

1. "Did you manage to cook the sausages?" asked Tom.
2. The princess arrived in a carriage for her marriage.
3. It is an advantage to speak many languages.

- In sentence 1, remind them to use speech marks with the correct punctuation (see pages 16–17). *Tom* is a proper noun and needs a capital letter.

36

Grammar: Parts of Speech and Parsing

Aim
- Revise all the parts of speech learnt so far (nouns, pronouns, adjectives, verbs, adverbs, prepositions and conjunctions) and how to identify them in a piece of writing (parsing) (see page 20).

Introduction
- Make sure the children know these parts of speech:
  - Nouns are the names of people, places and dates (proper nouns) or things (common nouns). Common nouns can be concrete, abstract or collective. Nouns can also be possessive, as in *Tom's bike* or *the horses' saddles*. Possessive nouns always act as adjectives in a sentence.
  - Pronouns are the small words that replace nouns. Those learnt so far are personal pronouns (as in *I/me* and *we/us*) and possessive pronouns (as in *mine* and *ours*).
  - Adjectives are words that describe nouns and pronouns. These include possessive adjectives (such as *my* and *our*) and comparatives and superlatives (formed by adding ‹-er› and ‹-est›, or by putting other words like *more* and *most*, *less* and *least* in front).
  - Verbs are 'doing words' that describe the past, present and future. They can be conjugated, some have 'tricky' pasts and others, like the verb *to be*, are very irregular and need to be learnt. The tenses introduced so far are the simple tenses and continuous tenses.
  - Adverbs are words that describe verbs by showing how, where, when, how much or how often something happens. Adverbs often end in the suffix ‹-ly›, as in *quickly* and *lately*.
  - Prepositions are words that relate one noun or pronoun to another, as in *on* and *under*. Many prepositions also act as adverbs if they do not come before a noun or pronoun, as in *We went in*.
  - Conjunctions are words used to join parts of a sentence together to create longer, less repetitive sentences, such as *and*, *but*, *or*, *so* and *because*.

Main Point
- Identifying the different parts of speech in a sentence is called parsing. Many words can act as different parts of speech, depending on how they are being used.
- It helps to identify the nouns and verbs first, underlining them in the appropriate colours, as this makes it easier to find the adjectives and adverbs.
- Although the articles (*a*, *an* and *the*) are really special sorts of adjectives, the children are not expected to underline them.
- Write the following sentences on the board and parse them with the children:
  The boy greedily ate the last chocolate cookie.
  I will be walking my dog in the park.
  The large and rebellious army captured the English king's castle.
- Point out other grammar features, such as the tricky past *ate*, the different tenses and how they are formed, the nouns acting as adjectives (*chocolate* and *king's*, which is a possessive noun), and the adverb *greedily*, formed by adding ‹-ly› to the adjective *greedy* (when 'shy ‹i›' returns to replace 'toughy ‹y›').

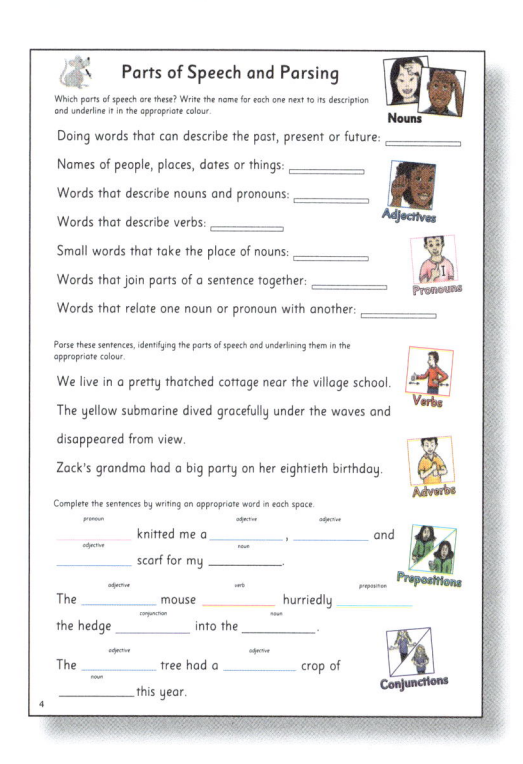

Activity Page
- The children write the parts of speech that are being described (verbs, nouns, adjectives, adverbs, pronouns, conjunctions, prepositions) and underline them in the appropriate colour.
- Then they parse the sentences.
  We live in a pretty thatched cottage near the village school.
  The yellow submarine dived gracefully under the waves and disappeared from view.
  Zack's grandma had a big party on her eightieth birthday.
- Finally they complete the last three sentences, choosing words that are the correct part of speech and which make sense.

Extension Activity
- Write more sentences with missing words for the class to complete.

Rounding Off
- Go over the activity page with the class, discussing their answers.

GRAMMAR 5 PUPIL BOOK: PAGE 5 & 6

Spelling: ‹nge›

Spelling Test
- The children turn to the backs of their books and find the column labelled *Spelling Test 1*.
- In any order, call out the spelling words learnt last week. The children write the words on the lines.

Revision
- Revise these spellings of the long vowel sounds. Flash cards can be used for reading and sound dictation for spelling.
- Ask the class to suggest words for each one: /ai/ ‹ai›, ‹ay›, ‹a_e›, ‹ei›, ‹eigh›, ‹a›; /ee/ ‹ee›, ‹ea›, ‹e_e›, ‹y›, ‹ey›, ‹ie›, ‹e›; /ie/ ‹ie›, ‹y›, ‹igh›, ‹i_e›, ‹i›; /oa/ ‹oa›, ‹ow›, ‹o_e›, ‹o›; /ue/ ‹ue›, ‹ew›, ‹u_e›, ‹u›.

Spelling Point
- Revise the spellings of the /j/ sound that have been taught so far. The main ones are ‹j› and the soft ‹g› spellings: ‹ge›, ‹gi› and ‹gy›. There is also ‹dge›, which is usually used after a single vowel letter saying a short vowel sound, as in *badge*, *hedge*, *ridge*, *dodge* and *fudge*.
- Point out that although the children learnt the ‹ege› and ‹age› spellings for words ending in /ij/ in the previous lesson, another common spelling pattern is ‹idge›, as in *bridge*, *porridge* and *partridge*. If they are not sure which to use, the children should check the spelling in the dictionary.
- Now introduce the spelling pattern ‹nge›, which children sometimes spell incorrectly because they do not hear the ‹n›, as is often the case with consonant blends.

Spelling List
- Read the words with the class, identify the stressed syllables and discuss the meaning of any unfamiliar words.
- Ask the children to find and highlight the ‹nge› saying /nj/ in each word.
- Discuss any other spelling features, including the schwas (*challenge* and *avenge*, for example), the ‹a› as /ai/ in *change*, *strange*, *exchange*, *arrange* and *interchange*, the ‹a› in *orange* and first ‹e› in *revenge* saying /i/, the ‹o› as /u/ in *sponge* and the ‹y› as /i/ in *syringe*.
- It is a good idea to blend and sound out the spelling words quickly every day with the class, emphasising the /n/ in ‹nge› each time.

change
strange
challenge
orange
plunge
sponge
exchange
arrange
lounge
fringe
revenge
cringe
syringe
avenge
twinge
singe
scavenge
interchange

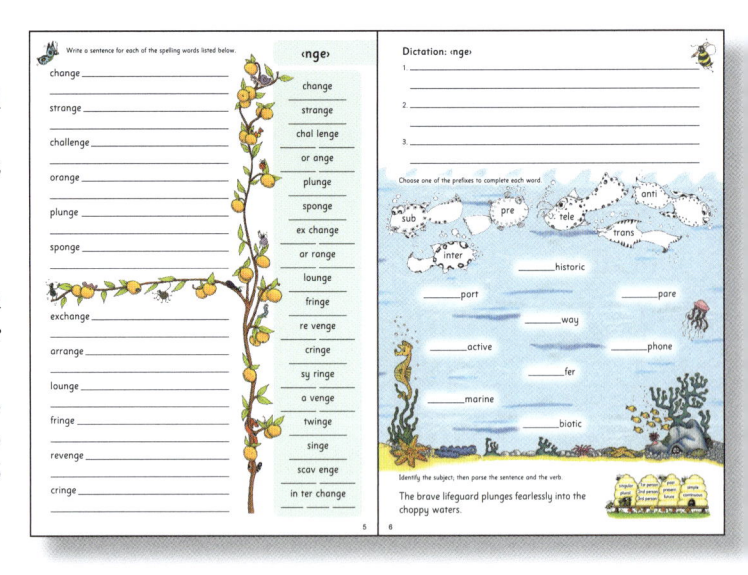

Activity Page 1
- The children copy out the syllables of each spelling word.
- They then write a sentence for each of the first twelve spelling words. Encourage the children to use a dictionary if they are unsure of any words.

Activity Page 2
- The children choose a prefix from one of the fish to complete each word (*prehistoric*, *transport/teleport*, *subway*, *prepare*, *interactive*, *transfer/prefer*, *telephone*, *submarine*, *antibiotic*).
- They then parse the sentence, underlining each part of speech in the correct colour, identify the subject (*lifeguard*) and parse the verb (3rd person singular, simple present).
- Point out that *fearlessly* is an adverb made by adding ‹-ly› to the adjective *fearless*.

The brave lifeguard plunges fearlessly into the choppy waters.

Dictation
- Dictate the following sentences for the children to write down:

1. "The fringe is singed!" exclaimed the stranger.
2. The children had sponge cake and a drink of orange.
3. They arranged to exchange messages on the internet.

- Remind the children to use speech marks with the correct punctuation in sentence 1.

Grammar: One Word – Different Parts of Speech

Aim
- Develop the children's understanding that many words can act as more than one part of speech, depending on how they are being used in a sentence.

Introduction
- Briefly revise the parts of speech learnt so far: nouns (the names of people, places, dates or things), pronouns (small words that take the place of nouns), adjectives (words that describe nouns and pronouns), verbs ('doing' words that describe the past, present or future), adverbs (words that describe verbs), prepositions (words that relate one noun or pronoun with another, often indicating direction or position) and conjunctions (words that join parts of a sentence together).

Main Point
- When the children parse a sentence, they must look at each word in context before deciding which part of speech it is.
- This is because words can often act as more than one part of speech and their function (or job) is determined by how they are being used in a sentence.
- For example, without extra information we cannot tell whether the word *light* is being used as a noun (as in *the light of the moon*), a verb (as in *she will light the fire*) or as an adjective (as in *she wore a light blue dress*).
- It is only by analysing the word's use within a sentence that its function can be identified.
- Write the word *cry* on the board and ask the children how they could use it in a sentence.
- Then decide which part of speech it represents: it could either act as a verb (as in *I heard the baby cry*) or as a noun (as in *the baby's cry was loud and strong*).
- Look at some more words and discuss which parts of speech they can be.
- Examples include words that could be nouns or verbs: *brush, jump, dress, cook, puzzle, itch, cough, flower, cheer, lift, drink, work*; or words that can act as either adjectives or nouns: *square, round, blue* (as in *a blue shirt* or *the colour blue*), *orange, Chinese, English, grave*; or words that are either adverbs or prepositions: *in, on, off, under, over, up, down*.
- Remind the children that they can use a dictionary to check what parts of speech a word can be, although they have to work it out for themselves when nouns act as adjectives (as in *He ate the **apple** pie* or *I found the **dog's** toy*).

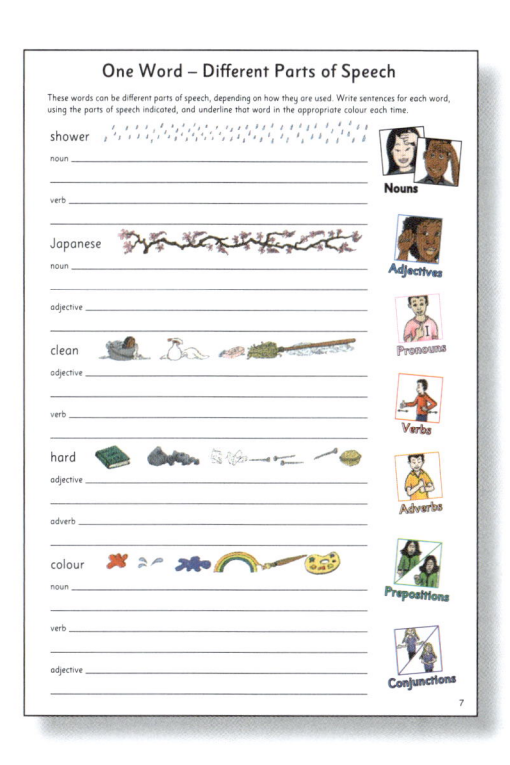

Activity Page
- The children look at the words in turn and write a different sentence for each part of speech indicated. So, for example, they should write two sentences for the word *shower*: one using *shower* as a noun (as in *I like to sing in the shower*) and one using it as a verb (as in *I like to shower every morning*).
- Then they underline the noun in black and the verb in red.
- Encourage the children to use a dictionary if they need some help using some of the harder words.

Extension Activity
- The children write some more pairs of sentences for words that can be different parts of speech, choosing from the words discussed earlier in the lesson.

Rounding Off
- Go over the activity page with the children, discussing their answers.
- If they have done the extension activity, ask some of the children to read out their sentences.

GRAMMAR 5 PUPIL BOOK: PAGE 8 & 9

Spelling: ‹-ance›

Spelling Test
- The children turn to the backs of their books and find the column labelled *Spelling Test 2*.
- In any order, call out the spelling words learnt last week. The children write the words on the lines.

Revision
- Revise these spellings of the long vowel sounds and ask the class to suggest words for each one: /ai/ ‹ai›, ‹ay›, ‹a_e›, ‹ei›, ‹eigh›, ‹a›; /ee/ ‹ee›, ‹ea›, ‹e_e›, ‹y›, ‹ey›, ‹ie›, ‹e›; /ie/ ‹ie›, ‹y›, ‹igh›, ‹i_e›, ‹i›; /oa/ ‹oa›, ‹ow›, ‹o_e›, ‹o›; /ue/ ‹ue›, ‹ew›, ‹u_e›, ‹u›.
- Flash cards can be used for reading and sound dictation for spelling.

Spelling Point
- Revise the soft ‹c› spellings for the /s/ sound: ‹ce›, ‹ci› and ‹cy›. Then remind the class of the suffix ‹-ant›, which makes adjectives and nouns, like *important* and *assistant*.
- Write these examples on the board, replace the final ‹t› in each word with ‹ce› and introduce the spelling ‹-ance›.
- As a suffix, it makes abstract nouns with the quality, state or action of the root word (so if something is *important*, you can say it has *importance*, and if you *assist* someone, you are giving them *assistance*). This happens when the suffix is used with adjectives ending in ‹-ant› or is added to verbs.
- If the root verb ends in ‹e›, then the usual spelling rules apply and the ‹e› is dropped before adding ‹ance›, so *ignore* becomes *ignorance* and *guide* becomes *guidance*.
- Remind the class that abstract nouns are things that do not exist in a physical form, like ideas, feelings or actions.

Spelling List
- Read the words with the class and discuss the meaning of any unfamiliar words.
- Ask the children to find and highlight every ‹ance› spelling.
- Point out any other spelling features, such as the schwas (apart from *advance* and *chance*, all the words have an unstressed final syllable, so the ‹a› is swallowed), the hard ‹c› followed by soft ‹c› in *acceptance*, the ‹oy› spelling of /oi/ in *annoyance*, the ‹ear› in *clearance*, the ‹ur› in *disturbance*, the ‹a› saying /ai/ in *fragrance*, the soft ‹g› and ‹e› saying /ee/ in *allegiance*, the silent letter digraph ‹gu› in *guidance*, the ‹ui› and soft ‹c› in *nuisance* and the ‹cqu› in *acquaintance*.

distance
advance
balance
entrance
chance
acceptance
admittance
annoyance
assistance
clearance
disturbance
fragrance
allegiance
guidance
nuisance
hindrance
irrelevance
acquaintance

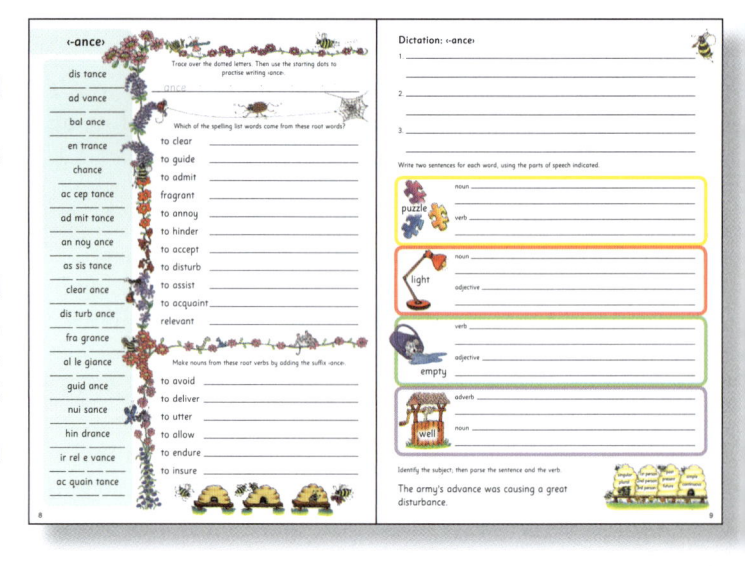

- It is a good idea to blend and sound out the spelling words quickly every day with the class, emphasising the /a/ in ‹ance› to help remember the spelling.

Activity Page 1
- The children copy out the syllables of each spelling word.
- They then practise writing ‹ance›, first tracing over the dotted letters before writing them along the line with the help of the starting dots.
- Then they match the root words to the spelling words (*clearance, guidance, admittance, fragrance, annoyance, hindrance, acceptance, disturbance, assistance, acquaintance, irrelevance*) and make abstract nouns by adding the suffix to the verbs, using the spelling rules listed on pages 28–29 (*avoidance, deliverance, utterance, allowance, endurance, insurance*).

Activity Page 2
- The children write two sentences for each word, using the part of speech indicated. They could also underline the word each time in the appropriate colour.
- They then parse the sentence, underlining each part of speech in the correct colour, identify the subject (*advance*) and parse the verb (3rd person singular, past continuous).
- *Army's* is a possessive noun; these act as adjectives in a sentence and should be underlined in blue. All parts of the verb should be underlined in red.
  The army's advance was causing a great disturbance.

Dictation
- Dictate the following sentences for the children to write down:

1. The cottage was seriously damaged during the disturbance.
2. They saw the entrance to the college in the distance.
3. "The flowers have an elegant fragrance," the florist observed.

- Remind the children to use speech marks with the correct punctuation in sentence 3.

GRAMMAR 5 PUPIL BOOK: PAGE 10

Grammar: Sentence Walls

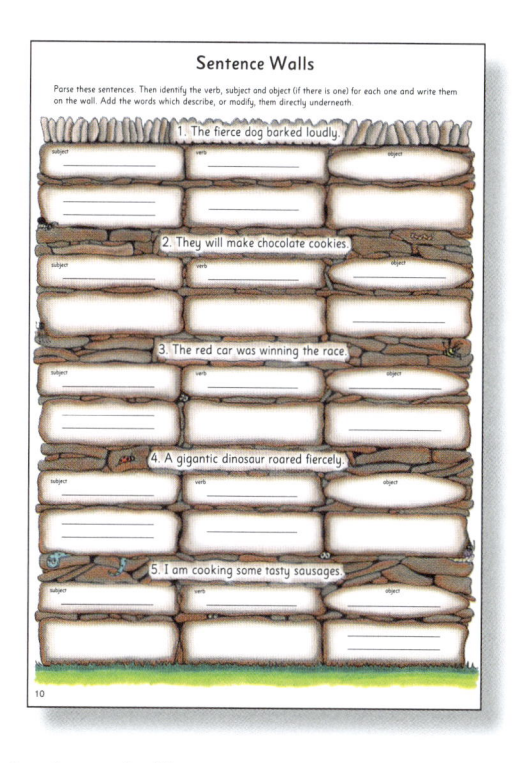

Aim
- Introduce the idea of sentence walls (a simplified form of sentence diagramming) to help understand more about sentence structure.

Introduction
- Write this sentence on the board and parse it with the children: The little boy kicked a red ball.
- Then ask the children to identify the verb, subject (the noun or pronoun that does the verb action) and object, if there is one (the noun or pronoun that receives the verb action).
- Draw a box around the subject, *boy*, with a small ‹s› in the corner, and a ring around the object, *ball*, with a small ‹o› inside.
- The children might say that the subject is *the little boy* and the object is *a red ball*. This is not wrong, but remind the class that only the noun or pronoun is highlighted and not the adjectives or articles that go with it.

Main Point
- Add the word *hard* to the end of the sentence and ask what part of speech it is. Although *hard* is an adverb telling us more about how the ball is kicked, it does not end in ‹-ly› and is not next to the verb in the sentence, so its function may not be obvious.
- Explain that there is a way to organise a sentence visually that helps show how the different words relate to each other. It is called a sentence wall.
- Draw the diagram below on the board. Begin by drawing a long horizontal line across the board, intersected by a short vertical line a third of the way along. Then draw a rectangular box in the top left section, with a small ‹s› in its corner and write the word *boy* inside. Then draw a box on the right hand side of the line, but this time put a small ‹v› in the corner and write the word *kicked*. Then draw an oval to the right of the verb, put a small ‹o› inside and write *ball*. Add three more boxes beneath the line, directly underneath, and put the words associated with the subject, verb and object in the correct box, so it looks like this:

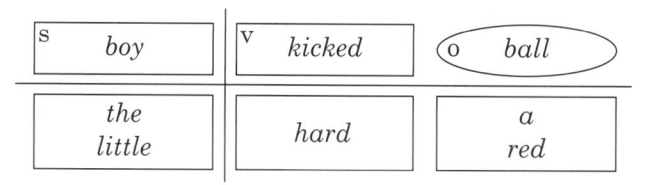

s boy	v kicked	o ball
the little	hard	a red

- Explain that at its most basic level, a sentence has two parts: what the sentence is about (the subject, plus the words that modify it) and then everything else (the verb and any extra information), known as the predicate.
- The vertical line separates the subject and predicate.
- The horizontal line separates all the essential information at the top (rather like a newspaper headline: *boy kicked ball*) from the extra information below.

Activity Page
- The children parse the sentences and complete the wall:
  1. The fierce dog barked loudly.
     Top: *dog - barked - (blank)*
     Bottom: *The fierce - loudly - (blank)*
  2. They will make chocolate cookies.
     Top: *They - will make - cookies*
     Bottom: *(blank) - (blank) - chocolate*
  3. The red car was winning the race.
     Top: *car - was winning - race*
     Bottom: *The red - (blank) - the*
  4. A gigantic dinosaur roared fiercely.
     Top: *dinosaur - roared - (blank)*
     Bottom: *A gigantic - fiercely - (blank)*
  5. I am cooking some tasty sausages.
     Top: *I - am cooking - sausages*
     Bottom: *(blank) - (blank) - some tasty*

Extension Activity
- The children identify the verb tenses in the sentences on the activity page (1. simple past, 2. simple future, 3. past continuous, 4. simple past, 5. present continuous).

Rounding Off
- Go over the activity page with the children, discussing their answers.

41

GRAMMAR 5 PUPIL BOOK: PAGE 11 & 12

Spelling: ‹-ancy›

Spelling Test
- The children turn to the backs of their books and find the column labelled *Spelling Test 3*.
- In any order, call out the spelling words learnt last week. The children write the words on the lines.

Revision
- Revise these spellings of the long vowel sounds and ask the class to suggest words for each one: /ai/ ‹ai›, ‹ay›, ‹a_e›, ‹ei›, ‹eigh›, ‹a›; /ee/ ‹ee›, ‹ea›, ‹e_e›, ‹y›, ‹ey›, ‹ie›, ‹e›; /ie/ ‹ie›, ‹y›, ‹igh›, ‹i_e›, ‹i›; /oa/ ‹oa›, ‹ow›, ‹o_e›, ‹o›; /ue/ ‹ue›, ‹ew›, ‹u_e›, ‹u›.
- Flash cards can be used for reading and sound dictation for spelling

Spelling Point
- Revise the soft ‹c› spellings for the /s/ sound: ‹ce›, ‹ci› and ‹cy›.
- Write the adjective *relevant* and noun *relevance* on the board. Ask the children to suggest how each word could be used in a sentence.
- Now add *relevancy* to the list and underline the suffix.
- Explain that, just like ‹-ance›, this suffix makes abstract nouns with the quality, state or action of the root word when it is added either to verbs or to adjectives ending in ‹-ant› (so if a hotel has a *vacancy*, it has a *vacant* room). However, words ending in ‹-ance› are much more common.
- Occasionally, the noun exists in both forms, as in *relevance* and *relevancy*.
- Discuss how the three words on the board are very similar in form and meaning. Explain that groups of words like this are called word families.

Spelling List
- Read the words with the class, discuss the meaning of any unfamiliar words and ask the children to find and highlight every ‹ancy› spelling.
- Point out any other spelling features, such as the schwa in the unstressed final syllable of each word, the ‹a›, ‹i› and ‹u› saying their long vowel sound in *vacancy*, *vibrancy* and *occupancy*, the ‹gn› saying /ny/ in *poignancy*, the ‹u› saying /oo/ in *truancy*, the soft ‹c› and ‹qu› saying /c/ in *piquancy* and the ‹ouy› saying /oi/ in *bouyancy*.
- It is a good idea to blend and sound out the spelling words quickly every day with the class, emphasising the /a/ in ‹ancy› to help remember the spelling.

infancy
vacancy
vibrancy
constancy
hesitancy
relevancy
consultancy
discrepan cy
flippancy
pregnancy
expectancy
dormancy
poignancy
truancy
occupancy
piquancy
buoyancy
malignancy

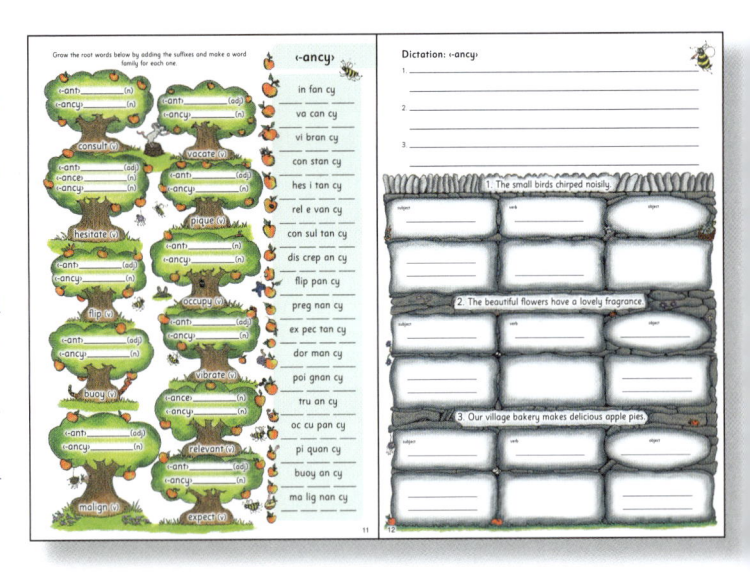

Activity Page 1
- The children copy out the syllables of each spelling word.
- They then complete the word family tree for each root word. To add the suffixes correctly, it will help the children if they refer to the spelling words to see how the suffix is added to each root word.

Activity Page 2
- The children parse the sentences, underlining each part of speech in the correct colour. In sentence 3, *our* is a possessive adjective, and *village* and *apple* are nouns acting as adjectives, so they should all be underlined in blue.
  1. The small birds chirped noisily.
  2. The beautiful flowers have a lovely fragrance.
  3. Our village bakery makes delicious apple pies.
- Then they complete the wall, putting each subject, verb and object (if there is one) in the top row and the words which describe (or modify) them directly underneath.
  1. Top: *birds - chirped -* (blank)
     Bottom: *The small - noisily -* (blank)
  2. Top: *flowers - have - fragrance*
     Bottom: *The beautiful -* (blank) *- a lovely*
  3. Top: *bakery - makes - pies*
     Bottom: *Our village -* (blank) *- delicious apple*

Dictation
- Dictate the following sentences for the children to write down:

1. There is a vacancy for an assistant in the village library.
2. She waited with great expectancy during her pregnancy.
3. "There is a discrepancy in the accounts," said the accountant.

- Remind them to use speech marks with the correct punctuation in sentence 3.

Grammar: Verb Tenses

Aim
- Revise the simple and continuous (or progressive) tenses. Ensure the children's understanding is secure before introducing the perfect tenses later (see page 49).

Introduction
- Write *to play* on the board. Discuss what kind of word it is (a verb) and how we know this (*to play* is the infinitive form or name of the verb).
- Verbs can be written in different tenses, describing what is happening in the past, present or future. By now the children should be able to identify and write the simple and continuous tenses.
- Draw a grid of six boxes on the board and add the tenses as you talk about them (each box should be large enough to include a simple sentence beneath the heading).

simple past	simple present	simple future
past continuous	present continuous	future continuous

- Discuss how the tenses are formed (see *Verbs*, pages 10–11). Sometimes a suffix is added, like ‹-ed› or ‹-ing›, sometimes an auxiliary verb is used, like *shall* or *will*, and sometimes both are used.
- Remind the children that when ‹-ing› is added to the verb it is called the present participle and that this form of the verb, along with the auxiliary verb *to be*, is used to make the continuous tenses. Remind them that some verbs have a tricky or irregular past tense, but *to be* is also tricky in the present tense.
- Conjugate *to be* with the class in the simple present, past and future, doing the pronoun actions.

Main Point
- Say *I play the flute* and ask which tense the sentence is in (the simple present). Write it in the correct box.
- Call out the sentence in another tense for the children to identify. Again, write it in the correct box.
- Do this in all six tenses, reminding the children of the spelling rules for adding ‹-ed› and ‹-ing› (see Spelling Rules, pages 28–29).

simple past	simple present	simple future
I played the flute	I play the flute	I shall/will play the flute
past continuous	**present continuous**	**future continuous**
I was playing the flute	I am playing the flute	I shall/will be playing the flute

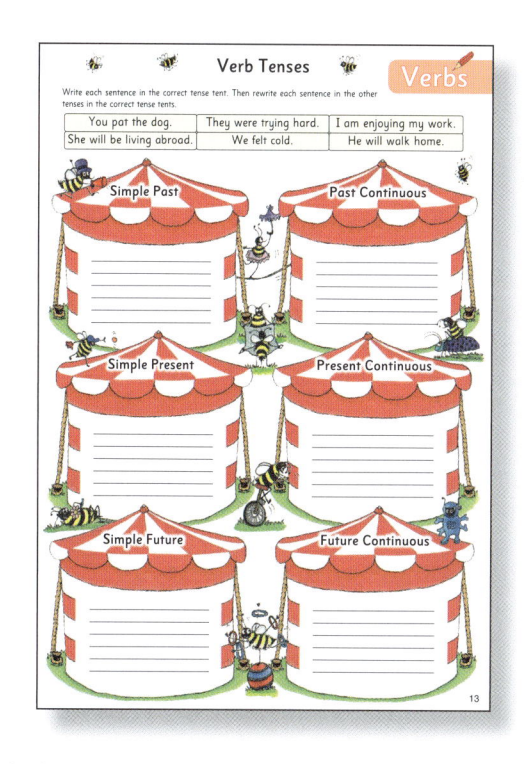

- Remind the class that the simple tenses describe an action which started and finished within a specific time, while the continuous tenses describe an action that has started and is still happening.
- The simple present also tends to describe actions that are repeated or usual, as in *I play the flute every day*.

Activity Page
- The children write each sentence in the correct tense tent:
  You pat the dog. (simple present)
  They were trying hard. (past continuous)
  I am enjoying my work. (present continuous)
  She will be living abroad. (future continuous)
  We felt cold. (simple past)
  He will walk home. (simple future)
- They then rewrite these sentences in the other tenses, putting them in the correct tense tents.

Extension Activity
- The children draw a grid like the one on the board and think of some simple sentences of their own to write in the six tenses.

Rounding Off
- Go over the activity page with the children, discussing their answers.
- If they have done the extension activity, ask some of the children to read out their sentences.

GRAMMAR 5 PUPIL BOOK: PAGE 14 & 15

Spelling: ‹-ence›

Spelling Test
- The children turn to the backs of their books and find the column labelled *Spelling Test 4*.
- In any order, call out the spelling words learnt last week. The children write the words on the lines.

Revision
- Revise these spellings of the long vowel sounds and ask the class to suggest words for each one: /ai/ ‹ai›, ‹ay›, ‹a_e›, ‹ei›, ‹eigh›, ‹a›; /ee/ ‹ee›, ‹ea›, ‹e_e›, ‹y›, ‹ey›, ‹ie›, ‹e›; /ie/ ‹ie›, ‹y›, ‹igh›, ‹i_e›, ‹i›; /oa/ ‹oa›, ‹ow›, ‹o_e›, ‹o›; /ue/ ‹ue›, ‹ew›, ‹u_e›, ‹u›.
- Flash cards can be used for reading and sound dictation for spelling.

Spelling Point
- Revise the soft ‹c› spellings for the /s/ sound: ‹ce›, ‹ci› and ‹cy›.
- Remind the children of the suffix ‹-ent›, which makes adjectives and nouns, like *independent* and *student*.
- Now introduce the spelling ‹-ence›. Like ‹-ance›, this suffix makes abstract nouns with the quality, state or action of the root word (so if two things are *different*, you can say there is a *difference*, and if you *prefer* one thing to another, that is your *preference*). This happens when the suffix is used with adjectives ending in ‹-ent› or added to verbs. If the root verb ends in ‹e›, then the usual spelling rules apply and the ‹e› is dropped before adding ‹ence›, so *confide* becomes *confidence* and *emerge* becomes *emergence*.
- The suffixes ‹-ance› and ‹-ence› are usually unstressed and have a neutral vowel sound, the schwa. This makes it difficult to hear the difference between words ending in ‹ance› and ‹ence›, and the spellings have to be learnt.
- Remind the children that if they are unsure of how to spell a word, they should look it up in a dictionary.

Spelling List
- Read the words with the class and discuss the meaning of any unfamiliar words.
- Ask the children to find and highlight every ‹ence› spelling.
- Point out any other spelling features, such as the letters saying their long vowel sound in s*i*lence, c*oi*ncidence and conv*e*nience, the ‹ex› saying /igz/ in *existence*, the ‹au› in *audience*, the soft ‹c› in *coincidence* and the soft ‹g› in *emergence* and *intelligence*.
- A useful spelling strategy is to 'say it as it sounds', emphasising, for example, the pure vowel sound of any schwas, as in *diff*e*rence* and *eloqu*e*nce*.

absence
silence
sentence
evidence
difference
fence
existence
coherence
confidence
eloquence
preference
audience
coincidence
emergence
experience
opulence
intelligence
convenience

- It is a good idea to blend and sound out the spelling words quickly every day with the class, emphasising the /e/ in ‹ence› to help remember the spelling.

Activity Page 1
- The children copy out the syllables of each spelling word.
- They then match the spelling words with their root words (*absence/absent, evidence/evident, difference/differ, existence/exist, coherence/cohere, confidence/confide, eloquence/eloquent, preference/prefer, coincidence/coincide, emergence/emerge, opulence/opulent*).
- Then they add either ‹-ance› or ‹-ence› to the root words to make abstract nouns, remembering to cross out the final ‹e› in *guide* before adding the suffix (*clearance, confidence, annoyance, assistance, guidance, preference, acceptance, difference, emergence, existence*).

Activity Page 2
- The children decide which suffix is needed to complete the words (*audience, disappearance, disturbance, attendance, eloquence, opulence, acquaintance, coincidence, coherence, absence, brilliance, advance*).
- Then they parse the sentence and complete the wall.
The hesitant cat slowly climbs a tall tree.
Top: *cat - climbs - tree*
Bottom: *The hesitant - slowly - a tall*

Dictation
- Dictate the following sentences for the children to write down:

1. "The orange dress is my preference," admitted the customer.
2. They waited in silence during her absence.
3. He spoke with great eloquence about his recent experience.

- Remind them to use speech marks with the correct punctuation in sentence 1.

Grammar: Irregular Verb 'To Have'

Aim
- Ensure the children can conjugate the irregular verb *to have* in the past, present and future, in both the simple and continuous tenses.

Introduction
- Briefly revise personal pronouns. Remind the children that a pronoun can change depending on whether the noun it replaces is the subject or the object of the sentence.
- Practise the pronouns with the class, saying them in order as you do the actions: *I/me* (point to yourself); *you/you* (point to someone else); *he/him* (point to a boy), *she/her* (point to a girl); *it/it* (point to the floor); *we/us* (point to yourself and others in a circle); *you/you* (point to two other people); *they/them* (point to the class next door).
- Subject pronouns are used when conjugating verbs. They can be divided into three groups, known as first, second and third person, which can be singular or plural: *I* is the first person singular and *we* is the first person plural. This is why a verb is always conjugated by saying *I* first, *you* second and *he/she/it* third for the singular and then *we*, *you* and *they* for the plural.

Main Point
- Remind the children that some verbs do not form the past tense by adding ‹-ed› to the root. Instead, the verb roots change when they are put into the past to form irregular (or tricky) pasts.
- The verb *to have* has the tricky past *had* and it is also slightly irregular in the present tense, as the third person singular is *has*.
- Like the verb *to be*, children can sometimes find *to have* difficult to identify as the verb in a sentence. However, it is important for the children to overcome this problem as *to have* is one of the most commonly used verbs and is used as an auxiliary verb to form the perfect tenses.
- Starting with the simple present, conjugate the verb *to have* as a class and write it on the board. Then do the same for the simple past.
- The children should be able to work out the future tense for themselves, as it is formed in the regular way with the auxiliary *shall* or *will* before *have* (*will* can be used with all the pronouns, but *shall* is only used with *I* and *we*). Write the future tense on the board, as the children conjugate the verb.

simple past	simple present	simple future
I had	I have	I shall/will have
you had	you have	you will have
he/she/it/had	he/she/it has	he/she/it will have
we had	we have	we shall/will have
you had	you have	you will have
they had	they have	they will have

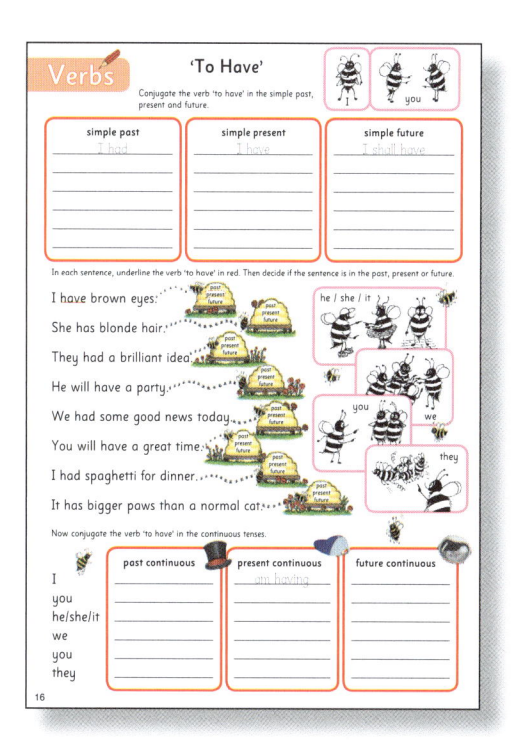

- Explain that the continuous tenses of *to have* are formed in the regular way, and ask the children to conjugate the verb in the past, present and future continuous.

Activity Page
- The children write inside the outlined word *Verbs*, using a red pencil.
- Then they conjugate the verb *to have* in the simple past, present and future.
- Next they identify *to have* in each sentence, underlining it in red, and identifying the tense (*have/present*, *has/present*, *had/past*, *will have/future*, *had/past*, *will have/future*, *had/past*, *has/present*).
- Finally, they conjugate *to have* in the continuous tenses, using the different forms of *to be* as the auxiliary verb, followed by the present participle, *having*.

Extension Activity
- Write some simple sentences on the board, such as *He has chocolate cake*.
- Ask the children to rewrite them in the other tenses.

Rounding Off
- Go over the children's work, checking their answers.
- If they have done the extension activity, ask some of the children to read out their sentences.

GRAMMAR 5 PUPIL BOOK: PAGE 17 & 18

Spelling: ‹-ency›

Spelling Test
- The children turn to the backs of their books and find the column labelled *Spelling Test 5*.
- In any order, call out the spelling words learnt last week. The children write the words on the lines.

Revision
- Revise these spellings of the long vowel sounds and ask the class to suggest words for each one: /ai/ ‹ai›, ‹ay›, ‹a_e›, ‹ei›, ‹eigh›, ‹a›; /ee/ ‹ee›, ‹ea›, ‹e_e›, ‹y›, ‹ey›, ‹ie›, ‹e›; /ie/ ‹ie›, ‹y›, ‹igh›, ‹i_e›, ‹i›; /oa/ ‹oa›, ‹ow›, ‹o_e›, ‹o›; /ue/ ‹ue›, ‹ew›, ‹u_e›, ‹u›.
- Flash cards can be used for reading and sound dictation for spelling.

Spelling Point
- Revise the soft ‹c› spellings for the /s/ sound: ‹ce›, ‹ci› and ‹cy›.
- Write the adjective *resident* and the nouns *residence* and *residency* on the board and underline the suffixes. Then introduce ‹-ency›. Explain that, just like ‹-ence›, this suffix makes abstract nouns with the quality, state or action of the root word when it is added either to verbs or to adjectives ending in ‹-ent› (so if a job is *urgent*, it must be done with *urgency*).
- Occasionally, the noun exists in both forms, as in *residence* and *residency*, but there can be subtle differences in meaning. Sometimes the meaning will be very different, as in *emergence* and *emergency*.
- Remind the class that groups of similar words like the ones on the board are called word families.
- Also point out that the syllables in ‹-ancy› and ‹-ency› are nearly always unstressed and have a neutral vowel sound, the schwa. This makes it difficult to hear the difference between words ending in the two suffixes, and the spellings have to be learnt.
- Remind the children that if they are unsure of how to spell a word, they should look it up in a dictionary.

Spelling List
- Read the words with the class and discuss the meaning of any unfamiliar words.
- Ask the children to find and highlight every ‹ency› spelling.
- Point out any other spelling features, such as the schwa in ‹-ency›, as well as in *interdependency*, the letters saying their long vowel sound (as in *agency*, *potency* and *frequency*, for example), the ‹e› saying /i/ in *emergency*, *efficiency* and *interdependency*, the soft ‹g› (examples include *regency* and

agency
currency
emergency
potency
tendency
urgency
regency
fluency
frequency
pungency
residency
efficiency
coherency
incompetency
proficiency
consistency
contingency
interdependency

pungency), the ‹ci› as /sh/ in*efficiency* and *proficiency*, the ‹ur› as /er/ in *urgency*, the ‹u› as /oo/ in *fluency*, the ‹s› as /z/ in *residency* and the ‹er› as /ear/ in *coherency*.
- It is a good idea to blend and sound out the spelling words quickly every day with the class, emphasising the /e/ in ‹ency› to help remember the spelling.

Activity Page 1
- The children copy out the syllables of each spelling word.
- They then complete the word family trees. To add the suffixes correctly, it will help the children if they refer to the spelling words to see how the suffix is added to each root word.

Activity Page 2
- The children conjugate the verb *to have* in the simple and continuous tenses. Remind them that, in the future tense, *shall* is only used in the first person singular and plural, but *will* can be used with all the pronouns.
- Then they parse the sentence and complete the wall.
- Point out that *beautifully* is an adverb made by adding ‹-ly› to the adjective *beautiful*.

He sang the old song beautifully.
Top: *He - sang - song*
Bottom: (blank) - *beautifully - the old*.

Dictation
- Dictate the following sentences:

1. The manager has a tendency to work late at the agency.
2. The audience left the building by the emergency exit.
3. "Will you want to exchange any currency?" asked the travel agent.

- Remind them to use speech marks with the correct punctuation in sentence 3.

Grammar: Present and Past Participles

Aim
- Revise the present participle and introduce the children to the past participle, which is used to form the perfect tenses.

Introduction
- Revise the present participle, discussing how it is formed by adding the suffix ‹-ing› to a root verb.
- By now, the children should know that the present participle helps form the continuous tenses (as in *I was running; I am running; I will be running*).
- They may also remember that it can be used as an adjective, as in *the galloping horse disappeared from view*.
- Ask the children to call out some verbs and conjugate each one in the continuous tenses.
- Then ask them to think of some sentences or phrases that use a present participle as an adjective (such as *the screaming baby*, *a winding road* or *an interesting book*).
- Present participles also take the same form as gerunds (which act as nouns, as in *dancing is fun*), but the children can learn about these when they are older.

Main Point
- Explain that there is another participle, the past participle, which is also used in verb tenses or as an adjective. If the verb is regular, the past participle is formed in the same way as the simple past tense: by adding the suffix ‹-ed›.
- Revise the rules for adding ‹-ing› and ‹-ed›, depending on how the root verb is spelt:
  - If the root verb ends in a consonant which is not immediately after a short vowel sound, simply add the suffix (as in *dreaming* and *dreamed*).
  - If the root verb ends in ‹e›, remove it before adding the suffix (as in *baking* and *baked*), except when adding ‹-ing› to a word like *tie*. In this case, ‹ie› is replaced by ‹y› to avoid having two ‹i›s next to each other: so the present participle is *tying*, but the past participle is *tied*.
  - If the root verb ends in a consonant immediately after a short, stressed vowel sound, double the final consonant before adding the suffix (as in *chatting* and *chatted*)
  - If a root verb ends in ‹y›, simply add the suffix, unless you are adding ‹-ed› to a verb which has a consonant immediately before the ‹y›, like *worry*. Normally, we would expect 'shy ‹i›' to return when a suffix is added, as it is no longer on the end of the word; it does so in the past participle *worried* but not in *worrying* (where it would look odd to have two ‹i›s together), nor in *played* (where the ‹y› is part of the digraph).
- Write the verbs *test, wave, lie, clap, try* and *stay* on the board and create two columns, one for each participle.
- Ask some of the children to come and add the suffixes, using the spelling rules and putting them in the correct column (*testing/tested, waving/waved, lying/lied, clapping/clapped, trying/tried, staying/stayed*).

Activity Page
- The children write the present and past participle for each verb in the butterfly house, using the spelling rules for adding ‹-ing› and ‹-ed› (*accepting/accepted, entering/entered, dying/died, marrying/married, annoying/annoyed, damaging/damaged, disturbing/disturbed, copying/copied, chopping/chopped, permitting/permitted, competing/competed, applauding/applauded, spraying/sprayed, exercising/exercised, terrifying/terrified, worrying/worried, unwrapping/unwrapped, disapproving/disapproved*).

Extension Activity
- The children use some present participles from the activity page to write sentences in the continuous tenses or use them as adjectives in phrases.

Rounding Off
- Go over the children's work, checking their answers.
- If they have done the extension activity, ask some children to read out their sentences or phrases.

GRAMMAR 5 PUPIL BOOK: PAGE 20 & 21

Spelling: ‹multi-›

Spelling Test
- The children turn to the backs of their books and find the column labelled *Spelling Test 6*.
- In any order, call out the spelling words learnt last week. The children write the words on the lines.

Revision
- Revise prefixes, which are one or more syllables added at the beginning of a word to change or add meaning.
- The word *prefix* itself is a good example: the prefix ‹pre› means *before*, so *prefix* means *fixed before*.
- Write these words on the board, identify the prefixes, and discuss how they modify the meaning: **mid**day, **mid**night, **mid**summer, **semi**circle, **semi**-final, **semi**-conscious.
- The prefix ‹mid-› means *in the middle* and ‹semi-› literally means *half*, but can also mean *partly* or *almost*.
- Look at the last two words and remind the children that sometimes a hyphen separates the prefix and root word.
- There is no useful rule for knowing whether there will be a hyphen or not, so encourage the children to use a dictionary if they are not sure.

Spelling Point
- Write *multitude*, *multiply* and *multipurpose* on the board and ask the children whether they know what the letters ‹multi› mean: the word *multitude* can mean a crowd of many people, if your problems *multiply* you have many more problems than before and if something is *multipurpose* it can be used in more than one way.
- Explain that ‹multi-› is a prefix meaning *many* or *more than one* and comes from the Latin *multus*, meaning *much* or *many*.
- Ask the children if they can think of any words beginning with the prefix ‹multi-›.

Spelling List
- Go through the list, look at how the prefix changes or adds meaning to each word and discuss the meaning of any unfamiliar words.
- Ask the children to find and highlight the ‹multi› spelling each time.
- Point out other spelling features, such as the ‹ck› after the short /a/ in *multipack*, the ‹ay› spelling of /ai/ in *multiplayer* and *multilayered*, the ‹y› saying /ie/ in *multiply*, the ‹u_e› in *multitude*, the letters saying their long vowel sound in *multimedia* and *multiplication*, the ‹o› saying /u/ in *multicoloured*, the ‹ur› in *multipurpose*, the soft ‹c› in *multiplicity*, the ‹tion› saying

multitask
multipack
multiplayer
multiplex
multiply
multitude
multiple
multimedia
multilayered
multicoloured
multitalented
multipurpose
multiplicity
multiplication
multimillionaire
multinational
multicultural
multisyllabic

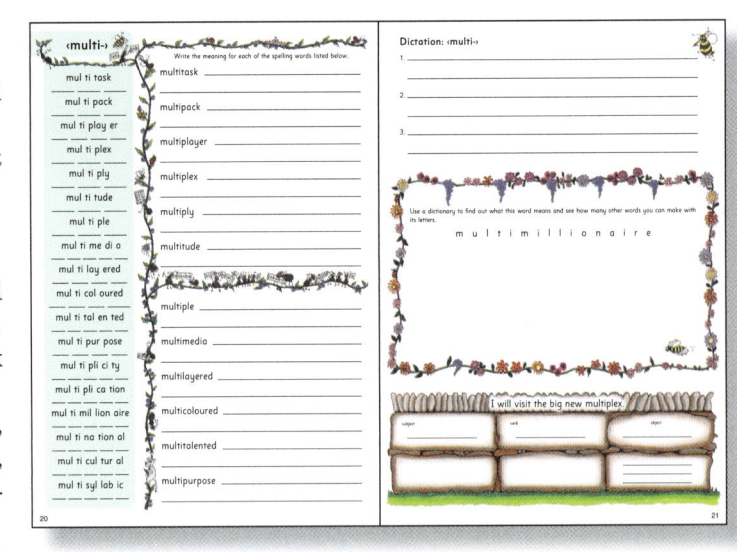

/shun/ in *multiplication*, the ‹aire› spelling of /air/ in *multimillionaire*, the ‹tur› saying /cher/ in *cultural* and the ‹y› saying /i/ in *multisyllabic*.
- Also point out the different spellings of /ool/ at the end of *multip**le***, *multination**al*** and *multicultur**al***.
- It is a good idea to blend and sound out the spelling words quickly every day with the children, using the 'say it as it sounds' strategy where appropriate, or you could break down the words into prefix and root word.

Activity Page 1
- The children copy out the syllables of each spelling word.
- They then write the meaning for the listed spelling words.
- Encourage them to look up a word in the dictionary if they are unsure of its meaning.

Activity Page 2
- The children look up the word *multimillionaire* in the dictionary to check its meaning. They make as many other words as they can with its letters.
- Then they parse the sentence and complete the wall.
- All parts of the verb should be underlined in red.
  I will visit the big new multiplex.
  Top: *I - will visit - multiplex*
  Bottom: (blank) - (blank) - *the big new*

Dictation
- Dictate the following sentences:

1. "I know my multiplication tables!" exclaimed the boy.
2. The convenience store sells multipacks of orange juice
3. A multitude of stars were shining in the night sky.

- In sentence 1, remind them to use speech marks with the correct punctuation

Grammar: Perfect Tenses

Aim
- Develop the children's understanding of verbs and introduce the perfect tenses.
- Explain how the perfect tenses are formed by using an auxiliary verb, *to have*, followed by the past participle.

Introduction
- Briefly revise the simple and continuous tenses. Discuss how they are formed and when they may be used (see page 43).
- Then conjugate the verb *to have* with the class in the simple present, past and future, doing the pronoun actions (see page 45).

Main Point
- The perfect tenses, like the simple and continuous tenses, can happen in the past, present and future.
- Write these sentences on the board and ask the children to identify the verb in each one: *I had walked* to school, *I have walked* to school and *I will have walked* to school.
- Explain that these are called the perfect tenses, which are formed by adding the past participle (in this case *walked*) to the simple past, present or future of the auxiliary verb *to have*.
- Remind the class that the simple tenses describe actions that start and finish within a specific time (the simple present also tends to describe actions that are repeated or usual, as in *I walk to school every day*).
- The continuous tenses describe actions that have started and are still happening, either at that very moment or as a longer action in progress (as in *I am learning to play the flute*).
- The perfect tenses are used to describe actions that have already been completed. They usually describe general experiences or unspecified points in the past (as in *I have stayed at that hotel several times*), or actions that, although complete, still have some connection to the present (as in *I have just finished my homework*).
- Starting with the present perfect, conjugate the verb *to look* with the class:

past perfect	present perfect	future perfect
I had looked you had looked he/she/it had looked we had looked you had looked they had looked	I have looked you have looked he/she/it has looked we have looked you have looked they have looked	I shall/will have looked you will have looked he/she/it will have looked you will have looked they will have looked

Activity Page
- The children conjugate the verb *to finish* in the past perfect, present perfect and future perfect, writing the verbs in the correct tense tents.
- The children need to remember to use the correct form of the verb *to have* in the third person singular of the present perfect (*has*) and to only use *shall* in the first person singular and plural for the future perfect.
- They then write a sentence at the bottom of each tent, using the verb in its correct tense.

Extension Activity
- Make flashcards with the following infinitives on: *to accept, to destroy, to marry, to unlock, to identify, to behave, to scrub, to compare, to weigh, to slip, to confess, to copy, to empty, to applaud, to decorate, to compete, to fix, to beg, to ban, to annoy, to judge, to introduce, to juggle, to laugh, to stay, to amuse, to chop, to permit, to provide, to multiply*.
- Ask each child to pick a card. They then use the verb they have chosen to write a sentence in each of the perfect tenses.
- They can do this on a separate sheet of paper, using a different pronoun each time.
- The verbs selected allow plenty of practice in using the spelling rules for adding ‹-ed› to form the past participle.

Rounding Off
- Go over the activity page with the children, checking their answers.
- If they have done the extension activity, ask some of the children to read out their sentences.

GRAMMAR 5 PUPIL BOOK: PAGE 23 & 24

Spelling: ‹auto-›

Spelling Test
- The children turn to the backs of their books and find the column labelled *Spelling Test 7*.
- In any order, call out the spelling words learnt last week. The children write the words on the lines.

Revision
- Revise prefixes, which are one or more syllables added at the beginning of a word to change or add meaning.
- Write these words on the board, identify the prefixes ‹un-› and ‹dis-› and discuss how they modify the meaning: **un**afraid, **un**pleasant, **un**popular, **dis**please, **dis**comfort, **dis**approve.
- Both prefixes are used to make antonyms or opposites of the root word so they both mean *not*; ‹dis-› often has the particular meaning of *undo* or *remove*.

Spelling Point
- Write *autograph*, *autobiography* and *automatic* on the board and ask the children whether they know what the letters ‹auto› mean: famous people's *autographs* are prized for being in their own handwriting, people write about themselves in *autobiographies*, and if a machine is *automatic* it does the work itself, so we don't have to.
- Explain that ‹auto-› is a prefix meaning *self*, as in *our own* or *by ourselves/itself*, and comes from the Greek *autos*.
- It is also commonly used in words like *automobile*, which relate to cars and similar vehicles. When they were first invented, cars were remarkable for moving by themselves, rather than being pulled by horses.
- Ask the children if they can think of any words beginning with the prefix ‹auto-›.

Spelling List
- Go through the list, look at how the prefix changes or adds meaning to each word and discuss the meaning of any unfamiliar words.
- Ask the children to find and highlight the ‹auto› spelling each time.
- Point out the ‹au› spelling and ‹o› as /oa/ in *auto*, the schwas (as in *aut*o*matic*), the suffixes in *automatic* and *automatically*, the ‹y› as /ee/ in *autonomy*, *autopsy*, *autocracy*, *automatically* and *autobiography*, the long vowel sounds in *autopilot*, *automation*, *automobile*, *automotive*, *autofocus* and *autobiography*, the ‹tion› in *automation*, the ‹i_e› as /ee/ in *automobile*, the ‹ph› in *autograph* and *autobiography*, the ‹ive› as /iv/ in *automotive* and the soft ‹c› in *autocracy*.

Spelling List
auto
automatic
autonomy
automated
automaton
autopilot
automation
automobile
autograph
automotive
autopsy
autocrat
autoimmune
autofocus
autocracy
autonomous
automatically
autobiography

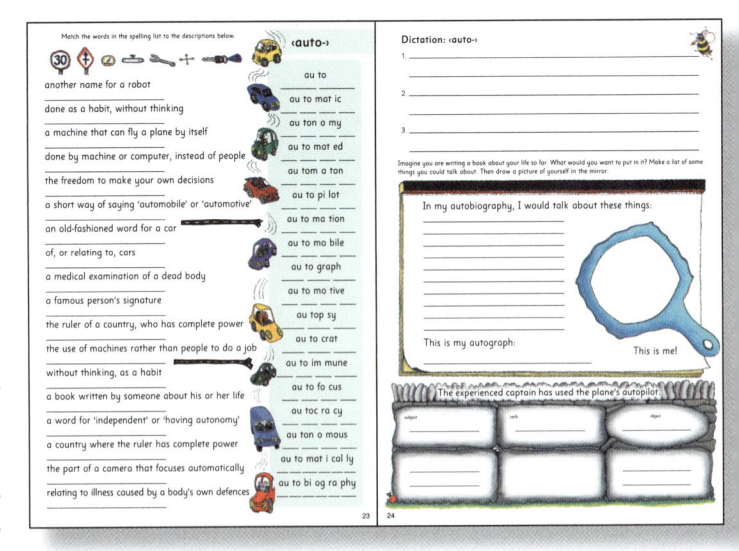

- Blend and sound out the spelling words quickly every day with the class, using the 'say it as it sounds' strategy where appropriate, or you could break down the words into prefix and root word.

Activity Page 1
- The children copy out the syllables of each spelling word.
- They then read the phrases and decide which spelling words they describe (*automaton*, *automatic*, *autopilot*, *automated*, *autonomy*, *auto*, *automobile*, *automotive*, *autopsy*, *autograph*, *autocrat*, *automation*, *automatically*, *autobiography*, *autonomous*, *autocracy*, *autofocus*, *autoimmune*).
- If they are unsure of any words, encourage the children to use a dictionary.

Activity Page 2
- The children make a list of things they might talk about if they were writing their autobiography.
- They then sign their autograph and draw a picture of themselves.
- Then they parse the sentence and complete the wall.
- Possessive nouns always act as adjectives, so *plane's* should be underlined in blue. All parts of the verb should be underlined in red.
  The experienced captain has used the plane's autopilot.
  Top: *captain - has used - autopilot*
  Bottom: *The experienced - (blank) - the plane's*

Dictation
- Dictate the following sentences:

1. "This camera has autofocus," explained the assistant.
2. The doors opened automatically as we reached the multiplex.
3. She was confident she could get the actor's autograph.

- In sentence 1, remind the children to use speech marks with the correct punctuation.

Grammar: Contractions and the Verb 'To Have'

Aim
- Revise the use of the apostrophe in contractions. Explain how the auxiliary verb *to have* is often contracted in the perfect tenses.

Introduction
- Briefly revise the verb *to have*, conjugating it with the class in the simple and continuous tenses.
- Like *to be*, this is a commonly used verb, but it can be difficult for children to recognise because it has tricky or irregular parts.
- Write some sentences on the board and ask the children to identify the verb in each one: *He **has** big feet; I **had** a large lunch; We **will be having** a rest soon; She **is** taller than me; You **were** being very good; They **will be** late for school.*

Main Point
- Remind the children that the verb *to have* can be used as an auxiliary verb to make the perfect tenses.
- Ask them to suggest some sentences using the perfect tenses and write them on the board.
- Explain that while this is how we would write these sentences in a formal piece of writing, it is probably not how we would say them if we were speaking to someone.
- It is more likely we would shorten a sentence like *I have walked here* by joining together the words *I* and *have* to make *I've*.
- Write the sentence out in full on the board and ask the children which letters need to be taken out to make *I have*.
- Rub out ‹ha› and put an apostrophe in its place. Then ask the children what we call this (a contraction).
- Go through the other contractions for the perfect tenses with the class:

past perfect (had)	present perfect (have/has)	future perfect (shall/will have)
I'd walked	I've walked	I'll have walked
you'd walked	you've walked	you'll have walked
he'd walked	he's walked	he'll have walked
she'd walked	she's walked	she'll have walked
it'd walked	it's walked	it'll have walked
we'd walked	we've walked	we'll have walked
you'd walked	you've walked	you'll have walked
they'd walked	they've walked	they'll have walked

- Point out that in *I'll* and *we'll* the letters that have been removed could be either the ‹sha› from *shall* or the ‹wi› from *will*.
- *He's*, *she's* and *it's* can also stand for *he is*, *she is* and *it is* and the children need to read the sentence to decide which verb is being contracted.
- For this reason, these contractions are never used when *to have* is acting as the main verb: we would never say, for example, *He's blue eyes* for *He has blue eyes*.

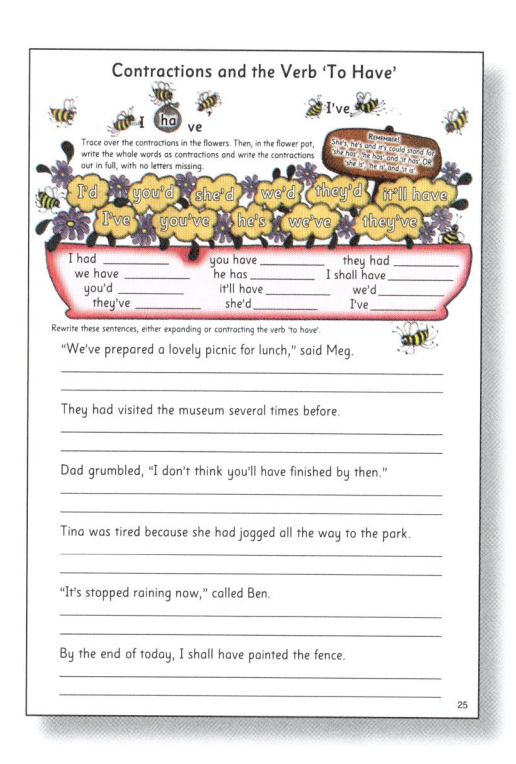

Activity Page
- The children practise the contractions for *to have*. First they write inside the outlined contractions in the flowers.
- They then look at the words in the flower pot and write the whole words as contractions and the contractions as whole words (*I'd, you've, they'd, we've, he's, I'll have, you had, it will have, we had, they have, she had, I have*).
- Then they rewrite the sentences below, either expanding or contracting the verb in each one (*We have prepared, They'd visited, you will have finished, she'd jogged, It has stopped, I'll have painted*).

Extension Activity
- Make pairs of flashcards: *they had/they'd, it has/it's, she will have/she'll have, I shall have/I'll have, you had/you'd, we have/we've, she had/she'd, I have/I've, they will have/they'll have, you have/you've, he had/he'd, we will have/we'll have, I had/I'd, they have/they've, he will have/he'll have, she has/she's, you will have/you'll have, we had/we'd, it will have/it'll have, he has/he's, it had/it'd.*
- Give the children a selection of the cards. They then match the pairs.
- They could then work in pairs, taking it in turns to choose a card and read it to their partner. If the card shows a contraction, the partner has to say it aloud as whole words. If it shows full words, the partner has to say the corresponding contraction and spell it. To turn this into a morning or filler activity, add more pairs of cards and laminate the whole set.

Rounding Off
- Go over the activity page with the children, checking their answers.

GRAMMAR 5 PUPIL BOOK: PAGE 26 & 27

Spelling: ‹mega-›, ‹micro-›

Spelling Test
- The children turn to the backs of their books and find the column labelled *Spelling Test 8*.
- In any order, call out the spelling words learnt last week. The children write the words on the lines.

Revision
- Revise prefixes, which are one or more syllables added at the beginning of a word to change or add meaning.
- Write these words on the board, identify the prefix ‹im-› and discuss how it modifies the meaning: **im**possible, **im**mortal, **im**proper, **im**mobile, **im**personal, **im**balance.
- This is another prefix meaning *not*, so it makes antonyms or opposites of the root words.
- Ask the children what these root words have in common: they begin with one of three letters: ‹m›, ‹p› or ‹b›.
- Explain that the prefix ‹im-› is an alternative spelling of ‹in-› (as in *invisible, incomplete, incapable, inactive* and *incorrect*) when the prefix comes before the letters ‹m›, ‹p› or ‹b›.

Spelling Point
- Write the words *megaphone* and *microscope* on the board.
- Ask the children whether they know what the letters ‹mega› and ‹micro› mean: a *megaphone* is something you talk into to make your voice sound much louder, and a *microscope* is used by scientists to see extremely small things.
- Explain that both these prefixes have a Greek origin, with ‹mega-› (from *megas*) meaning *great* and ‹micro-› (from *mikros*) meaning *small*. They both also have specific technical meanings: as a measurement, ‹mega-› means *million* (a *megawatt* is a million units of electrical power) and ‹micro-› means *millionth*.
- Ask the children if they can think of any words beginning with these prefixes.

Spelling List
- Go through the list, look at how each prefix changes or adds meaning to the word and discuss the meaning of any unfamiliar words.
- Ask the children to find and highlight the ‹mega› or ‹micro› spelling each time.
- Point out the schwas (such as the swallowed ‹a› in *mega*), the ‹ck› after the short /u/ in *megabucks*, the letters saying their long vowel sound in the prefix *micro-*, *microbiology, microprocessor* and *megalomania*, the ‹ph› saying /f/ in *microphone* and *megaphone*, the ‹wa› saying /wo/ and double

megastar
megabit
megabucks
microchip
microfilm
megalith
microscope
microbe
microwave
microphone
megaphone
megawatt
microscopic
microbiology
microprocessor
megabyte
megahertz
megalomania

‹t› in *megawatt*, the suffix in *microscopic*, the ‹y› saying /ee/ and soft ‹g› in *microbiology*, the soft ‹c› in *microprocessor*, the ‹y_e› saying /ie/ in *megabyte* and the ‹tz› in *megahertz*.
- It is a good idea to blend and sound out the spelling words quickly every day with the children, using the 'say it as it sounds' strategy where appropriate, or you could break down the words into prefix and root word.

Activity Page 1
- The children copy out the syllables of each spelling word.
- They then write out some of the spelling words in the prefix fish, putting the prefixes in the fish's heads and the root words in the bodies.

Activity Page 2
- The children rewrite the two sentences in the past, present and future perfect (*had played/copied, has played/have copied, will have played/copied*).
- Then they parse the sentence and complete the wall. *College* is a noun acting as an adjective and should be underlined in blue. *Previously* is an adverb made by adding ‹-ly› to the adjective *previous*.
  The college student previously studied microbiology.
  Top: *student - studied - microbiology*
  Bottom: *The college - previously -* (blank)

Dictation
- Dictate the following sentences:

1. "Can I exchange the megaphone for a microphone?" asked Jane.
2. The multitalented megastar has written his autobiography.
3. The microbiologist looked at the microbes down the microscope.

- In sentence 1, remind them to use speech marks with the correct punctuation. *Jane* is a proper noun and needs a capital letter.

Grammar: Irregular Past Participles

Aim
- Develop the children's understanding of past participles and introduce the idea that many past participles are irregular or tricky and need to be learnt.

Introduction
- Briefly revise the past participle, discussing how it is formed by adding the suffix ‹-ed› to a regular verb root.
- Ask the children when the past participle is used and see if they can think of any examples.
- They have recently learnt that it helps form the perfect tenses (as in *I had waited*; *I have waited*; *I will have waited*).
- They may also remember that it can be used as an adjective (in the same way that the present participle can, as in *the frightened boy*).
- Discuss how the perfect tenses are formed and write examples on the board, using regular verbs like *walk*, *play* and *like* (see page 49).

Main Point
- Whereas the present participle is always formed by adding ‹-ing› to the root verb, the past participle of irregular verbs can be formed in a variety of ways with no clear rules for which verbs take which spellings.
- Children who are native speakers of English will be using these forms quite naturally in their written and spoken language, even if they do not know what a past participle is.
- Children who are non-native speakers will need a lot more practice to know which one to use.
- A good dictionary will always list the irregular past tense and past participle of a verb, so if the children are not sure which form to use in their writing, encourage them to look it up.
- Although there are many ways to form irregular past participles, there are some common patterns that the children may recognise.
- Write *swim*, *swam*, *swum* on the board and ask the children to put these into sentences.
- These different forms come from Old English, where a change in vowel letter indicates a change in tense.
- *Swim* is the verb name used in the infinitive and present tense form. *Swam* – where the ‹i› changes to ‹a› – is the irregular past tense form. *Swum* – where the vowel changes again, this time to ‹u› – is the irregular past participle. So we would say *I swim every day*, *I swam yesterday* and *I have swum at the pool recently*.
- Ask the children if they can suggest other examples and put them on the board.
- Now write *write, wrote, written* and *fall, fell, fallen* on the board. Ask the children if they can see the pattern in these different verb forms.
- Like before, the vowel sound changes in the past tense, but the past participle is formed by adding either ‹-n› or ‹-en› to the present tense form.

- Point out also that in the past participle *written*, the doubling rule is used to change the long vowel into the short vowel sound.
- Look at other examples from the activity page and discuss their formation with the class.

Activity Page
- The children write the verb forms for the simple present, simple past and past participle in the two greenhouses, remembering to use the doubling rule when ‹-en› follows a short vowel sound.
Top: *swim/swam/swum, ring/rang/rung, sink/sank/sunk, begin/began/begun, drink/drank/drunk, sing/sang/sung, stink/stank/stunk, spring/sprang/sprung, shrink/shrank/shrunk*
Bottom: *grow/grew/grown, bite/bit/bitten, draw/drew/drawn, write/wrote/written, fall/fell/fallen, know/knew/known, take/took/taken, give/gave/given, shake/shook/shaken, hide/hid/hidden*

Extension Activity
- The children choose some irregular verbs from the activity page (one from each greenhouse) and write sentences for each verb form. For example, *I grow carrots every year*, *I grew carrots last year* and *I have grown carrots in the past*.

Rounding Off
- Go over the activity page with the children, discussing their answers.
- If they have done the extension activity, ask some children to read out their sentences.

Grammar 5 Pupil Book: Page 29 & 30

Spelling: ‹super-›

Spelling Test
- The children turn to the backs of their books and find the column labelled *Spelling Test 9*.
- Call out the spelling words learnt last week.

Revision
- Revise prefixes, which are one or more syllables added at the beginning of a word to change or add meaning.
- Write these words on the board, identify the prefixes ‹il-› and ‹ir-›, and discuss how they modify the meaning: *illegal*, *illogical*, *illiterate*, *irrational*, *irregular*, *irresponsible*.
- The prefixes ‹il-› and ‹ir-› are two more alternative spellings of the prefix ‹in-›, meaning *not*, and they are used before words starting with ‹l›, for ‹il-›, and ‹r›, for ‹ir-›.

Spelling Point
- Write *superstar*, *superior* and *superimpose* on the board. Ask the children whether they know what the letters ‹super› mean: a *superstar* is an extremely famous actor or musician, a *superior* officer has a higher rank, and if you *superimpose* one image on another, you put it on top of the other so that both can be seen.
- Explain that ‹super-› comes from the Latin for *above* or *beyond* and is used to indicate a higher position, degree or quality.
- Ask the children if they can think of any words beginning with the prefix ‹super-›.

Spelling List
- Go through the list, look at how the prefix changes or adds meaning to each word and discuss the meaning of any unfamiliar words.
- Ask the children to find and highlight the ‹super› spelling each time.
- Point out the schwas (as in *super* and *supermodel*), the suffix in *supersonic*, the ‹e› saying /ear/ and the ‹i› saying /ee/ in *superiority* and its root word *superior*, the ‹ow› spelling of /ou/ in *superpower*, the ‹s› saying /z/ in *supervise*, the ‹ive› saying /iv/ in *superlative*, the ‹ture› saying /cher/ in *superstructure*, the ‹sion› saying /zhun/ in *supervision*, the soft ‹c› in *supercilious*, the ‹k› spelling in *supermarket* and the long vowel sound of ‹u› in *superfluous*.
- It is a good idea to blend and sound out the spelling words quickly every day with the children, using the 'say it as it sounds' strategy where appropriate, or you could break down the words into prefix and root word.

super
superb
superstar
supersonic
superglue
supermodel
superior
supersede
superimpose
superpower
supervise
superlative
superiority
superstructure
supervision
supercilious
supermarket
superfluous

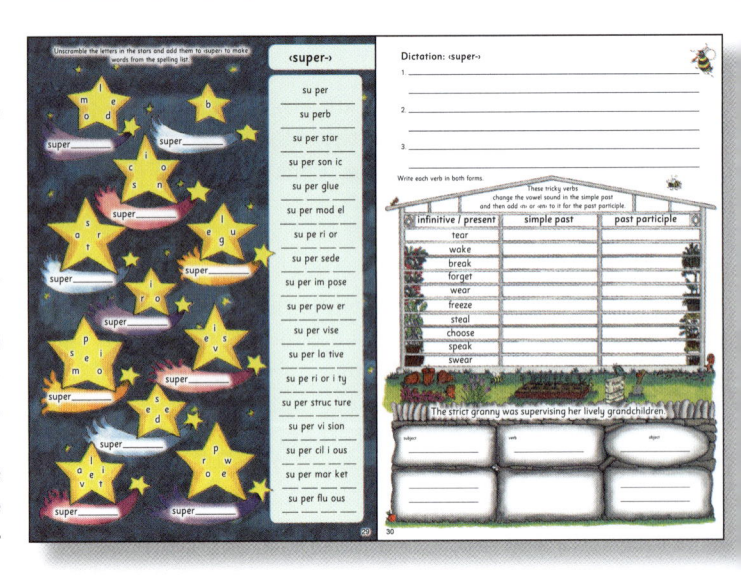

Activity Page 1
- The children copy out the syllables of each spelling word.
- They then unscramble the letters in the stars and add them to ‹super-› to make some of the spelling words (*supermodel*, *superb*, *supersonic*, *superstar*, *superglue*, *superior*, *superimpose*, *supervise*, *supersede*, *superlative*, *superpower*).

Activity Page 2
- The children write out the simple past and past participles for each verb (*tear*: *tore/torn*, *wake*: *woke/woken*, *break*: *broke/broken*, *forget*: *forgot/forgotten*, *wear*: *wore/worn*, *freeze*: *froze/frozen*, *steal*: *stole/stolen*, *choose*: *chose/chosen*, *speak*: *spoke/spoken*, *swear*: *swore/sworn*).
- Then they parse the sentence and complete the wall.
- All parts of the verb should be underlined in red. Although *lively* ends in ‹-ly›, it is an adjective describing the children and should be underlined in blue. *Her* is a possessive adjective describing who the granchildren belong to.

The strict granny was supervising her lively grandchildren.

Top: *granny - was supervising - grandchildren*
Bottom: *The strict - (blank) - her lively*

Dictation
- Dictate the following sentences:

1. "Is it a supersonic plane?" asked the girl.
2. I bought some superglue at the supermarket.
3. The superstar gave a superb performance.

- Remind the children to use speech marks with the correct punctuation in sentence 1.

Grammar: Identifying Verb Tenses

Aim
- Reinforce the children's understanding of the simple, continuous and perfect tenses, and develop their ability to identify the tenses in sentences.

Introduction
- Write *to unlock* on the board and ask what form of the verb this is (the infinitive).
- Discuss with the class how the infinitive is the name of the verb. Explain that without more information you cannot say who did the unlocking or when it was done.
- Draw the grid below on the board (leaving the white boxes empty for now), reminding the children that verbs describe what is happening in the past, present or future. Add the column labels as you do this.
- Ask the children what tenses they have learnt so far and label each row as they call them out: simple, continuous and perfect.
- Discuss how the tenses are formed (see pages 10–11). Ask some of the children to come up to the board and write the verb *unlock* in one of the nine tenses, putting it in the correct box:

	Past	Present	Future
Simple	I unlocked	I unlock	I shall unlock
Continuous	I was unlocking	I am unlocking	I shall be unlocking
Perfect	I had unlocked	I have unlocked	I shall have unlocked

Main Point
- Write the sentence *He will be unlocking the gate at eight o'clock* on the board. Ask a child to come up, identify the verb (*will be unlocking*) and underline it in red.
- Ask the class which tense they think this is (the future continuous) and discuss how they know this (the continuous tenses are formed by using the auxiliary verb *to be* with the present participle, and the future tense of *to be* is *shall/will be*).
- Erase *will be unlocking* and replace it with *had unlocked*, ask which tense this is (past perfect) and discuss again how the children know this (the perfect tenses are formed by using the auxiliary verb *to have* with the past participle, and the past tense of *to have* is *had*).
- Change the tense a few more times, in each case asking the children to identify the tense and discussing how they came to that decision.

Activity Page
- The children write inside the outlined word *Verbs*, using a red pencil.
- They then read each sentence and identify the verb, underlining it in red.
- They then decide which tense is being used, and write it in the long tense tent (*am balancing*: present continuous, *were scavenging*: past continuous, *has damaged*: present perfect, *will be going*: future continuous, *change*: simple present, *will have written*: future perfect, *had grown*: past perfect, *will emerge*: simple future, *received*: simple past).

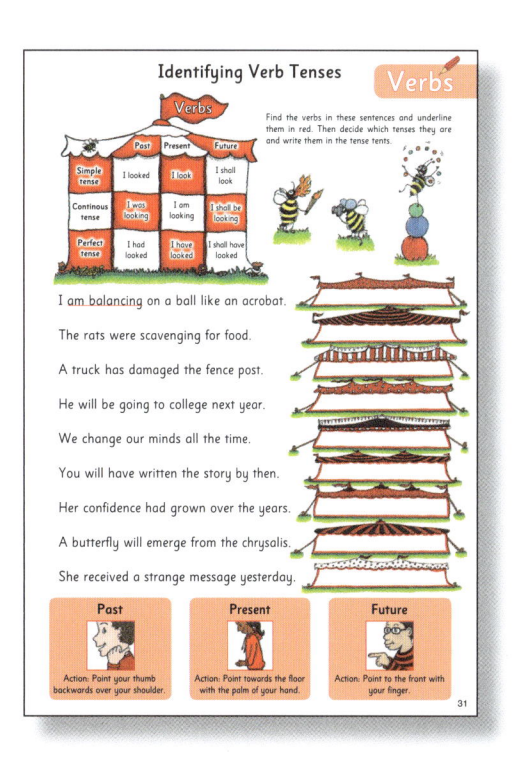

Extension Activity
- The children practise writing sentences in the nine tenses they now know on a separate sheet of paper.
- They could choose one of the sentences from the activity page and write it out in each tense.
- Alternatively, some small cards with the tenses written on them could be given to the children. The children can then pick a card and rewrite the first sentence from the activity page in the tense selected. They then pick another card and write the second sentence in that tense, and so on.

Rounding Off
- Go over the activity page with the children, discussing their answers.
- If they have done the extension activity, ask some of the children to read out their sentences.

GRAMMAR 5 PUPIL BOOK: PAGE 32 & 33

Spelling: ‹cent-›, ‹kilo-›, ‹milli-›

Spelling Test
- The children turn to the backs of their books and find the column labelled *Spelling Test 10*.
- Call out the spelling words learnt last week.

Revision
- Revise prefixes, which are one or more syllables added at the beginning of a word to change or add meaning.
- Write these words on the board, identify the prefixes and discuss how they modify the meaning: **sub**marine (under), **anti**freeze (opposite or against), **pre**fix (before), **trans**port (across), **tele**phone (at a distance), **inter**national (between).

Spelling Point
- Write the words *century*, *kilogram* and *millisecond* on the board and underline the prefix in each word.
- Ask the children whether they know what the prefixes mean. Explain that they all relate to numbers: a *century* is a period of one hundred years, a *kilogram* weighs one thousand grams, a *millisecond* is a thousandth of a second and a *million* is a thousand thousands.
- The prefixes ‹cent-›/‹centi-› and ‹milli-› are of Latin origin and mean a hundred and a thousand respectively (*million* in Latin means *a big thousand*).
- The prefix ‹kilo-› comes from the Greek word *khilioi* and also means *a thousand*.
- Ask the children if they can think of any words beginning with these prefixes.

Spelling List
- Go through the list, look at how the prefix changes or adds meaning to each word and discuss the meaning of any unfamiliar words.
- Ask the children to find and highlight the prefix in each word.
- Point out the soft ‹c› in ‹cent›, the schwas (as in *century* and *kilogram*), the ‹y› saying /ee/ on the end of *century* and *centenary*, the spelling of /ee/ in *kilo*, *millilitre* and *centenary*, the letters saying their long vowel sound in *kilo* and *metre*, the ‹re› spelling of /er/ in *metre* and *litre* (adopted from the French spelling), the ‹a› saying /air/ in *centenarian*, the double ‹n› in *centennial* and the suffix in *centenary*.
- Explain that *centennial* is another word for *centenary* and means *the hundredth anniversary*.
- It is a good idea to blend and sound out the spelling words quickly every day with the children, using the 'say it as it sounds' strategy where appropriate, or you could break down the words into prefix and root word.

cent
century
kilo
million
kilogram
milligram
centigrade
centipede
millisecond
centimetre
millimetre
millipede
centenarian
centennial
centenary
kilometre
millilitre
millionth

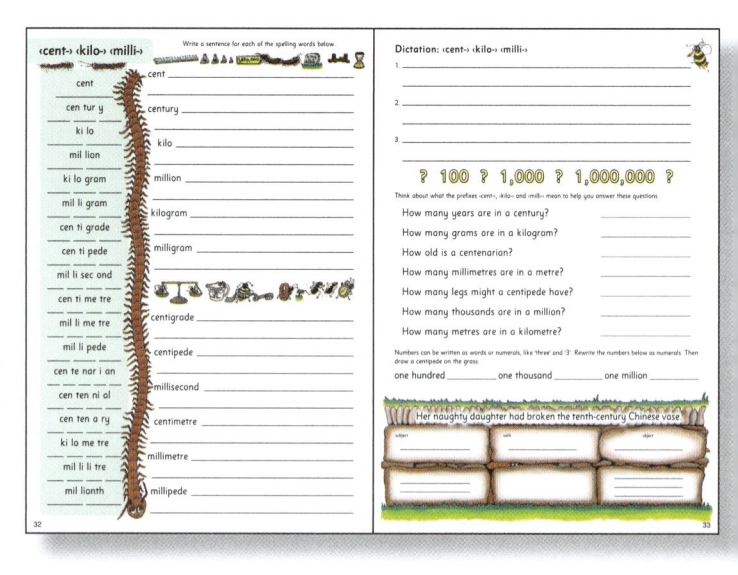

Activity Page 1
- The children copy out the syllables of each spelling word.
- They then write a sentence for each of the first twelve spelling words.
- Encourage the children to use a dictionary if they are unsure of any words.

Activity Page 2
- The children answer the questions (*a hundred, a thousand, a hundred years old, a thousand, a hundred, a thousand, a thousand*).
- They then write the numbers as numerals (*100; 1,000; 1,000,000*) and draw a centipede.
- Then they parse the sentence and complete the wall.
- *Her* is a possessive adjective describing who the daughter belongs to and *Chinese* is a proper adjective so both should be underlined in blue. All parts of the verb should be underlined in red.

Her naughty daughter had broken the tenth-century Chinese vase.

Top: *daughter - had broken - vase*
Bottom: *Her naughty - (blank) - the tenth-century Chinese*

Dictation
- Dictate the following sentences:

1. "The orphanage is ten kilometres away," said Miss Smith.
2. Fresh water freezes at zero degrees centigrade.
3. Does a millipede really have one thousand legs?

- In sentence 1, remind the children to use speech marks with the correct punctuation.
- *Miss Smith* is a proper noun and needs capital letters at the start of both words.

Grammar: Adverb Placement

Aim
- Reinforce the children's understanding of adverbs. Develop their ability to identify adverbs wherever they are in a sentence.

Introduction
- Revise adverbs with the class. An adverb is similar to an adjective but rather than describing (or modifying) a noun, it usually describes a verb instead; it tells us more about how, where, when, how much or how often something happens.
- The children should already know that adverbs can be made by adding the suffix ‹-ly› to many adjectives, as in *bravely*, *loudly* and *carelessly*, or by adding ‹-ally› if the adjective ends in ‹-ic› (as in *artistically* or *energetically*).
- However, it is important that the children remember that some adverbs – such as *just*, *too* and *soon*, for example – do not end in ‹-ly› and that some words, like *lovely*, *silly* and *friendly*, are not adverbs but adjectives.
- In order to identify the adverb, the children need to look at the verb in the sentence and think about which word is describing it.
- The children will learn later that adverbs can modify other adverbs and also adjectives (see pages 91 and 93).
- Ask the children to call out some adverbs, or write some verbs on the board and discuss which adverbs could describe them.

Main Point
- Write the sentence *He drove carefully around the corner* on the board. Ask the children to identify the verb and adverb (*drove/carefully*).
- Point out that *drove* is a tricky or irregular past tense verb and that the adverb has been made by adding ‹-ly› to the adjective *careful*.
- Look at the position of the adverb, which is next to the verb it is describing, and explain that the adverb could be put elsewhere in the sentence and still make sense: *He carefully drove around the corner*; *He drove around the corner carefully*; *Carefully, he drove around the corner*.
- Write these examples on the board and read them with the children. Discuss how the sentences still carry the same meaning, but the emphasis changes subtly in each one from **who** was doing the driving, to **how** the driving was done, to **where** the careful driving took place.
- However, sometimes the placement of the adverb is crucial to the meaning of the sentence.
- Write *She only grazed her knee* and *She grazed only her knee* on the board and discuss these with the class. In the first sentence she only grazed her knee rather than doing something more serious, whereas in the second sentence only the knee was grazed and nothing else.
- The children need to listen to how the sentence sounds and check that the correct meaning is given.
- Now write *He had carefully driven around the corner* on the board and ask where the adverb is now.
- Point out that if you want to put the adverb next to the verb and there is both an auxiliary and a main verb, then the adverb usually goes between the two.
- This is always the case with the adverb *not*, which is used to make a word, statement or question negative, so it has the opposite meaning: *He has not driven carefully around the corner*.

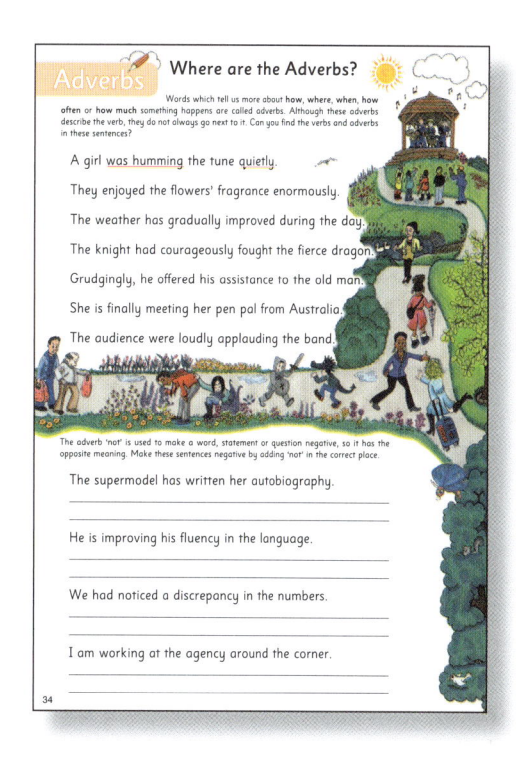

Activity Page
- The children write inside the outlined word *Adverbs*, using an orange pencil.
- They then read each sentence and identify the verb and adverb, underlining them in their appropriate colours (*was humming/quietly*, *enjoyed/enormously*, *has improved/gradually*, *had fought/courageously*, *offered/grudgingly*, *is meeting/finally*, *were applauding/loudly*).
- They then make the sentences negative by adding the adverb *not* in the correct position between the auxiliary and main verb (*has not written*, *is not improving*, *had not noticed*, *am not working*).

Extension Activity
- Give the children some more sentences in the continuous and perfect tenses and ask them to make them negative.

Rounding Off
- Go over the sheet with the children, discussing their answers. If they have done the extension activity, ask some children to read out their sentences.

Spelling: ⟨post-⟩

Spelling Test
- The children turn to the backs of their books and find the column labelled *Spelling Test 11*.
- Call out the spelling words learnt last week.

Revision
- Revise prefixes, which are one or more syllables added at the beginning of a word to change or add meaning.
- Write these words on the board, identify the prefixes and discuss how they modify the meaning: **sub**way (*under*), **anti**septic (*against*), **pre**view (*before*), **trans**plant (*across*), **tele**gram (*at a distance*), **inter**lock (*between*).

Spelling Point
- Write *postpone*, *postscript* and *posterity* on the board and ask the children whether they know what the letters ⟨post⟩ mean.
- Explain that the prefix ⟨post-⟩ comes from the Latin for *after* or *behind*, so if you postpone something, you arrange to do it at a later date, a postscript is a set of notes added at the end of a letter or book (*PS* is short for *postscript*), and *posterity* means all future generations of people.
- However, some other words with *post*, like *postcard* and *postmaster*, come from the Latin for *to place* and often relate to sending letters (although the word *posture* refers to how we place or position ourselves).
- Ask the children if they can think of any words beginning with ⟨post⟩.

Spelling List
- Go through the list, look at how the prefix changes or adds meaning to each word and discuss the meaning of any unfamiliar words.
- Ask the children to find and highlight the ⟨post⟩ spelling each time.
- Point out the letters saying their long vowel sound in *post*, *post*n*a*tal, *postgradu*ate and *post-haste*, the schwas (as in *postn*a*tal* and *postmod*e*rn*), the ⟨ture⟩ saying /cher/ in *posture*, the ⟨ar⟩ saying /or/ in *postwar*, the ⟨e⟩ saying /ear/ in *posterior*, the silent ⟨h⟩ in *posthumous*, the ⟨ive⟩ saying /iv/ in *postoperative* and the suffix in *postponement*.
- It is a good idea to blend and sound out the spelling words quickly every day with the children, using the 'say it as it sounds' strategy where appropriate, or you could break down the words into prefix and root word.

post
postcard
posture
postpone
postwar
postdate
postscript
postnatal
posterity
posterior
postmodern
postmaster
posthumous
postmortem
post-operative
postponement
postgraduate
post-haste

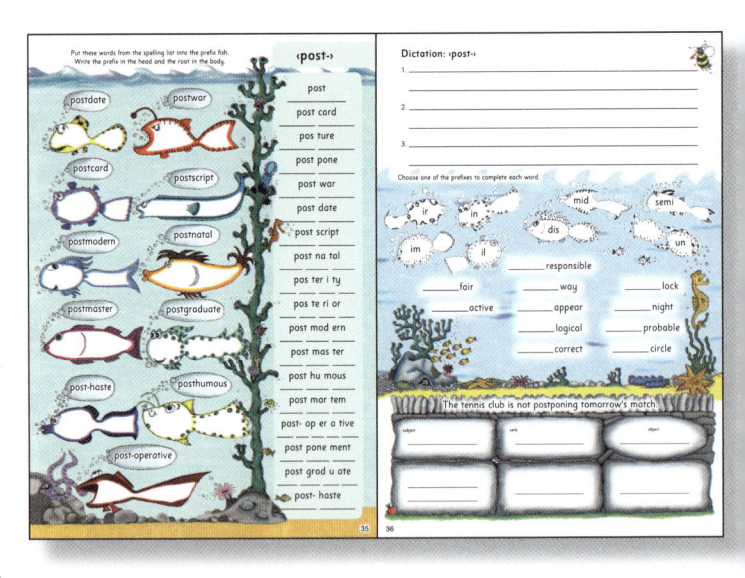

Activity Page 1
- The children copy out the syllables of each spelling word.
- They then write out some of the spelling words in the prefix fish, putting the prefixes in the fish's heads and the root words in the bodies.

Activity Page 2
- The children choose a prefix from one of the fish to complete each word (*irresponsible*, *unfair*, *midway*, *unlock*, *inactive*, *disappear*, *midnight*, *illogical*, *improbable*, *incorrect*, *semicircle*).
- Then they parse the sentence and complete the wall.
- All parts of the verb (*is postponing*) should be underlined in red, while *not* is an adverb modifying the verb and should be underlined in orange.
- *Tennis* is a noun acting as an adjective and should be underlined in blue.
- Possessive nouns always act as adjectives, so *tomorrow's* should also be underlined in blue.
  The tennis club is not postponing tomorrow's match.
  Top: *club - is postponing - match*
  Bottom: *The tennis - not - tomorrow's*

Dictation
- Dictate the following sentences:

1. The author added a postscript at the end of the book.
2. "My son is a postgraduate student," the woman said proudly.
3. The art critic hates postmodernist paintings.

- Remind the children to use speech marks with the correct punctuation in sentence 2.

Grammar: Proofreading

Aim
- Encourage the children to always proofread their work, checking for themselves that they have used correct spelling and punctuation to write complete sentences with a subject and verb that agree and which make sense to the reader.

Introduction
- Remind the children that a sentence starts with a capital letter and must make sense.
- It ends in a full stop, question mark or exclamation mark and always has a verb and subject, but not necessarily an object.
- It can be written in the first, second or third person, with the person being singular or plural:
  - The first person refers to the author and uses the pronoun *I* for the singular and *we* for the plural.
  - The second person addresses someone directly with the pronoun *you* for both singular and plural.
  - The third person refers to someone else and uses the pronoun *he/she/it* for the singular and *they* for the plural.
- With the class, conjugate the verbs *to be* and *to have* in the simple present and past tenses, doing the pronoun actions. Point out how the verb itself can change, depending on the grammatical person.
- Briefly revise the simple, continuous and perfect tenses and the spelling rules for creating present and past participles, and make sure the children know how to form the past tense of some commonly used irregular verbs.

Main Point
- Write 'That cat were chaseing an mous' on the board and ask the children to read it and comment on how it has been written.
- They will hopefully point out the following: it should be *was chasing* rather than *were chasing* because the verb needs to agree with the singular subject *cat*; the ‹e› on the end of *chase* should have been removed before adding the suffix ‹-ing›; 'an mous' should be *a mouse* because *an* is only used before words starting with a vowel sound and the noun has an ‹e› on the end; and the sentence needs closing with some punctuation (in this case a full stop, as the sentence is a statement rather than a question or exclamation).
- Now write 'she had droped a stitch in the skarf she will be knitting' and put a full stop on the end.
- Again, ask the children to say what is wrong, and discuss the following: *She* should have a capital letter because it is at the beginning of the sentence; the doubling rule should be applied to *drop* and *knit* before adding ‹-ed› and ‹-ing› in *dropped* and *knitting*; *skarf* has been misspelt and should be *scarf*; and the use of the future continuous in *she will be knitting* does not make sense after the past perfect of *she had dropped*: a stitch cannot have already been dropped in a scarf that is yet to be made.
- It should read *She had dropped a stitch in the scarf she **was** knitting*.

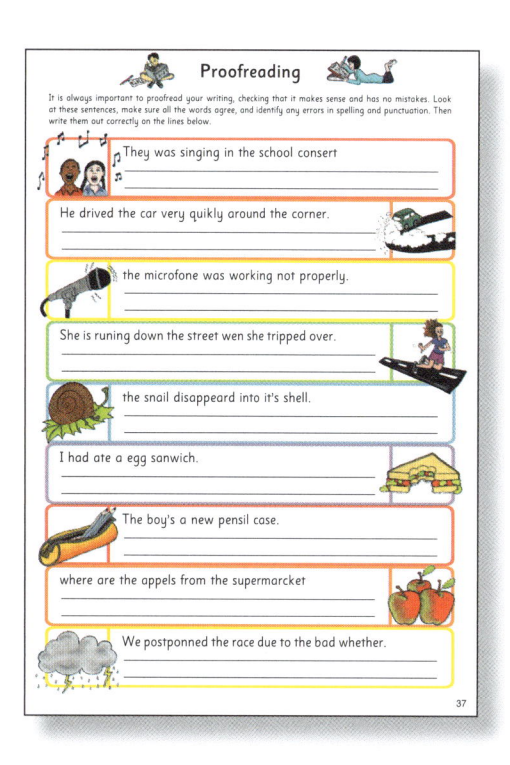

Activity Page
- The children read the sentences and decide what is wrong with each one.
- Remind the children to look at the punctuation and spelling, check that the tenses have been formed correctly and make sure that everything else makes sense.
- They can mark the mistakes by either correcting them with a coloured pencil or putting a ring around them. They then write out the sentences correctly on the lines below. (*They **were** singing in the school con**c**ert. He **drove** the car very qui**c**kly around the corner. The microp**h**one was **not** working properly. She **was** ru**nn**ing down the street w**h**en she tripped over. The snail disappear**e**d into **its** shell. I had **eaten** a**n** egg sand**w**ich. The boy **has** a new pencil case. Where are the app**le**s from the supermarket? We postpo**n**ed the race due to the bad **wea**ther.*)

Extension Activity
- Each child writes a sentence with some spelling, punctuation and grammar mistakes.
- Then, working in pairs, they swap and proofread each other's work.

Rounding Off
- Go over the activity page with the children, discussing their answers.
- If they have done the extension activity, ask some of the children to read out their sentence and say how they corrected it.

GRAMMAR 5 PUPIL BOOK: PAGE 38 & 39

Spelling: ‹-tion›

Spelling Test
- The children turn to the backs of their books and find the column labelled *Spelling Test 12*.
- Call out the spelling words learnt last week.

Revision
- Revise prefixes, which are one or more syllables added at the beginning of a word to change or add meaning.
- Write these prefixes on the board and ask the class to think of words beginning with them: ‹post-› (*after/behind*), ‹cent(i)-› (*hundred*), ‹milli-› (*thousand*), ‹super-› (*above/beyond*), ‹mega-› (*great*), ‹micro-› (*small*), ‹auto-› (*self*) and ‹multi-› (*many/more than one*).
- Discuss how each prefix modifies the meaning.

Spelling Point
- Revise the ‹tion› spelling of /shun/ in words like *station* and *relation*.
- Remind the class that ‹ti› is making the /sh/ sound and that the ‹o› has lost its pure sound and has become a schwa.
- The suffix ‹-tion› is often added to verbs to make nouns meaning the act, state or result of doing the verb (so an *infection* is the result of being infected, for example).
- If the root word already ends in ‹t›, then only ‹-ion› is added, and if it ends in ‹e›, this is removed before the ‹-tion› is added (as in *produce* and *production*).
- Sometimes, the ‹e› changes to ‹i› before ‹-tion› is added (so *compete* becomes *competition* and *oppose* becomes *opposition*).
- Write the words *question* and *suggestion* on the board, and point out that in words ending in ‹-stion›, the ‹ti› often says /ch/ rather than /sh/.

Spelling List
- Go through the list, identify the syllables in each word and discuss the meaning of any unfamiliar words.
- Ask the children to find and highlight each ‹tion› spelling.
- Point out the schwas (as in p**o**sition and c**o**ndition) and any letters saying their long vowel sound (as in contrib**u**tion), the ‹qu› saying /kw/ in *question* and the double consonants in su**gg**estion, o**pp**osition and co**nn**ection.
- It is a good idea to blend and sound out the spelling words quickly every day with the children, using the 'say it as it sounds' strategy where appropriate, or you could break down the words into root (word) and suffix.

option
position
action
section
mention
question
direction
suggestion
infection
rejection
condition
function
competition
contribution
introduction
opposition
production
connection

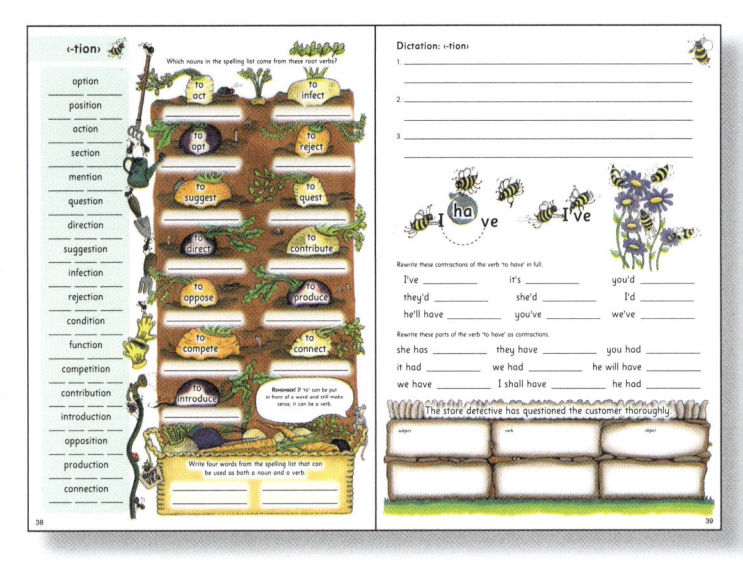

Activity Page 1
- The children split each spelling word into syllables (*op/tion, po/si/tion, ac/tion, sec/tion, men/tion, ques/tion, di/rec/tion, sug/ges/tion, in/fec/tion, re/jec/tion, con/di/tion, func/tion, com/pe/ti/tion, con/tri/bu/tion, in/tro/duc/tion, op/po/si/tion, pro/duc/tion, con/nec/tion*).
- They then match the root verbs to the spelling words (*action, infection, option, rejection, suggestion, question, direction, contribution, opposition, production, competition, connection, introduction*).
- They then write four spelling words that can be used either as a noun or a verb (the main ones are: *position, mention, question, function*).

Activity Page 2
- The children write the contractions in full (*I have, it has, you had, they had, she had, I had, he will have, you have, we have*); then they write the verbs as contractions (*she's, they've, you'd, it'd, we'd, he'll have, we've, I'll have, he'd*).
- They then parse the sentence and complete the wall.
- All parts of the verb should be underlined in red. *Store* is a noun acting as an adjective and should be underlined in blue. *Thoroughly* is an adverb made by adding ‹-ly› to the adjective *thorough* and should be underlined in orange.

The store detective has questioned the customer thoroughly.

Top: *detective - has questioned - customer*
Bottom: *The store - thoroughly - the*

Dictation
- Dictate the following sentences:

1. A section of the fence is in bad condition.
2. Did I mention my suggestion to have a competition?
3. "You have a post-operative infection," remarked the doctor.

- Remind them to use speech marks with the correct punctuation in sentence 3.

Grammar: Prepositions

Aim
- Reinforce the children's understanding that a preposition relates one noun or pronoun to another, often by describing where it is or where it is moving towards.
- Introduce the idea that as well as being a preposition of place, many can be prepositions of time.

Introduction
- Briefly revise the different parts of speech: nouns (proper, common, collective, concrete and abstract), pronouns (personal and possessive), adjectives (including comparatives and superlatives), verbs, adverbs, conjunctions and prepositions.
- Ask the children to think of different examples for each part of speech and, together, see if they can make a sentence using all the parts of speech, or as many as possible.
- For example, they could say something like:
Sally was running quickly along the hedge when she saw a large herd of cows in a muddy field.

Main Point
- Remind the children that a preposition is a word that relates one noun or pronoun to another, often by describing where it is or where it is moving towards.
- Look at the prepositions used in the children's sentence and discuss which words they are relating; in the example above, for instance, the preposition *along* describes where Sally is moving in relation to the hedge, *of* relates the collective noun *herd* to the *cows* it is describing, and *in* describes where the cows are in relation to the field.
- Point out that *pre* means *before* and *position* means *place*, so *preposition* means *placed before*.
- Look at the prepositions again and discuss how they are placed before the noun and also before any other words (like articles and adjectives) that describe (or modify) the noun, as in *along the hedge* and *in a muddy field*.
- Ask the children where else Sally might run and make a list of the different prepositions used in each example, such as *across*, *behind*, *under*, *among*, *between*, *into*, *around*, *down* and *through*. Other examples can be found on the activity page.
- Now say something like *Sally ran **in** the morning*, *Sally ran **during** the race* or *Sally ran **throughout** the summer* and ask the children if there is anything different about these sentences.
- In these examples, the prepositions are not describing a physical position or direction; instead they are relating Sally to the time or event in which she ran.
- Ask the children to think of other examples of prepositions of time.

Activity Page
- The children write inside the outlined word *Prepositions*, using a green pencil.
- They then find and ring the prepositions, using a green pencil, in the word search (Across: Row 1: *by/as/inside*, Row 2: *about/of*, Row 3: *below*, Row 4: *from/around*, Row 5: *outside*, Row 6: *past*, Row 7: *across/against*, Row 8: *opposite*, Row 9: *over*, Row 10: *in/with/onto*, Row 11: *beneath*, Row 12: *before/along*, Row 13: *off*, Row 14: *into*, Row 15: *until*, Row 16: *under/for*, Row 17: *during/beside*; Down: Column 1: *throughout*, Column 2: *following*, Column 4: *above/between*, Column 5: *on*, Column 6: *behind*, Column 8: *at/up/to*, Column 12: *near/after*, Column 14: *towards*, Column 15: *down*, Column 16: *through*, Column 17: *underneath*).

Extension Activity
- Make a set of preposition cards for each child. Each card should have one of the following prepositions on it: *aboard, about, above, across, after, against, along, amid, among, around, as, at, before, behind, below, beneath, beside, between, beyond, by, down, during, following, for, from, in, inside, into, near, of, off, on, onto, opposite, outside, over, past, through, throughout, to, towards, under, underneath, until, up, upon, with, without*.
- Make sure you give out the cards in a random order, which the children can then use to play games like Snap and Pairs with a partner.
- This can also be used as a morning or filler activity if the cards are laminated and extra words are added.

Rounding Off
- Go over the activity page with the children and check that they have been able to find all the prepositions.

GRAMMAR 5 PUPIL BOOK: PAGE 41 & 42

Spelling: ‹-sion›

Spelling Test
- The children turn to the backs of their books and find the column labelled *Spelling Test 13*.
- Call out the spelling words learnt last week.

Revision
- Revise prefixes, which are one or more syllables added at the beginning of a word to change or add meaning.
- Write these prefixes on the board and ask the class to think of words beginning with them: ‹mid-› (*in the middle*), ‹pre-› (*before*), ‹un-› (*not*), ‹sub-› (*under*), ‹anti-› (*opposite or against*), ‹semi-› (*half, partly or almost*), ‹trans-› (*across, through or changed*) and ‹inter-› (*between or among*).
- Discuss how each prefix modifies the meaning.

Spelling Point
- Revise the ‹-tion› spelling, which usually says /shun/ but can say /chun/ in words like *question* and *suggestion*.
- Ask the children if they know any other ways of writing /shun/.
- Write *mansion* on the board, underline the suffix and point out how ‹si› is making the /sh/ sound.
- Now write *version* on the board, ask what sound ‹si› is saying in this word and remind them that ‹si› can also make the /zh/ sound.
- Like ‹-tion›, the suffix ‹-sion› is often added to verbs to make nouns meaning the act, state or result of doing the verb (so a *collision* happens when two things *collide*).
- The suffix ‹-sion› is commonly added to verbs ending in ‹s›, ‹se›, ‹d› and ‹de›. These letters are removed before the suffix is added.
- Look at the spelling words and identify the root verbs where possible.

Spelling List
- Go through the list, identify the syllables in each word and discuss the meaning of any unfamiliar words.
- Ask the children to find and highlight each ‹sion› spelling.
- Point out the schwas (as in *a*version and *o*ccasion), any letters saying their long vowel sound (as in occ*a*sion and d*i*version), the ‹e› saying /i/ in pr*e*tension, *e*xtension and *e*xpansion, the double consonants in o*cc*asion, a*pp*rehension and misa*pp*rehension and the prefix in **mis**apprehension, meaning *wrongly* or *not*.
- It is a good idea to blend and sound out the spelling words quickly

version
mansion
tension
pension
aversion
pretension
occasion
compulsion
conversion
diversion
propulsion
extension
dimension
collision
expansion
apprehension
comprehension
misapprehension

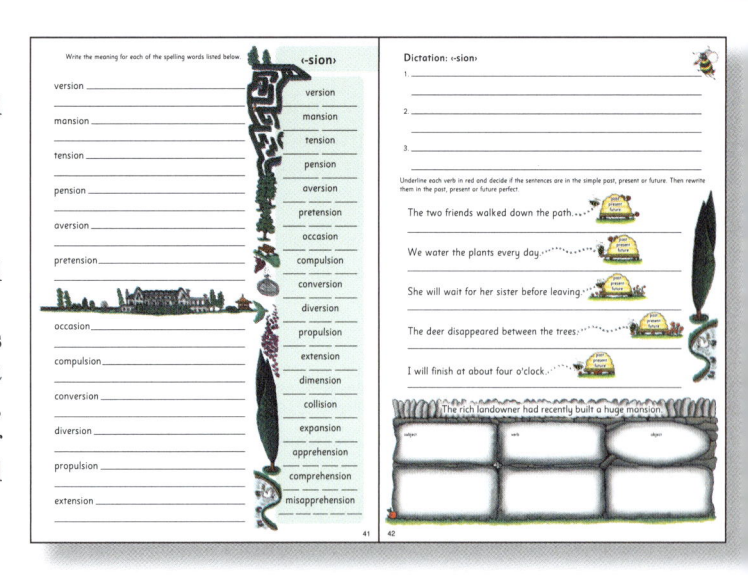

every day with the children, using the 'say it as it sounds' strategy where appropriate, or you could break down the words into root (word) and suffix.

Activity Page 1
- The children split each spelling word into syllables (*ver/sion, man/sion, ten/sion, pen/sion, a/ver/sion, pre/ten/sion, oc/ca/sion, com/pul/sion, con/ver/sion, di/ver/sion, pro/pul/sion, ex/ten/sion, di/men/sion, col/li/sion, ex/pan/sion, ap/pre/hen/sion, com/pre/hen/sion, mis/ap/pre/hen/sion*).
- They then write the meaning of the first twelve spelling words. Encourage the children to use a dictionary if they are unsure of any words.

Activity Page 2
- The children underline the verbs and decide whether the sentences are written in the simple past, present or future. They then rewrite them using the perfect tense rather than the simple tense (*had walked, have watered, will have waited, had disappeared, will have finished*).
- Then they parse the sentence and complete the wall.
- All parts of the verb (*had built*) should be underlined in red. *Recently* is an adverb made by adding ‹-ly› to the adjective *recent*.
The rich landowner had recently built a huge mansion.
Top: *landowner - had built - mansion*
Bottom: *The rich - recently - a huge*

Dictation
- Dictate the following sentences:

1. Her apprehension was causing a lot of tension.
2. They examined the wreckage after the collision.
3. "I need the exact dimensions of the room," replied the builder.

- Remind the children to use speech marks with the correct punctuation in sentence 3.

Grammar: Prepositional Phrases

Aim
- Refine the children's understanding of prepositions by introducing the term *prepositional phrase*, which is the name for a group of words that begins with a preposition and makes sense but has no verb or subject.

Introduction
- Briefly revise sentences and phrases.
- A sentence must make sense, start with a capital letter, contain a subject and verb and end in a full stop, question mark or exclamation mark.
- When a group of words makes sense but has no verb and subject, it is called a phrase.
- Remind the children that a noun, together with all the words that describe it, is called a noun phrase.
- Call out some examples of noun phrases and ask the children to turn them into simple sentences.

Main Point
- Write the phrases **in** the park, **on** the way, **around** the corner and **after** them on the board and ask the children what they have in common.
- These phrases all start with a preposition and are followed by a simple noun phrase or pronoun.
- Using a green pen, underline the prepositions, draw a green box around each phrase and explain that phrases like this are called prepositional phrases.
- Ask the children to call out examples of prepositions and write them on the board.
- Then look at each one in turn with the class and make it into a prepositional phrase.
- Possible examples include: *at home, into the dark, until the end, up the street, down the stairs, from my house, during the war, across the river, between the trees, under the sea, to the library, with the others, by train, for many years, over the rainbow, after breakfast, inside the box.*
- Remind the children to take care with the preposition *to*: when this word is followed by a verb it is the infinitive and not a prepositional phrase.

Activity Page
- The children write inside the outlined word *Prepositions*, using a green pencil.
- They then complete the first set of sentences by adding a suitable prepositional phrase.
- They can either think of the phrases themselves or use ones from the extension activity.
- Then they identify the prepositions in the second set of sentences, underlining them in green, and put a green box around all the words in each prepositional phrase (**across** the park, **at** a standstill, **from** her sister, **to** Carla's party, **with** his key, **by** two o'clock, **in** time, **on** the right, **under** arrest, **for** my birthday).

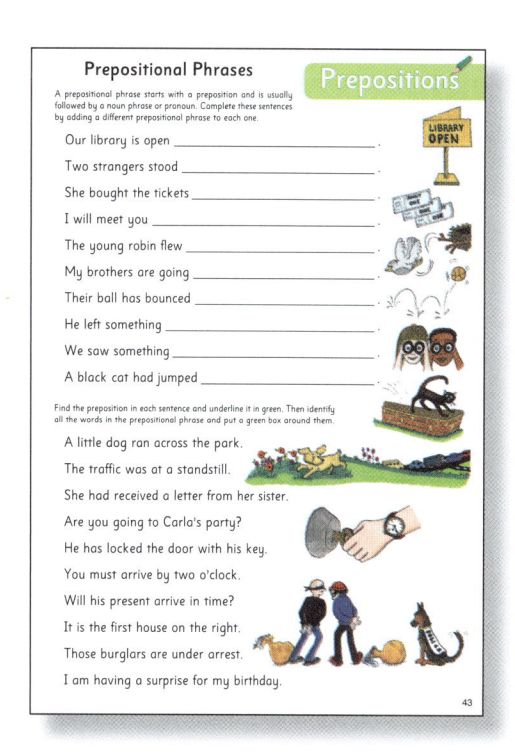

Extension Activity
- The children can either think of as many prepositional phrases as possible, or they can put some of the following prepositional phrases into sentences: *behind the tree, aboard the ship, in the air, during the holidays, through the window, with some friends, around the corner, under the bridge, at the back, after lunch, into the garden, over the fence, without delay, among the leaves, by the fireplace, for a long time, at midday, onto the roof, inside the house, near the pond, across the street, in an hour, up the road, before ten o'clock, on Monday morning, opposite the bus stop.*
- In either case, the children will need a seperate sheet of paper. The extension activity can also be used to create a morning or filler activity.
- The children take it in turns to pick a card and say a sentence using the prepositional phrase on the card.
- When they come to the phrase, the children should hold up the card to help reinforce the idea that this phrase is a distinct part of the sentence.

Rounding Off
- Go over the activity page with the children, discussing their answers.
- If they have done the extension activity, ask some of the children to read out their phrases and sentences.

GRAMMAR 5 PUPIL BOOK: PAGE 44 & 45

Spelling: ‹ssion›

Spelling Test
- The children turn to the backs of their books and find the column labelled *Spelling Test 14*.
- Call out the spelling words learnt last week.

Revision
- Write these words on the board and identify the suffixes: ac*tion*, man*sion*, ques*tion*, conver*sion*, compe*tition*, colli*sion*.
- These suffixes usually say /shun/, but ‹-tion› can say /chun/ and ‹-sion› can say /zhun/.
- Blend and sound out the words with the class and discuss how the suffix is said in each one.

Spelling Point
- Introduce ‹ssion›, which is an alternative spelling of ‹-sion›. It is added to verbs to make nouns meaning the act, state or result of doing the verb (so if you give permission for something, you permit it to happen).
- It is usually added to verbs ending in ‹ss›, ‹mit› or ‹ede› and ‹eed›. If the root word already ends in ‹ss›, then only ‹-ion› is added, (as in *express* and *expression*) and if it ends in ‹mit›, the ‹t› is removed before the ‹ssion› is added (as in *admit* and *admission*).
- If the root word ends in ‹ede› or ‹eed›, the last two letters are removed before ‹ssion› is added (so *succeed* becomes *succession* and *concede* becomes *concession*).
- Look at the spelling words and point out that the spelling always follows a short vowel sound, as in the word *mission*, which can be found in several of the words.
- Explain that if the children want to write a word ending in /shun/ and it has either the word *mission* in it, or a short vowel directly before the /shun/ (making a long soft /sh/ sound), then the word is probably spelt with ‹ssion›.

Spelling List
- Go through the list, identify the syllables in each word and discuss the meaning of any unfamiliar words.
- Ask the children to find and highlight each ‹ssion› spelling.
- Point out any schwas, the double consonants in *aggression*, the ‹cc› saying /ks/ in *succession* and the soft ‹c› in *concession*.
- It is a good idea to blend and sound out the spelling words quickly every day with the children, using the 'say it as it sounds' strategy where appropriate, or you could break down the words into root (word) and suffix.

session
passion
mission
permission
submission
admission
expression
impression
profession
aggression
progression
obsession
discussion
depression
succession
concession
omission
percussion

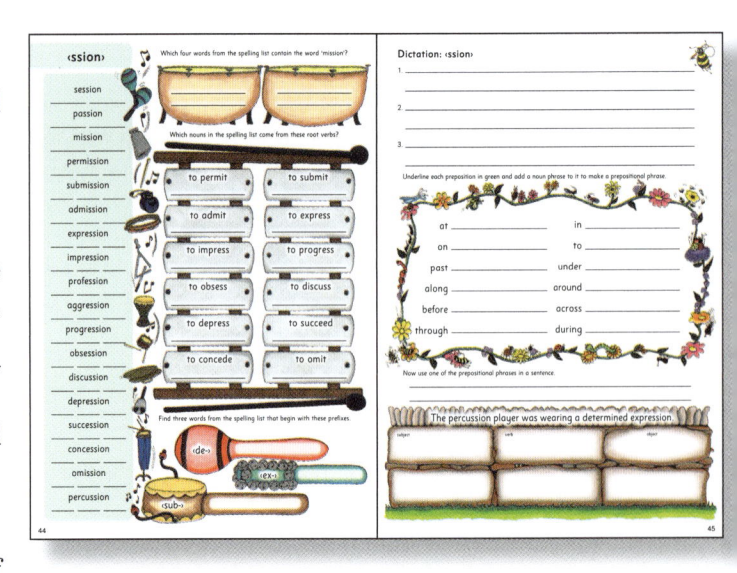

Activity Page 1
- The children split each spelling word into syllables (*ses/sion, pas/sion, mis/sion, per/mis/sion, sub/mis/sion, ad/mis/sion, ex/pres/sion, im/pres/sion, pro/fes/sion, ag/gres/sion, pro/gres/sion, ob/ses/sion, dis/cus/sion, dep/res/sion, suc/ces/sion, con/ces/sion, o/mis/sion, per/cus/sion*).
- They then write four spelling words containing the word *mission* (*permission, submission, admission, omission*) and match the root verbs to the spelling words (*permission, submission, admission, expression, impression, progression, obsession, discussion, depression, succession, concession, omission*).
- Finally, they write three spelling words with the prefixes (***de**pression*, ***ex**pression*, ***sub**mission*).

Activity Page 2
- The children underline each preposition in green and add a noun phrase to it to make a prepositional phrase.
- They then choose one and use it in a sentence.
- Then they parse the sentence and complete the wall.
- All parts of the verb should be underlined in red. *Percussion* is a noun acting as an adjective and should be underlined in blue.
  The percussion player was wearing a determined expression.
  Top: *player - was wearing - expression*
  Bottom: *The percussion - (blank) - a determined*

Dictation
- Dictate the following sentences:

1. We had a long discussion about all the options.
2. The spy hid the microfilm during his mission.
3. "You need permission to leave the session early," he explained.

- Remind them to use speech marks with the correct punctuation in sentence 3.

Grammar: Noun Phrases as Subjects and Objects

Aim
- Develop the children's understanding of how noun phrases can act as the subject or object of a sentence. Introduce the terms *simple subject* and *simple object*.

Introduction
- Write *the fierce Viking warriors* on the board and discuss whether it is a phrase or a sentence.
- As it makes sense but does not have a verb with a subject, it must be a phrase.
- Now ask the children whether it is a noun phrase or prepositional phrase: it does not start with a preposition but it does have a noun (*warriors*) and some words that describe it (the definite article *the* and the adjectives *fierce* and *Viking*), so it is a noun phrase.
- Underline *warriors* in black and draw a black box around the whole phrase.
- Ask the children to suggest some nouns, or give them pictures of nouns, which could be connected to a topic they are studying.
- Using these words, think of some noun phrases with the class and write them on the board.
- Some of the children can then come up and underline each noun and draw a black box around the noun phrase.

Main Point
- Use the first noun phrase in a sentence and write it on the board. Parse it with the children: The fierce Viking warriors had raided their village.
- Identify the subject (the noun or pronoun that does the verb action) and object (the noun or pronoun that receives the verb action).
- Draw a box around the subject, *warriors*, with a small ‹s› in the corner, and a ring around the object, *village*, with a small ‹o› inside.
- Remind the class that although we only highlight the main noun or pronoun, we could in fact say that *the fierce Viking warriors* is the subject and *their village* is the object.
- To understand this better, try replacing the noun phrases with the pronouns *they* and *it*, so the sentence reads *They had raided it*.
- The sentence still makes sense but now *they* (replacing *the fierce Viking warriors*) is the subject and *it* (replacing *their village*) is the object.
- Now draw a sentence wall on the board and put the sentence into the boxes:

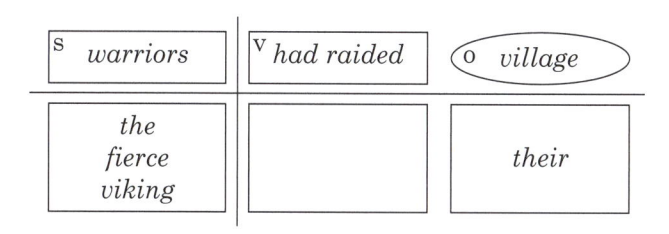

s warriors	v had raided	o village
the fierce viking		their

- The nouns and the words describing (or modifying) them are all in or under the subject or object box, so a noun phrase can be considered as the subject or object. However, when we want to refer to the main noun only, we call it the simple subject or object.

Activity Page
- The children parse each sentence and complete the wall.
1. Two savage lions roared loudly.
Top: *lions - roared -* (blank)
Bottom: *Two savage - loudly -* (blank)
2. We recently visited a new French restaurant.
Top: *We - visited - restaurant*
Bottom: (blank) *- recently - a new French*
3. The multitalented megastar has mysteriously disappeared.
Top: *megastar - has disappeared -* (blank)
Bottom: *The multitalented - mysteriously -* (blank)
- Then, under each wall, they write the noun phrase acting as the subject or object and the simple subject or object (*two savage lions/lions, the new French restaurant/restaurant, the multitalented megastar/megastar*).

Extension Activity
- Give each child a sheet of paper and ask them to draw some sentence walls.
- Write some more sentences on the board, using the noun phrases from the start of the lesson. Make sure they are simple sentences following the pattern of those on the activity page, otherwise the children will find it difficult to use them.
- The children complete the sentence walls and identify the noun phrases as well as the simple subjects or objects.

Rounding Off
- Go over the children's work, discussing their answers.

GRAMMAR 5 PUPIL BOOK: PAGE 47 & 48

Spelling: ‹cian›

Spelling Test
- The children turn to the backs of their books and find the column labelled *Spelling Test 15*.
- Call out the spelling words learnt last week.

Revision
- Write these words on the board and identify the suffixes: men**tion**, pen**sion**, mi**ssion**, direc**tion**, diver**sion**, progre**ssion**.
- These suffixes usually say /shun/ and can be added to verbs to make nouns.
- However, ‹-tion› can also say /chun/ and ‹-sion› can say /zhun/.
- Ask the class to suggest other words and discuss how each suffix is said.

Spelling Point
- Introduce the ‹cian› spelling, which, like ‹-tion›, ‹-sion› and ‹ssion›, says /shun/.
- Write *musician*, *magician* and *politician* on the board and ask what these words have in common.
- The children may notice that all the words end in ‹cian›, where the ‹ci› says /sh/ rather than the /s/ of the soft ‹c›.
- But they might also notice that these three words describe people with a particular skill or occupation: a musician is a person who plays music, a magician performs magic and a politician works in politics. (The spelling word *patrician* and adjective *Grecian* are exceptions to this.)
- Furthermore, the root words – *music*, *magic* and *politics* – all end in ‹ic› or ‹ics›.
- Explain that if the children want to write a word ending in /shun/ and it describes a person or occupation, then it is probably spelt ‹cian›.
- Look at the spelling words and identify the root verbs where possible.

Spelling List
- Go through the list, identify the syllables in each word and discuss the meaning of any unfamiliar words.
- Ask the children to find and highlight each ‹cian› spelling.
- Point out the long vowel sound in m**u**sician and d**ie**tician, the ‹s› saying /z/ in mu**s**ician, the soft ‹g› in ma**g**ician, the schwas (as in di**e**tician and p**a**trician), the ‹ch› spelling of /k/ in te**ch**nician, the ‹ph› saying /f/ and ‹y› saying /i/ in **phy**sician, the ‹eau› saying /ue/ in b**eau**tician and the ‹ae› saying /ee/ in p**ae**diatrician.
- It is a good idea to blend and sound out the spelling words quickly

musician
magician
dietician
optician
tactician
technician
clinician
mortician
patrician
politician
physician
electrician
beautician
statistician
arithmetician
mathematician
obstetrician
paediatrician

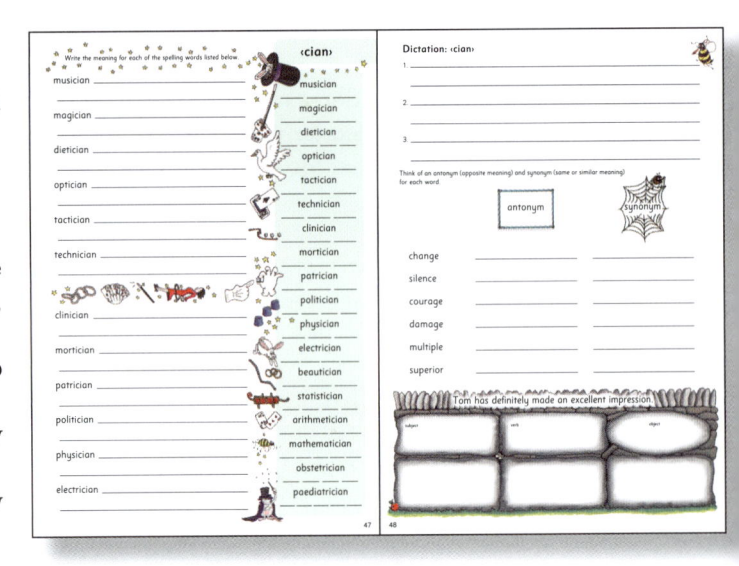

every day with the children, 'saying it as it sounds' where appropriate, or you could break down the words into root (word) and suffix. The mnemonic **b**ig **e**lephants **a**re **u**sual can be used to help remember the spelling of ‹beau› in *beautician*.

Activity Page 1
- The children split the spelling words into syllables (mu/si/cian, ma/gi/cian, di/e/ti/cian, op/ti/cian, tac/ti/cian, tech/ni/cian, cli/ni/cian, mor/ti/cian, pa/tri/cian, pol/i/ti/cian, phy/si/cian, e/lec/tri/cian, beau/ti/cian, sat/is/ti/cian, a/rith/me/ti/cian, math/e/ma/ti/cian, ob/ste/tri/cian, pae/di/a/tri/cian).
- They then write the meanings for the first twelve spelling words, using a dictionary if they are unsure of any words.

Activity Page 2
- The children write an antonym and synonym for each word, using a thesaurus if they need to. Possible answers are: *keep/replace* (change), *noise/hush* (silence), *cowardice/bravery* (courage), *repair/ruin* (damage), *few/many* (multiple), *better/worse* (superior).
- Then they parse the sentence and complete the wall.
- *Tom* is a proper noun and should be underlined in black. All parts of the verb *has made* should be underlined in red. *Definitely* is an adverb made by adding ‹-ly› to the adjective *definite*.
Tom has definitely made an excellent impression.
Top: *Tom - has made - impression*
Bottom: (blank) - *definitely - an excellent*

Dictation
- Dictate the following sentences:

1. The politician exclaimed, "We won the election!"
2. The musician had studied percussion at his old college.
3. The electrician is very proud of his profession.

- Remind them to use speech marks with the correct punctuation in sentence 1.

GRAMMAR 5 PUPIL BOOK: PAGE 49

Grammar: Compound Subjects and Objects

Aim
- Refine the children's ability to identify the subject and object of a sentence correctly by introducing the idea that in a sentence there can be more than one subject or object.

Introduction
- Remind the children that all sentences must have a subject, and they can also have an object.
- Write this sentence on the board and identify the verb: *Ann **had painted** a beautiful sunset.*
- With the children, decide who (or what) is doing the verb action and draw a box around the subject (*Ann*), with a small ‹s› in the corner.
- Then decide who or what is receiving the verb action and draw a ring around the object (*sunset*), with a small ‹o› inside.
- Remind the children that although we usually identify just the simple subject or object (the noun or pronoun on its own), a whole noun phrase can be considered to be the subject or object too.
- For example, if *a beautiful sunset* was replaced by the pronoun *it*, the sentence *Ann painted it* would still make sense and the object of the sentence would be *it*.
- As *it* has replaced the whole phrase, *a beautiful sunset* can therefore be considered the object too.

Main Point
- Write this sentence on the board and parse it with the children: Inky and Bee are hungrily eating jam sandwiches.
- Now draw a sentence wall on the board and put the sentence into the boxes.
- Deciding where the verb, adverb and object *sandwiches* go should be relatively straightforward. The children should be able to work out that the word *jam* is describing *sandwich* and goes in the box beneath.
- However, the subject of the sentence is slightly different; both Inky and Bee are doing the action, so they both belong in the subject box, and there is also the question of where to put *and*.
- Explain that when there is more than one subject or object, it is called a compound subject or object, and it is written in the boxes like this (Figure 1):

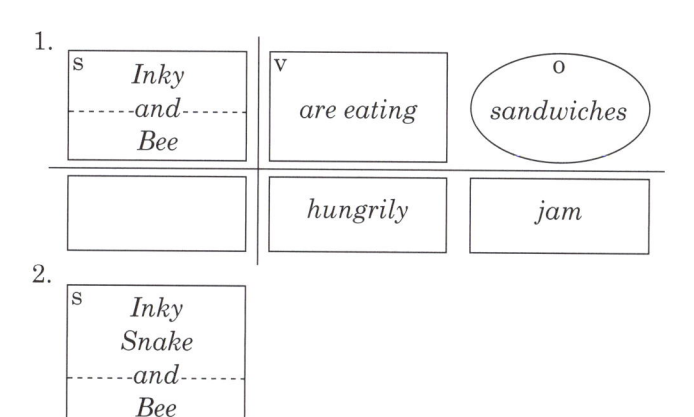

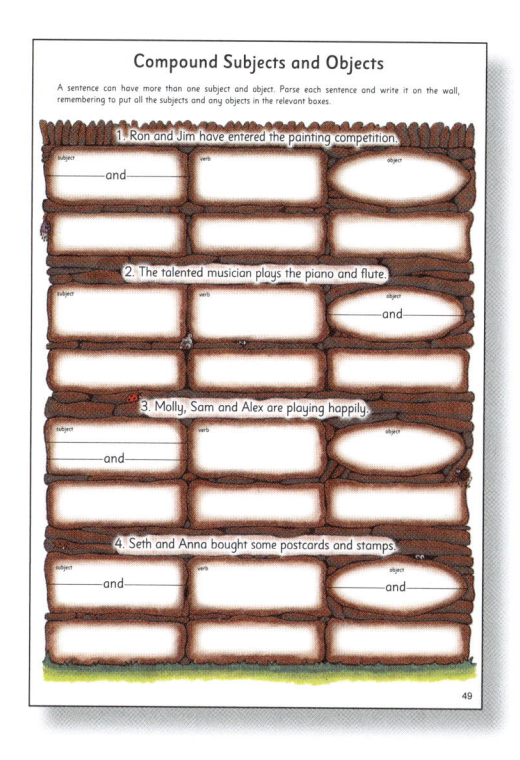

1.

s Inky ------and------ Bee	v are eating	o sandwiches
	hungrily	jam

2.

| s Inky Snake ------and------ Bee |

- Explain that the conjunction *and* joins the two compound subjects, but it is not actually the subject itself. This is why it is shown with the dotted line separating the two subjects.
- Now amend the original sentence on the board so it reads *Inky, Snake and Bee are hungrily eating jam sandwiches*. Ask the children how they would write this in the boxes.
- In this sentence, the subject box would be completed as above (see Figure 2).

Activity Page
- The children parse the sentences, underlining each word in the appropriate colour, and complete the walls.
1. Ron and Jim have entered the painting competition.
   Top: *Ron (and) Jim - have entered - competition*
   Bottom: (blank) - (blank) - *the painting*
2. The talented musician plays the piano and flute.
   Top: *musician - plays - piano (and) flute*
   Bottom: *The talented* - (blank) - *the*
3. Molly, Sam and Alex are playing happily.
   Top: *Molly, Sam (and) Alex - are playing* - (blank)
   Bottom: (blank) - *happily* - (blank)
4. Seth and Anna bought some postcards and stamps.
   Top: *Seth (and) Anna - bought - postcards (and) stamps*
   Bottom: (blank) - (blank) - *some*

Extension Activity
- Give each child a sheet of paper and ask them to draw some sentence walls.
- Write some more simple sentences on the board, following the pattern of those on the activity page.
- The children then parse the sentences and complete the sentence walls.

67

Grammar 5 Pupil Book: Page 50 & 51

Spelling: ‹-ation›

Spelling Test
- The children turn to the backs of their books and find the column labelled *Spelling Test 16*.
- Call out the spelling words learnt last week.

Revision
- Write these words on the board and identify the spellings: op*tion*, aver*sion*, permi*ssion*, beauti*cian*, introduc*tion*, exten*sion*, depre*ssion*, musi*cian*.
- These spellings usually say /shun/, but ‹-tion› can also say /chun/ and ‹-sion› can say /zhun/.
- Ask the class to suggest other words with these spellings and discuss how the suffix changes or adds meaning in each word.

Spelling Point
- Introduce the suffix ‹-ation›, which, like ‹-tion›, ‹-sion› and ‹ssion›, is often added to verbs to make nouns meaning the act, state or result of doing the verb (so if a surgeon *operates* on a patient, s/he performs an *operation*, and if you *locate* something, you find its *location*).
- Remind the children that the most common way of spelling /shun/ is ‹tion› and sometimes it is preceded by ‹a› saying its long vowel sound.
- Look at the spelling list and point out that the root verbs for many of these words end in ‹-ate›.

Spelling List
- Go through the list, identify the syllables in each word and discuss the meaning of any unfamiliar words.
- Ask the class to find and highlight each ‹ation› spelling.
- Ask the children to identify the root verb of each word.
- Point out the letters saying their long vowel sound in *cr*e*ation*, *ass*o*ciation* and *id*e*ntification*, the schwas (as in *op*e*ration* and *expl*o*ration*), the prefix ‹ex-› in *exploration* and *explanation*, the double consonants in *association* and *cancellation*, the soft ‹c› in *association*, *celebration*, *cancellation* and *pronunciation*.
- It is a good idea to blend and sound out the spelling words quickly every day with the children, using the 'say it as it sounds' strategy where appropriate, or you could break down the words into root (word) and suffix.

nation
creation
operation
education
relation
location
exploration
explanation
conversation
information
quotation
association
celebration
investigation
cancellation
identification
pronunciation
observation

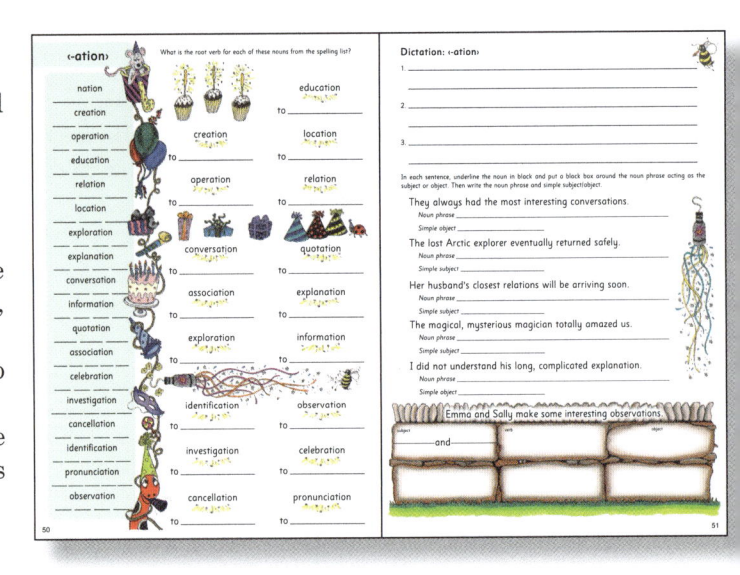

Activity Page 1
- The children split each spelling word into syllables (*na/tion*, *cre/a/tion*, *op/er/a/tion*, *ed/u/ca/tion*, *re/la/tion*, *lo/ca/tion*, *ex/plor/a/tion*, *ex/plan/a/tion*, *con/ver/sa/tion*, *in/form/a/tion*, *quo/ta/tion*, *as/so/ci/a/tion*, *cel/e/bra/tion*, *in/ves/ti/ga/tion*, *can/cel/la/tion*, *i/den/ti/fi/ca/tion*, *pro/nun/ci/a/tion*, *ob/ser/va/tion*).
- They then write the root verb for each spelling word (*educate*, *create*, *locate*, *operate*, *relate*, *converse*, *quote*, *associate*, *explain*, *explore*, *inform*, *identify*, *observe*, *investigate*, *celebrate*, *cancel*, *pronounce*).

Activity Page 2
- In each sentence, the children underline the noun in black and put a black box around the noun phrase acting as the subject or object.
- They then write the noun phrase and simple subject/object (*the most interesting **conversations***, *The lost Arctic **explorer***, *her husband's closest **relations***, *The magical, mysterious **magician***, *his long, complicated **explanation***).
- Then they parse the sentence and complete the wall.
- *Interesting* is an adjective that takes the present participle form.
  Emma and Sally make some interesting observations.
  Top: *Emma/Sally - make - observations*
  Bottom: (blank) - (blank) - *some interesting*

Dictation
- Dictate the following sentences:

1. I invited my relations to my birthday celebrations.
2. "Your operation has been postponed," confirmed the doctor.
3. They discovered important evidence during the investigation.

- Remind the children to use speech marks with the correct punctuation in sentence 2.

Grammar: Transitive and Intransitive Verbs

Aim
- Refine the children's knowledge of verbs, and introduce the terms *transitive* and *intransitive*.
- A transitive verb takes an object, while an intransitive verb does not take an object.

Introduction
- Write *The brother and sister made gingerbread and muffins* on the board and ask the children to identify the simple subject and object of the sentence.
- To find the subjects, *brother* and *sister*, the children should ask themselves who or what is doing the verb action and to find the objects, *gingerbread* and *muffins*, who or what is receiving the verb action.
- Ask some children to come up and draw a box with a small ‹s› in the corner around each of the subjects, and a ring with a small ‹o› inside around each of the objects.
- Remind the class that when two or more words come together to make a new word it is called a compound word (as in *blackbird*) and when two or more simple sentences are joined together by a conjunction it is called a compound sentence.
- Similarly, when there is more than one subject or object in a sentence, it is called a compound subject or object.

Main Point
- Now write *The children are reading quietly* on the board. Ask the children to find the simple subject and object of the sentence.
- This is a trick question, as this sentence has a subject (*children*), but does not have an object.
- Some of the children may think that *quietly* is the object because it comes after the verb (in English, the order of a sentence is often subject–verb–object) and is connected to it.
- However, an object is always a noun or pronoun that receives the action of the verb, whereas *quietly* is an adverb describing how the action was done.
- Remind the children that although a sentence always has a verb and subject, it does not necessarily have an object.
- Verbs that do have an object are said to be transitive, while those which do not (like the last example on the board) are called intransitive.
- Write the two terms on the board and underline the prefixes. Remind the children that ‹trans-› means *across* and so a transitive verb sends its action across to the object, while the prefix ‹in-› means *not* and so an intransitive verb does not send its action to an object.
- Now write *The children are reading their books* on the board and ask the children whether this is transitive or intransitive (there is an object, *books*, so it is transitive).
- Point out that in the first sentence the verb *to read* is transitive and in the other it is intransitive. Explain that many verbs can be both.

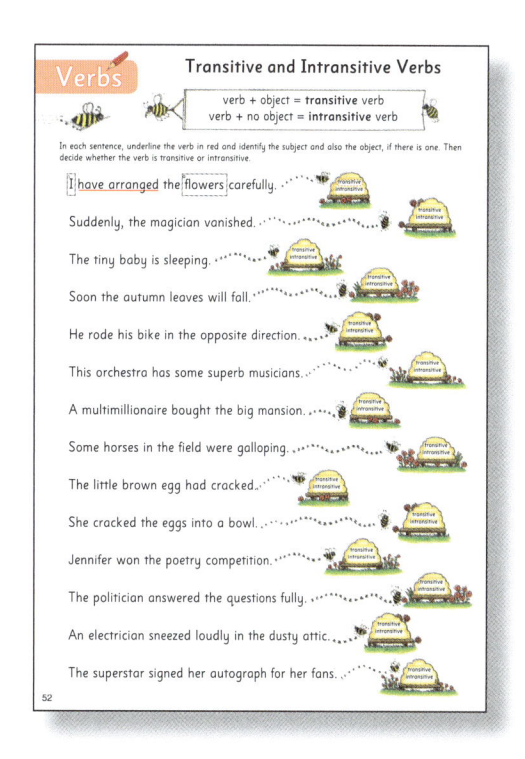

Activity Page
- The children write inside the outlined word *Verbs*, using a red pencil.
- They then read each sentence and identify the verb, underlining it in red.
- Then they identify the subject, drawing a box around it with a small ‹s› inside, and find the object, if there is one, putting a ring around it with a small ‹o› inside.
- Now they can decide whether the verb is transitive and takes an object, or is intransitive and does not take an object, and ring the appropriate word in each beehive.

I / have arranged / flowers / transitive
magician / vanished / intransitive
baby / is sleeping / intransitive
leaves / will fall / intransitive
He / rode / bike / transitive
orchestra / has / musicians / transitive
multimillionaire / bought / mansion / transitive
horses / were galloping / intransitive
egg / had cracked / intransitive
She / cracked / eggs / transitive
Jennifer / won / competition / transitive
politician / answered / questions / transitive
electrician / sneezed / intransitive
superstar / signed / autograph / transitive

Extension Activity
- The children write pairs of sentences in which the verb is transitive in one and intransitive in the other, such as *Anna paints a picture* (transitive) and *Anna paints beautifully* (intransitive).

Rounding Off
- Go over the activity page with the children, discussing their answers. If they have done the extension activity, ask some of the children to read out their sentences.

GRAMMAR 5 PUPIL BOOK: PAGE 53 & 54

Spelling: ‹ch›, ‹che›

Spelling Test
- The children turn to the backs of their books and find the column labelled *Spelling Test 17*.
- Call out the spelling words learnt last week.

Revision
- Write these words on the board and identify the spellings: *informa**tion***, *ver**sion***, *expre**ssion***, *magi**cian***, *identifi**cation***, *compre**hension***, *submi**ssion***, *physi**cian***.
- Words with these spellings usually end in /shun/, but ‹-tion› can also say /chun/ and ‹-sion› can say /zhun/.
- Ask the class to suggest similar words and discuss their meanings.

Spelling Point
- Revise the spellings of /shun/: ‹tion›, ‹sion›, ‹ssion›, ‹cian›.
- Write the word *chef* on the board and explain that another way to write /sh/ is ‹ch› or ‹che›.
- Many words with these spellings have been borrowed from French and are now used in the English language.
- In French, ‹ch› and ‹che› usually make a /sh/ sound and the French origin of the spelling words explains why some of the spellings are not usual in English.

Spelling List
- Go through the list, identify the syllables in each word and discuss the meaning of any unfamiliar words.
- Ask the class to find and highlight the ‹ch› or ‹che› spelling in each word.
- Point out the ‹f› at the end of *chef* (which is not doubled even though it comes at the end of the word and follows a short vowel), the ‹et› saying /ai/ in *chalet* and *crochet*, the ‹i_e› saying /ee/ in *machine*, *chenille* and *cliche*, the schwas (as in *pa**r**achute*, *m**o**ustache* and *broch**u**re*), the ‹eau› saying /oa/ in *chateau* and *chauffeur*, the ‹o› saying its long vowel sound in *brochure* and *crochet*, the ‹eur› saying /er/ in *chauffeur* (although the /er/ can be swallowed and become a schwa), the ‹e› saying /ai/ in *cliche* and ‹ier› saying /ear/ in *chandelier*.
- Point out that *cliché* and *châteu* can also be written with accents, as they would be in French.
- It is a good idea to blend and sound out the spelling words quickly every day with the children, using the 'say it as it sounds' strategy where appropriate.

chef
chute
chalet
chevron
chiffon
machine
parachute
moustache
chateau
brochure
crochet
cache
chivalry
chenille
chauffeur
cliche
chandelier
chaperone

Activity Page 1
- The children split each spelling word into syllables (*chef*, *chute*, *cha/let*, *chev/ron*, *chif/fon*, *ma/chine*, *pa/ra/chute*, *mous/tache*, *chat/eau*, *bro/chure*, *cro/chet*, *cache*, *chiv/al/ry*, *che/nille*, *chauf/feur*, *cli/che*, *chan/de/lier*, *chap/er/one*).
- They then match the phrases and spelling words, with the help of a dictionary if needed (*chalet*, *chef*, *chute*, *machine*, *chevron*, *chiffon*, *brochure*, *chateau*, *moustache*, *parachute*, *chauffeur*, *chandelier*, *chivalry*).
- They then look up the five spelling words in the dictionary and draw a different moustache on each chef.

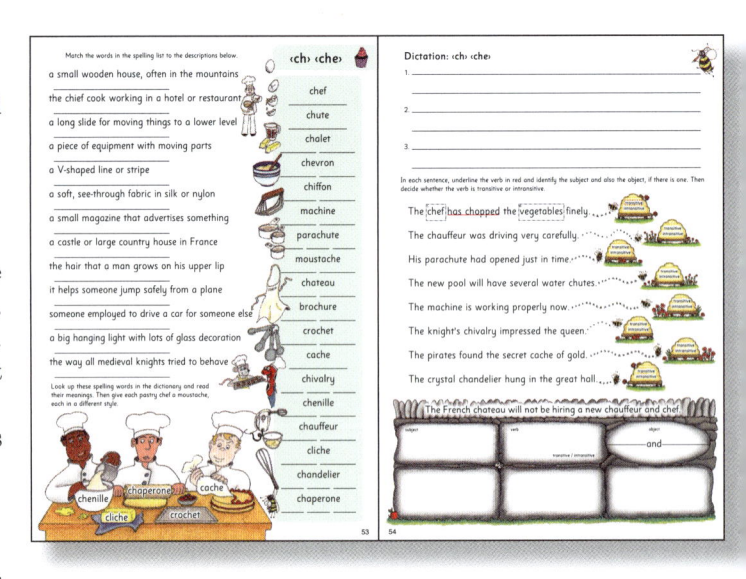

Activity Page 2
- The children find each subject and object, if there is one, and decide if the verb is transitive or intransitive.
  *chef/has chopped/vegetables/*transitive
  *chauffeur/was driving/*intransitive
  *parachute/had opened/*intransitive
  *pool/will have/chutes/*transitive
  *machine/is working/*intransitive
  *chivalry/impressed/queen/*transitive
  *pirates/found/cache/*transitive
  *chandelier/hung/*intransitive
- Then they parse the sentence and complete the wall.
- All parts of the verb (*will be hiring*) should be underlined in red. *French* is a proper adjective and should be underlined in blue.
  The French chateau will not be hiring a new chauffeur and chef.
  Top: *chateau - will be hiring - chauffeur/chef*
  Bottom: *The French - not - a new*
  Verb: transitive

Dictation
- Dictate the following sentences:

1. "Do you know how to crochet?" asked the chaperone.
2. My cousin is doing a parachute jump for charity.
3. The brochure had lots of information on the chalets.

- Remind them to use speech marks with the correct punctuation in sentence 1.

Grammar: Prepositional Phrases as Adverbs

Aim
- Develop the children's understanding of prepositional phrases by introducing the idea that they can act as adverbs within a sentence.

Introduction
- Briefly revise prepositional phrases, which are phrases that begin with a preposition, followed (often) by a noun phrase or pronoun.
- Ask the children to call out some prepositions and discuss with the class how they can be turned into prepositional phrases.
- Write a few of these on the board and ask some children to come up and underline the prepositions in green and draw a green box around the phrases.
- Now write *to walk* on the board and remind the children that this is not a prepositional phrase, but the infinitive or *name* of the verb.

Main Point
- Write *She wore a sparkling diamond ring* on the board and look at the words describing the ring.
- *Sparkling* is a present participle, made by adding the suffix ‹-ing› to the verb *sparkle*, and *diamond* is describing how the ring is decorated.
- One is normally a verb form and the other is a noun, but here they are acting as adjectives.
- Remind the class that a word can often be used as different parts of speech and we must always look at the context to decide what role it is playing.
- Now write *Zack and Jess had recently walked up the road* on the board, identify the verb (*had walked*) and ask whether the verb is transitive or intransitive.
- Transitive verbs have an object and intransitive verbs do not.
- A sentence always has a subject doing the verb (here it is a compound subject, *Zack* and *Jess*), but there is no object receiving the verb action, so the verb is intransitive.
- Now draw a sentence wall on the board and put the sentence into the boxes.
  Top: *Zack (and) Jess - had walked - (blank)*
  Bottom: *(blank) - recently - (blank)*
- Point out that the prepositional phrase *up the road* has not been put in yet and ask the children what its role is within the sentence. Explain that it is acting as an adverb by describing where Zack and Jess had walked.
- Put orange brackets around it in the sentence to show it is acting as an adverb and then write it under *recently* in the box below the verb on the sentence wall.

Activity Page
- The children write inside the outlined word *Adverbs* in orange.
- They then identify the prepositional phrase acting as an adverb and decide whether it says more about how, where or when the verb is happening (*up the hill*/where, *during the night*/when, *by airmail*/how, *without me*/how, *until 3pm*/when, *along the fence*/where, *at the table*/where, *in silence*/how, *with a big hug*/how, *for a long time*/when, *among the leaves*/where, *after breakfast*/when, *on the beach*/where).
- They can then choose one of the sentences and write it onto the sentence wall.
- If they have time, the children could draw some sentence walls on a separate piece of paper and do the same with the other sentences. 1. Top: *Jack (and) Jill - went - (blank)* / Bottom: *(blank) - up the hill - (blank)*, 2. Top: *Bats (and) owls - hunt - (blank)* / Bottom: *(blank) - during the night - (blank)*, 3. Top: *I - have sent - letter* / Bottom: *(blank) - by airmail - the*, 4. Top: *friends - have gone - (blank)* / Bottom: *My - without me - (blank)*, 5. Top: *We - visited - chateau* / Bottom: *(blank) - until 3pm - the French*, 6. Top: *cat - was creeping - (blank)* / Bottom: *A - along the fence - (blank)*, 7. Top: *family - were eating - (blank)* / Bottom: *The - at the table - (blank)*, 8. Top: *They - finished - homework* / Bottom: *(blank) - in silence - their*, 9. Top: *She - greeted - relations* / Bottom: *(blank) - with a big hug - her*, 10. Top: *dog - barked - (blank)* / Bottom: *the scruffy brown - for a long time - (blank)*, 11. Top: *hedgehog - built - nest* / Bottom: *The - among the leaves - its*, 12. Top: *We - will do - jump* / Bottom: *(blank) - after breakfast - the parachute*, 13. Top: *Milly (and) Zeena - built - sandcastle* / Bottom: *(blank) - on the beach - a*.

Extension Activity
- The children try putting more of the sentences into the word walls.

Grammar 5 Pupil Book: Page 56 & 57

Spelling: ‹sure›

Spelling Test
- The children turn to the backs of their books and find the column labelled *Spelling Test 18*.
- Call out the spelling words learnt last week.

Revision
- Write these words on the board and identify the ‹ch› saying /sh/ in each one: **ch**ef, para**ch**ute, ma**ch**ine, **ch**evron, bro**ch**ure, **ch**auffeur.
- Remind the class that many words with the ‹ch› spelling of /sh/ are originally French, but have been *borrowed* and are now used in English.

Spelling Point
- Revise the ‹ure› spelling, which is often preceded by ‹t› or ‹s›.
- In monosyllabic words like *pure* and *cure*, ‹ure› says /ue-r/, but when it follows ‹s› it can be said in several ways.
- At the end of multisyllabic words the vowel is swallowed and becomes a schwa: in words like *treasure* and *leisure*, ‹sure› says /zher/ and in *pressure* and *fissure* it says /sher/.
- In the monosyllabic word *sure*, however, the spelling usually says /shor/; this pronunciation is retained in longer words associated with it, such as *unsure* and *ensure*.
- Knowing examples of words that take each spelling will help the children in their writing; if they want to write a word ending in /zher/, /sher/ or /shor/, they can listen to the sounds and use analogy to work out the spelling.

Spelling List
- Go through the list, identify the syllables in each word and discuss the meaning of any unfamiliar words.
- Ask the class to find and highlight each ‹sure› spelling.
- Discuss which pronunciation of ‹sure› is being used in each word: /zher/, /sher/ or /shor/.
- Point out the ‹ea› saying /e/ in *measure*, *displeasure* and *countermeasure*, the letters saying their long vowel sound in r*ea*ssure, cl*o*sure, comp*o*sure, encl*o*sure, *o*verexp*o*sure and discl*o*sure, the soft ‹c› in *censure*, the ‹ei› saying /e/ in *leisurely* and the prefixes in **un**sure, **re**assure, **dis**closure and **dis**pleasure.
- It is a good idea to blend and sound out the spelling words quickly every day with the children, using the 'say it as it sounds' strategy where appropriate.

sure
unsure
ensure
assure
measure
insure
reassure
pressure
closure
censure
fissure
leisurely
composure
enclosure
overexposure
disclosure
displeasure
countermeasure

Activity Page 1
- The children split each spelling word into syllables (*sure, un/sure, en/sure, as/sure, mea/sure, in/sure, re/as/sure, pres/sure, clo/sure, cen/sure, fis/sure, lei/sure/ly, com/po/sure, en/clo/sure, o/ver/ex/po/sure, dis/clo/sure, dis/plea/sure, coun/ter/mea/sure*).
- They then write in the spelling word that completes each sentence (*ensure, measure, sure, unsure, assure, insure, closure, reassure, fissure, pressure, leisurely, censure*).
- Then they find the spelling words for the three prefixes ‹un›, ‹dis› and ‹re› (*unsure, displeasure/disclosure, reassure*).

Activity Page 2
- The children underline each preposition in green and add a noun phrase to make a prepositional phrase.
- They then choose one of the phrases and use it in a sentence so that the phrase is acting as an adverb, (describing how, where or when the verb is happening).
- Then they parse the sentence and complete the wall.
- *During his visit* is a prepositional phrase acting as an adverb, so orange brackets can be put around it.
The kind policeman had reassured the old couple (during his visit).
Top: *policeman - had reassured - couple*
Bottom: *The kind - during his visit - the old*
Verb: transitive

Dictation
- Dictate the following sentences:

1. Ensure that you are insured before driving the car.
2. "I'm sure that can't be true," she said with displeasure.
3. The dressmaker measured the chiffon carefully before she cut it.

- In sentence 2, remind the children to use speech marks with the correct punctuation and to place the apostrophe correctly in each contraction.

Grammar: Phrasal Verbs

Aim
- Introduce the idea of phrasal verbs, which consist of a verb and one or more other words, usually a preposition or adverb.
- Put together, these words make a new verb with a new meaning.

Introduction
- Briefly revise prepositions and prepositional phrases with the children.
- Remind them that a preposition is a word that relates one noun or pronoun to another.
- It usually does this by describing where the noun is or where it is moving towards, or by relating the noun to a time or event.
- Ask the children to call out some prepositional phrases and discuss whether they start with a preposition of time or place.

Main Point
- Write *Tom looked up a word in the dictionary* on the board. Ask the children to identify the preposition.
- The children should be able to identify *in*, which is describing the position of *word* in relation to *dictionary*.
- They may also say *up*, as this word can be either a preposition or an adverb.
- However, *up* in this sentence is not relating *Tom* to *word* as *up a word* by itself does not make sense. Nor is it acting as an adverb, as *up* is not describing the direction in which Tom is looking at the word.
- Instead it is part of the verb *to look up*, which means *to find*. (As the preposition or adverb no longer has its own meaning, it is also known as a particle, but the children can learn this later.)
- Explain that this kind of verb is called a phrasal verb and usually consists of a verb plus a preposition or adverb which, when put together, make a new verb with a new meaning.
- This is true of *to look up*, which has a different meaning to the verb *to look*. It is also true of the phrasal verb *to look up to*, which has a different meaning again.
- Ask the children if they know what this verb means and explain that if you look up to someone, you admire or respect them.
- Look at some other phrasal verbs and discuss how their meanings differ from the original words.
- Possible examples include: *blow up, break in, calm down, check in, fall apart, get away, give in, grow out of, hang back, hold on to, keep from, mix up, put up with, send for, sleep over, stick around, take after, work out.*
- Point out that in some of these examples, the extra words are adverbs (*apart, away, out, back*) rather than prepositions, and that the same phrasal verb can mean different things. For example you can *blow up* (destroy) something with dynamite, or *blow up* (inflate) a balloon, or *blow up* (enlarge) a photograph.

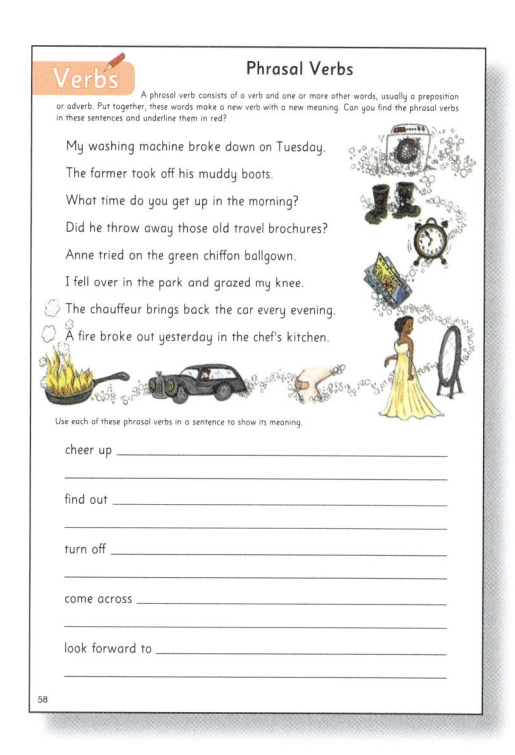

Activity Page
- The children write inside the outlined word *Verbs*, using a red pencil.
- They then identify the phrasal verb in each sentence, underlining all the words in red (*broke down*, meaning *stopped working*; *took off*, meaning *removed*; *get up*, meaning *get out of bed*; *throw away*, meaning *get rid of*; *tried on*, meaning *put on to see how it looks or fits*; *fell over*, meaning *fell onto the ground*; *brings back*, meaning *returns*; *broke out*, meaning *started suddenly*).
- Then they look at the phrasal verbs at the bottom of the activity page and use each one in a sentence to show its correct meaning.

Extension Activity
- The children can start a collection of phrasal verbs.
- Ask them to write down as many as they can think of, or give them some verbs (possible examples include: *break, call, cut, fall, get, give, go, hand, keep, look, put, take, turn*) along with the prepositions from page 40 of the *Pupil Book* to give them some ideas.

Rounding off
- Go over the activity page with the children, discussing their answers.
- If they have done the extension activity, ask some of the children to say some of their phrasal verbs and discuss what they mean.

GRAMMAR 5 PUPIL BOOK: PAGE 59 & 60

Spelling: ‹ture›

Spelling Test
- The children turn to the backs of their books and find the column labelled *Spelling Test 19*.
- Call out the spelling words learnt last week.

Revision
- Write these words on the board and identify the spellings: sugges**tion**, dimen**sion**, discu**ssion**, electri**cian**, celebra**tion**.
- Words with these suffixes usually end in /shun/, but ‹-tion› can also say /chun/ and ‹-sion› can say /zhun/.
- Ask the class to suggest other words with these spellings and discuss how the suffix changes or adds meaning in each word.

Spelling Point
- Revise the ‹ure› spelling, which is often preceded by ‹t› or ‹s›.
- In monosyllabic words like *pure* and *cure*, ‹ure› says /ue-r/ but when it follows ‹t› at the end of multisyllabic words, the ‹ture› usually sounds like /cher/, as in *picture* and *nature*: the ‹t› says /ch/ and the vowel is swallowed and becomes a schwa.
- Once children know that the sounds in /cher/ are usually written as ‹ture›, they can use analogy to spell these sounds in other words.

Spelling List
- Go through the list, identify the syllables in each word and discuss the meaning of any unfamiliar words.
- Ask the class to find and highlight each ‹ture› spelling.
- Point out other spelling features, such as the ‹x› in *mixture*, the soft ‹g› in *gesture*, the ‹ur› spelling of /er/ in *nurture* and *furniture*, the ‹u› saying its long vowel sound in *future*, the schwas (as in *temperature* and *literature*), the silent ‹a› in *miniature* and the ‹ch› saying ‹k› in *architecture*.
- Point out that *caricature* is the only word in the list which says /chooer/ or /chor/ instead of /cher/ and discuss the prefix ‹mini-› and its meaning in *miniature*.
- It is a good idea to blend and sound out the spelling words quickly every day with the children, using the 'say it as it sounds' strategy where appropriate.

mixture
gesture
nurture
culture
venture
future
structure
dentures
fracture
departure
temperature
literature
agriculture
caricature
miniature
furniture
signature
architecture

Activity Page 1
- The children split each spelling word into syllables (*mix/ture, ges/ture, nur/ture, cul/ture, ven/ture, fu/ture, struc/ture, den/tures, frac/ture, de/par/ture, tem/per/a/ture, lit/er/a/ture, ag/ri/cul/ture, car/i/ca/ture, min/ia/ture, fur/ni/ture, sig/na/ture, ar/chi/tec/ture*).
- They then write the meaning for each of the numbered spelling words.
- Encourage the children to use a dictionary if they are unsure of any words.

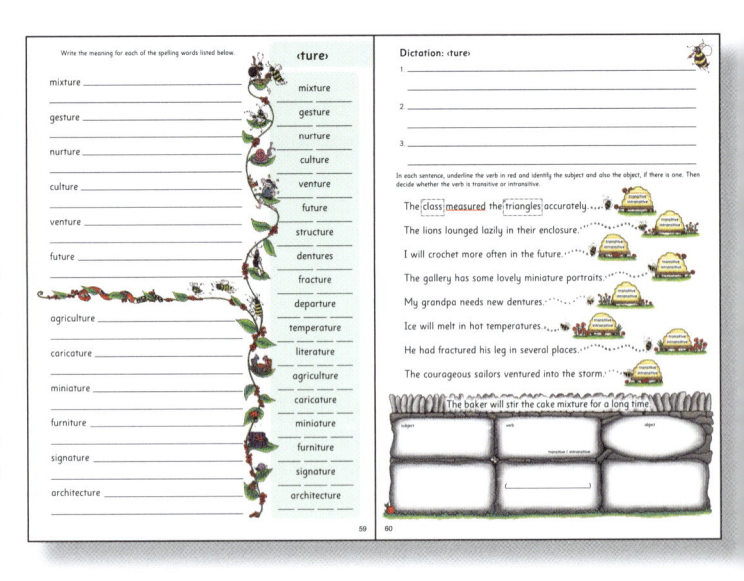

Activity Page 2
- The children find each subject and object, if there is one, and decide if the verb is transitive or intransitive.
  class / measured / triangles / transitive
  lions / lounged / intransitive
  I / will crochet / intransitive
  gallery / has / portraits / transitive
  grandpa / needs / dentures / transitive
  ice / will melt / intransitive
  he / had fractured / leg / transitive
  sailors / ventured / intransitive
- Then they parse the sentence and complete the wall.
- *Cake* is a noun acting as an adjective and should be underlined in blue. *For a long time* is a prepositional phrase acting as an adverb, so orange brackets can be put around it.
  The baker will stir the cake mixture (for a long time).
  Top: *baker - will stir - mixture*
  Bottom: *The - for a long time - the cake*
  Verb: transitive

Dictation
- Dictate the following sentences:

1. She studied Chinese culture and literature at college
2. The room had a mixture of different styles of furniture.
3. "The superstructure of the building is undamaged," assured the architect.

- Remind them to use speech marks with the correct punctuation in sentence 3. *Chinese* is a proper adjective and needs a capital letter.

Grammar: More Phrasal Verbs

Aim
- Develop the children's understanding of phrasal verbs, and introduce the idea that they can be separable or inseparable.

Introduction
- Briefly revise phrasal verbs with the class. Phrasal verbs consist of a verb and one or more other words (usually a preposition or adverb) which, put together, make a new verb with a new meaning.
- Ask the children to call out as many phrasal verbs they can think of, or give them some examples of verbs and prepositions to help them get started.
- Ask the children what some of the phrasal verbs mean and discuss whether they can have more than one meaning. (For example, *to break down* can mean *to stop working*, *to get upset* or *to divide into smaller parts*.)

Main Point
- Write *Jane looked up a word in the dictionary* on the board and ask the children to identify the phrasal verb.
- They should be able to remember from the previous lesson that it is *looked up*, which means *found*.
- Discuss what the subject and object of the sentence is. Invite two children to come up and draw a box (with a small ‹s› inside) around the simple subject, *Jane*, and a ring (with a small ‹o› inside) around the simple object, *word*.
- Ask the children whether the phrasal verb *to look up* is transitive or intransitive.
- They should know from the lesson on transitive and instransitive verbs (see page 52 of the *Pupil Book*) that it is transitive because the verb action is carried across to its object, whereas an intransitive verb does not have an object.
- Now write *Jane looked a word up in the dictionary* and ask the children what has changed. They should be able to see that the word order is different; the object (including *a*, its indefinite article) is now separating the two parts of the phrasal verb.
- When a phrasal verb is transitive it can usually be written in either way; it is separable. When the parts of the phrasal verb always stay together, it is called inseparable.
- Remind the children that the prefix ‹in-› means *not* and so *inseparable* means the opposite of its root: *not separable*.
- Write *James looked his dog after*, discuss why this does not sound right. Explain that *to look after* is an inseparable phrasal verb.
- Ask the children how it should be written and write it on the board: *James looked after his dog*.
- Now ask the children to look at the first sentence again and ask what would happen if the object *word* was replaced by the pronoun *it*. Even though *to look up* is a separable phrasal verb and can usually be written in both ways, we would never write *Jane looked up it*; a pronoun always separates a separable phrasal verb.

Activity Page
- The children write inside the outlined word *Verbs*, using a red pencil.
- They then look at the phrasal verbs in each honey pot and decide which one matches the description underneath (*get away*, *call out*, *look after*, *give up*, *put back*, *turn on*).
- Then they complete the sentences below by writing in the correct phrasal verb, choosing from the three options available (*take back*, meaning *return*; *break into*, meaning *enter without permission*; *pick up*, meaning *lift up*; *run out of*, meaning *have none left*; *drop off*, meaning *interrupt a car journey to let someone out*; *check in*, meaning *report that you have arrived*).

Extension Activity
- The children look at the second set of phrasal verbs on the activity page and decide whether they are separable or inseparable (separable, inseparable, separable, inseparable, separable, inseparable).

Rounding Off
- Go over the activity page with the children, discussing their answers.
- If they have done the extension activity, check the children's answers for this as well.

GRAMMAR 5 PUPIL BOOK: PAGES 62 & 63

Spelling: ‹-ible›

Spelling Test
- The children turn to the backs of their books and find the column labelled *Spelling Test 20*.
- Call out the spelling words learnt last week.

Revision
- Write these words on the board and identify the spellings ‹ture› and ‹sure›: *measure, pressure, insure, gesture, temperature, miniature*.
- Look at how each spelling is said – ‹sure› usually says /zher/, /sher/ or /shor/ and ‹ture› usually says /cher/ – and ask the class to suggest other words with these spellings.

Spelling Point
- Revise the suffix ‹-able›, which is often found in adjectives such as *breakable* and *lovable* and means *capable or worthy of being (the root word)*.
- Now write the word *visible* on the board and ask the class what it means (*able to be seen*).
- Explain that ‹-ible› and ‹-able› are suffixes with the same meaning. They only vary in spelling because of their Latin origins.
- However, knowing which spelling to use can be difficult because the vowel is often a schwa.
- As a general rule, the suffix ‹-able› is more common and is usually added to an identifiable root word. It always comes after words ending in a hard ‹c› or ‹g›, (avoiding the soft ‹ci› and ‹gi› spelling).
- The suffix ‹-ible› is more likely to be added to a root that is not a complete word; in *visible*, for example, *vis* comes from the Latin verb *videre* meaning *to see* and can be found in other English words like *vision, vista, visor* and *visual*.
- There will always be exceptions, of course, and the children should use a dictionary if they are not sure.

Spelling List
- Go through the list, identify the syllables in each word and discuss the meaning of any unfamiliar words.
- Ask the class to find and highlight each ‹ible› spelling.
- Point out the ‹x› in *flexible*, the soft ‹g› in *illegible, tangible* and *intelligible*, the ‹au› in *audible*, the schwa in *convertible*, the ‹s› saying /z/ in *visible* and *feasible*, the prefixes in *incredible, indestructible* and *reversible* (meaning *not* and *again*, respectively) and the variant spellings of ‹in-› in *illegible* and *irresponsible*.
- It is a good idea to blend and sound out the spelling words quickly every day with the class, using the

terrible
sensible
edible
horrible
possible
flexible
illegible
audible
tangible
convertible
visible
incredible
feasible
reversible
intelligible
indestructible
irresponsible
comprehensible

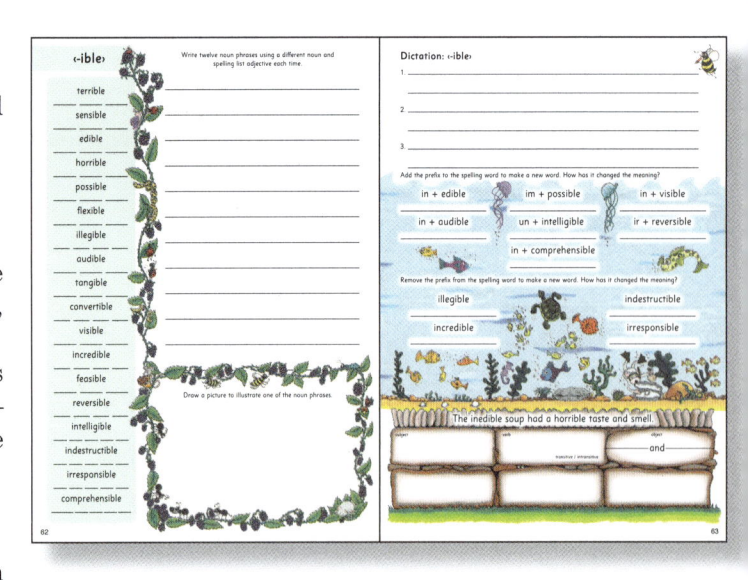

'say it as it sounds' strategy where appropriate, or you could break down the words into root (word) and suffix.

Activity Page 1
- The children split each spelling word into syllables (*ter/ri/ble, sen/si/ble, ed/i/ble, hor/ri/ble, pos/si/ble, flex/i/ble, il/le/gi/ble, au/di/ble, tan/gi/ble, con/ver/ti/ble, vis/i/ble, in/cre/di/ble, fea/si/ble, re/ver/si/ble, in/tel/li/gi/ble, in/de/struc/ti/ble, ir/re/spon/si/ble, com/pre/hen/si/ble*).
- They then choose twelve adjectives from the spelling list, write a noun phrase for each one and draw a picture to illustrate one of them.

Activity Page 2
- The children write out the new words formed when either adding or removing the prefixes from the spelling words. (The prefixes ‹il-›, ‹im-›, ‹in-›, ‹ir-› and ‹un-› all mean *not* and create words with the opposite meaning.)
- Then they parse the sentence and complete the wall.
The inedible soup had a horrible taste and smell.
Top: *soup - had - taste/smell*
Bottom: *The inedible - (blank) - a horrible*
Verb: transitive

Dictation
- Dictate the following sentences:

1. It is irresponsible to venture out alone at night.
2. The physician's handwriting is almost illegible.
3. "This convertible is an incredible automobile!" exclaimed the American.

- Remind them to use speech marks with the correct punctuation in sentence 3. *American* is a proper adjective and needs a capital letter.

Grammar: Making Nouns and Adjectives into Verbs

Aim
- Refine the children's knowledge of suffixes and how they change or add meaning to words.
- Introduce the suffixes ‹-ate›, ‹-ify›, ‹-ise› and ‹-ize›, which can be added to some nouns and adjectives to make verbs.

Introduction
- Remind the class that a suffix is usually one or more syllables added at the end of a word to change, or add to, its meaning: they can make plurals (bed**s**, sandwich**es**, diar**ies**), comparatives and superlatives (lat**er**, lat**est**), the simple past tense and regular past participle (watch**ed**/had watch**ed**), the present participle (watch**ing**) and irregular past participles (eat**en**/know**n**).
- They sometimes turn one type of word into another: ‹-y› turns nouns into adjectives (grass**y**) and ‹-ly› turns adjectives into adverbs (‹-ally› is used if the word ends in ‹-ic›, as in majestic**ally**); ‹-ful› and ‹-less› turn abstract nouns into adjectives with opposite meanings (care**less**, care**ful**); ‹-able› turns verbs into adjectives (believ**able**); and ‹-ance› and ‹-ence› can turn verbs into abstract nouns like guid**ance** and differ**ence**.
- Many have a particular meaning: ‹cian› and ‹-ist› are found in nouns describing people with a particular skill, interest or occupation, such as musi**cian** and tour**ist**.

Main Point
- Write the words decorate, simplify and apologise on the board and discuss how these are all verbs with different suffixes.
- Identify the suffixes with the class and underline them: decor**ate**, simpl**ify**, apolog**ise**.
- Explain that the suffix ‹-ise› is actually a variant of the older spelling ‹-ize› and either suffix can usually be used in British English, although ‹-ise› is often preferred. However, the children will learn later (see page 68 of the Pupil Book) that some words are only spelt ‹-ise› or ‹-ize› and have to be learnt.
- Point out that the root word for each of these verbs is either a noun or adjective (decor, simple, apology) and explain that these suffixes can be added to some nouns or adjectives to make verbs.
- Also remind the class that not every word ending in ‹ate› or ‹ise/ize› will be a verb: some words just take this spelling, such as climate, wise and prize. If the children are in any doubt they should try putting to in front of the word or look up the word in the dictionary.
- Look at the root words on the activity page and discuss how they can be made into verbs by adding the appropriate suffix:
  - In adjectives like invalid and solid and nouns like decor, origin, computer and item, the suffix is simply added to make invalid**ate**, solid**ify**, decor**ate**, origin**ate**, computer**ise** and item**ise**.
  - In words ending in ‹e› or ‹y›, the final letter is removed before adding the suffix, as in vaccinate, simplify and apologise.
  - In nouns like horror and terror, the letters ‹or› are removed before adding the suffix, to make horrify and terrify.
  - In the words drama and crystal, extra letters are added before adding the suffix, to make dramatise and crystallise.

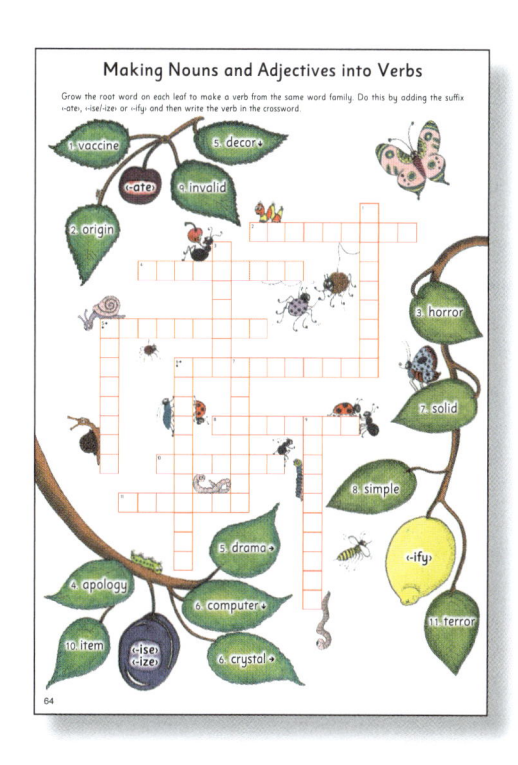

Activity Page
- The children add the suffixes in the way they were shown earlier and write the numbered verbs in the grid, like a crossword (1. vaccinate, 2. originate, 3. horrify, 4. apologise/ize, 5. dramatise/ize [across], decorate [down], 6. crystallise/ize [across], computerise/ize [down], 7. solidify, 8. simplify, 9. invalidate, 10. itemise/ize, 11. terrify).

Extension Activity
- On a separate sheet of paper, the children choose some of the verbs from the grid and use them in a sentence.

Rounding Off
- Go over the activity page with the children, discussing their answers.
- If they have done the extension activity, ask some of the children to read out their sentences.

GRAMMAR 5 PUPIL BOOK: PAGE 65 & 66

Spelling: ‹-ate›

Spelling Test
- The children turn to the backs of their books and find the column labelled *Spelling Test 21*.
- Call out the spelling words learnt last week.

Revision
- Write these words on the board and identify the ‹-ible› suffix: ter*rible*, vi*sible*, hor*rible*, comprehen*sible*, rever*sible*.
- Each time, ask the class to suggest some other words in that word family (that is, words that share the same root) and discuss their meanings.

Spelling Point
- Write the words *frustrate*, *complicate* and *vaccinate* on the board. Ask the class what they have in common.
- Following on from the previous grammar lesson, the children should recognise that they are all verbs which end in the suffix ‹-ate›.
- Remind the children that this suffix can be added to words to make either nouns or verbs. They can try adding *to* to check whether a word is a verb or not.
- When it appears in verbs, it means *to give or make something have the quality of* (the root word), so if you *frustrate* someone, you make them *frustrated*, if you *complicate* a situation, you make it more *complicated* and if you *vaccinate* people, you give them *vaccinations*.
- All the words in the spelling list are verbs with the suffix ‹-ate›.

Spelling List
- Go through the list, identify the syllables in each word and discuss the meaning of any unfamiliar words.
- Ask the class to find and highlight each ‹ate› spelling.
- Point out other spelling features, such as the schwas (as in *decorate* and *hibernate*), the ‹i› spelling in *pollinate* (in contrast to its root word *pollen*), the letters making their long vowel sound in *hibernate* and *appreciate*, the soft ‹c› in *circulate*, *vaccinate*, *participate* and *appreciate* (in this last word it is often pronounced /sh/), the soft ‹g› in *originate* and the prefix in *in*validate.
- Remind the children that the prefix ‹in-› means *not*, so *invalidate* means *to make something not valid*.
- It is a good idea to blend and sound out the spelling words quickly every day with the children, using the 'say it as it sounds' strategy where appropriate, or you could break down the words into root (word) and suffix.

negate
decorate
pollinate
frustrate
activate
captivate
hibernate
complicate
formulate
circulate
originate
aggravate
vaccinate
participate
invalidate
speculate
culminate
appreciate

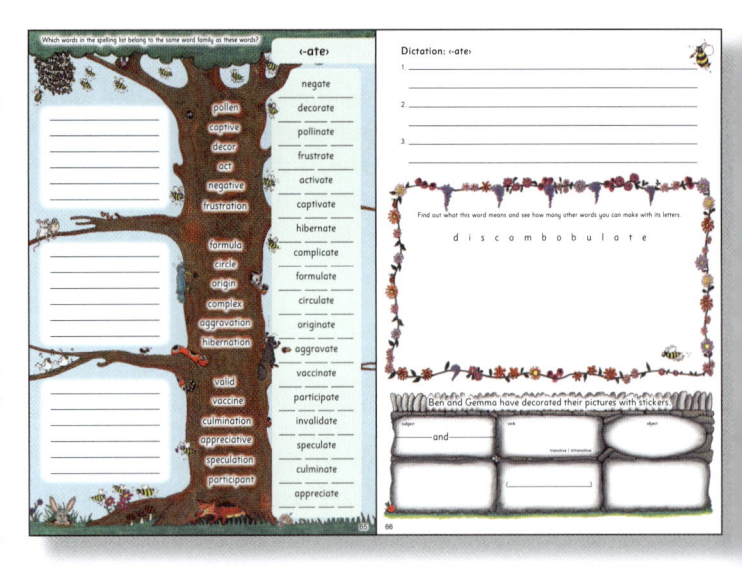

Activity Page 1
- The children split each spelling word into syllables (ne/gate, dec/o/rate, pol/li/nate, frus/trate, ac/ti/vate, cap/ti/vate, hi/ber/nate, com/pli/cate, for/mu/late, cir/cu/late, o/rig/i/nate, ag/gra/vate, vac/ci/nate, par/tic/i/pate, in/val/i/date, spec/u/late, cul/mi/nate, ap/pre/ci/ate).
- They then match each spelling list verb to the word from its word family (*pollinate, captivate, decorate, activate, negate, frustrate, formulate, circulate, originate, complicate, aggravate, hibernate, validate, vaccinate, culminate, appreciate, speculate, participate*).

Activity Page 2
- The children look up *discombobulate* in the dictionary and make as many words as they can with its letters.
- Then they parse the sentence and complete the wall.
- *Their* is a possessive adjective and should be underlined in blue. *With stickers* is a prepositional phrase acting as an adverb, so orange brackets can be put around it.

Ben and Gemma have decorated their pictures (with stickers).
Top: *Ben/Gemma - have decorated - pictures*
Bottom: (blank) - *with stickers - their*
Verb: transitive

Dictation
- Dictate the following sentences:

1. Honey bees pollinate the flowers in our cottage garden.
2. The paediatrician uses a syringe to vaccinate children.
3. "The hedgehogs are hibernating under the shed," announced Dad.

- Remind them to use speech marks with the correct punctuation in sentence 3. Here, *Dad* is used as a proper noun and needs a capital letter.

Grammar: Nouns or Verbs?

Aim
- Help the children develop their ability to choose the correct spelling for nouns and verbs that look and sound very similar, but can end in either ‹ce› or ‹se› or ‹cy› or ‹sy›.

Introduction
- Briefly revise these homophones with the children: *our* and *are*; *their*, *there* and *they're*; *your* and *you're*; *its* and *it's*; *to*, *two* and *too*; and *where*, *wear* and *were*.
- Make sure the children know which spellings take which meanings.
- *Our* is more properly pronounced /ou-r/ but in practice it is often pronounced /ar/ and can be confused with *are*.
- *Were* is not strictly a homophone of *where*, but their spellings are often confused so it helps to look at them together.
- Point out that some of these words are parts of the verb *to be* (*are*, *were*) and some are possessive adjectives (*our*, *your*, *their*, *its*), while others are contractions (*they're*, *you're*, *it's*).
- Children often find *its* and *it's* particularly difficult because apostrophe ‹s› can also be used to show possession.
- However, it is only used in this way to make possessive nouns and not possessive adjectives, and *its* is a possessive adjective.
- Remind the children that it is important to use the correct spelling when writing homophones, otherwise their writing will not make sense.

Main Point
- Remind the children that they have recently learnt the ‹-ise› or ‹-ize› suffix for verbs with a noun or adjective as their root word.
- For British English speakers, these verbs can take either spelling, although ‹-ise› is more usual.
- However, the children will learn in the next spelling lesson that certain verbs are only spelt ‹-ise› or ‹-ize› and have to be learnt; two of these are *advise* and *devise*.
- Write these words on the board and then write *advice* and *device* underneath. Ask the children what the difference is in each pair of words.
- The children should be able to say that the ‹s› has been replaced by ‹c› and therefore will be pronounced slightly differently; instead of ending in /iez/, the soft ‹c› spelling turns it into /ies/.
- Explain that these words are also different parts of speech.
- Write *I practise my spellings every day* and *We enjoyed our music practice yesterday* and ask what role they are playing in each sentence.
- *Practise* is a verb and takes the subject (*I*) and object (*spellings*). *Practice* is the object of the sentence and is described by *our* and *music* and so must be a noun.
- Explain that there are several pairs of nouns and verbs like this, where the nouns are spelt with a ‹c› and the verbs are spelt with an ‹s›.
- Two are pairs of homophones, which are spelt differently but sound the same (*practice/practise* and *licence/license*), and the other pair is *prophecy* and *prophesy*, where the noun ends in /see/ and the verb ends in /sie/.
- Discuss each of the words with the children, making sure they know what the words mean and can identify which is the noun and which is the verb. One way to remember is to connect the spelling ‹ice› with the noun *ice*, to help the children remember that the nouns are always spelt with a ‹c›.

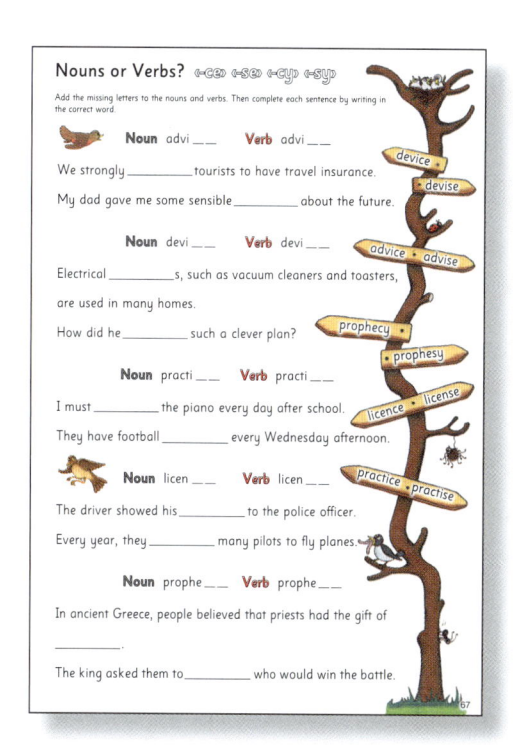

Activity Page
- The children add ‹ce› to all the nouns and ‹se› to all the verbs.
- They then read each pair of sentences, decide whether the missing word is the noun or the verb, and write it on the line (*advise*: verb, *advice*: noun, *device*: noun, *devise*: verb, *practise*: verb, *practice*: noun, *licence*: noun, *license*: verb, *prophecy*: noun, *prophesy*: verb).

Extension Activity
- The children write a sentence for each of the nouns and verbs, making sure they use the correct spelling each time.

Rounding Off
- Go over the activity page with the children, discussing their answers.
- If they have done the extension activity, ask some of the children to read out their sentences.

GRAMMAR 5 PUPIL BOOK: PAGE 68 & 69

Spelling: ‹-ise›, ‹-ize›

Spelling Test
- The children turn to the backs of their books and find the column labelled *Spelling Test 22*.
- Call out the spelling words learnt last week.

Revision
- Write these words on the board and identify the verb endings taught on page 64 of the *Pupil Book*: poll*inate*, decor*ate*, terr*ify*, ident*ify*, pr*ize*, disg*uise*.
- Ask the class to suggest other words with these suffixes, add them to the board and discuss their meanings.

Spelling Point
- Revise the spellings of verbs ending in /iez/: ‹ise› and ‹ize›.
- The suffix ‹-ise› is actually a variant of the older spelling ‹-ize› and either suffix can usually be used in British English (although ‹-ise› is often preferred).
- American English, however, only uses ‹-ise› in the small number of words that always take that spelling.
- The spelling list contains most of these words (the others are *demise, excise, surmise, franchise,* and *supervise*) and also the two words that always take ‹-ize›: *prize* and *capsize*.
- Words that always take the ‹-ise› spelling are words with a French origin.

Spelling List
- Go through the list, identify the syllables in each word and discuss the meaning of any unfamiliar words.
- Ask the class to find and highlight either the ‹ize› or ‹ise› spelling.
- Point out the schwas (as in *a*rise, *ad*vertise, *impro*vise, *exer*cise and *compro*mise), the ‹e› saying /i/ in *de*vise, *re*vise, *de*spise, *tele*vise, *en*franchise and *dis*enfranchise (in this last word, it can also be a schwa), the silent ‹u› in *disguise* (which is part of the silent letter digraph ‹gu›), the ‹ur› spelling in *surmise*, the soft ‹c› in *exercise* and the prefixes in *revise, disguise, televise* and *disenfranchise*.
- It is a good idea to blend and sound out the spelling words quickly every day with the children, using the 'say it as it sounds' strategy where appropriate, or you could break down the words into root (word) and suffix.

prize
capsize
arise
devise
advise
revise
advertise
comprise
despise
disguise
improvise
surmise
surprise
televise
exercise
compromise
enfranchise
disenfranchise

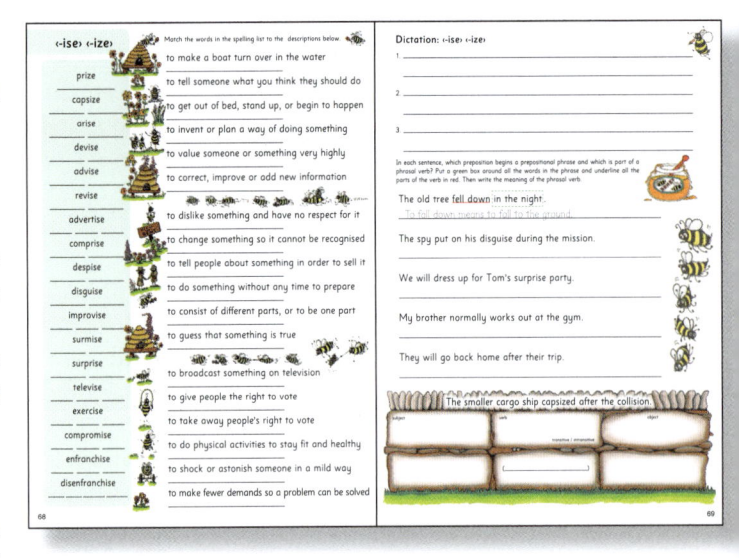

Activity Page 1
- The children split each spelling word into syllables (*prize, cap/size, a/rise, de/vise, ad/vise, re/vise, ad/ver/tise, com/prise, des/pise, dis/guise, im/pro/vise,* sur/mise, sur/prise, tel/e/vise, ex/er/cise, com/pro/mise, en/fran/chise, dis/en/fran/chise).
- They then match the phrases and spelling words (*capsize, advise, arise, devise, prize, revise, despise, disguise, advertise, improvise, comprise, surmise, televise, enfranchise, disenfranchise, exercise, surprise, compromise*).
- Encourage the children to use a dictionary if they are unsure of any words.

Activity Page 2
- The children identify the phrasal verbs and prepositional phrases and write the meaning of the verb.
  fell down [to fall to the ground]/in the night
  put on [to wear]/during the mission
  dress up [to put on nice clothes]/for Tom's surprise party
  works out [to exercise]/at the gym
  go back [to return to a place]/after their trip
- Then they parse the sentence and complete the wall.
- *Cargo* is a noun acting as an adjective and should be underlined in blue. *After the collision* is a prepositional phrase acting as an adverb, so orange brackets can be put around it.
  The smaller cargo ship capsized (after the collision).
  Top: *ship - capsized -* (blank)
  Bottom: *The smaller cargo - after the collision -* (blank)
  Verb: intransitive

Dictation
- Dictate the following sentences:

1. The doctor advised him to exercise more often.
2. Ron prized his collection of famous autographs.
3. "I'm advertising for a new assistant," said the magician.

- In sentence 3, remind the children to use speech marks with the correct punctuation and to place the apostrophe correctly in the contraction, *I'm. Ron* is a proper noun and needs a capital letter.

Grammar: The Order of Adjectives (1)

Aim
- Refine the children's understanding of adjectives, and introduce the idea that when we use more than one adjective to describe something, the adjectives tend to be written in a certain order.

Introduction
- Revise adjectives, which are words that describe nouns (a **blue** car or The car is **blue**) or pronouns (as in She is **happy**).
- Some adjectives show possession, as in I fed **my** cat or We put up **our** umbrellas and some describe something by comparing it to other items: a comparative compares a noun to one or more other items (He is **taller** than his brother and sister) and a superlative compares something to all the other items in its group (He is the **tallest** in the class).
- Ask the children to suggest some nouns (perhaps from a topic they are studying) and write them on the board.
- Look at each one in turn and ask the children to think of an adjective to describe it.
- Write the adjective next to the noun and underline it in blue.

Main Point
- Choose one of the nouns and adjectives from the board and ask the children to expand the noun phrase, adding more adjectives to it.
- For example, they could say *the little old Chinese lady*.
- Write this on the board and ask the children why they have put the words in this order.
- Try changing the order to *the Chinese old little lady* and ask them if it sounds right.
- Explain that adjectives can be grouped into certain categories, describing things like colour, size or what something is made of. These different types of adjective tend to be arranged in a certain order.
- Draw a large grid on the board with seven columns and write in the following headings, explaining what each one means. Ask the children to suggest adjectives for each category and write them in the appropriate column:
1. Determiners (special sorts of adjectives showing which thing is meant): for example, *a, an, the, these, this, some, this, that, those, these, one, two*.
2. Opinion: *beautiful, ugly, terrifying, tasty, lovely, interesting, boring*.
3. Size and shape (including weight and length): *big, little, large, heavy, wide, narrow, tall, short, light, deep, long, enormous, tiny, round, square*.
4. Condition and age: *old, young, new, antique, clean, dirty, wet, dry*.
5. Colour and pattern: *red, yellow, blue, orange, green, pink, purple, striped, spotty, checked, flowery*.
6. Origin (describing nationality or religion): *Scottish, Chinese, Indian, Russian*.
7. Material: *wooden, silky, metallic, furry*.

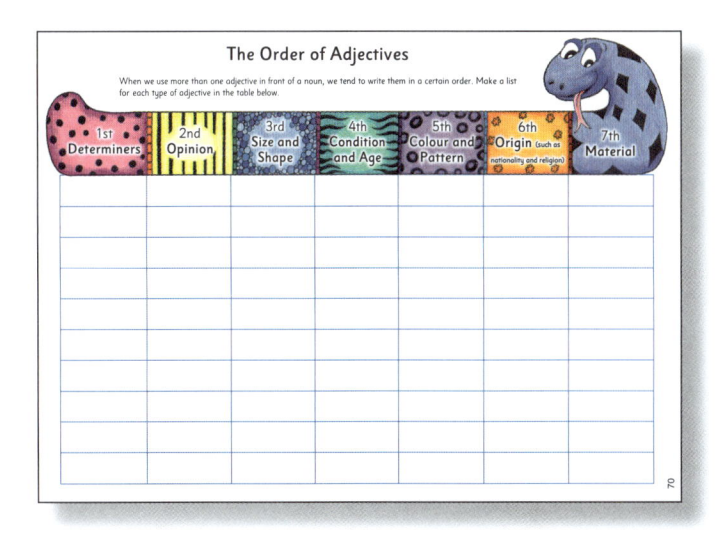

- Explain that this is only a general rule and sometimes the adjectives can go in a different order.
- For example, when describing something's shape and age, we tend to put shape second, as in *the old square box*.
- However, it can be a useful guide, especially for children who do not have English as their first language.

Activity Page
- They then fill in the column for each type of adjective, using some of the words on the board and then adding their own.
- If some of the children need extra support they could use some of the adjectives from the extension activity below, sorting them into the correct categories.

Extension Activity
- Write the following adjectives on the board: *brick, yellow, elderly, a, Roman, new, superb, flat, Australian, this striped, paper, Russian, clean, five, strange, big, Thai, glass, purple, African, short, flowery, friendly, ancient, the, plastic, orange, terrible, wooden, round, noisy, sponge, Japanese, thin, white, my, cotton, wide, hungry, kind, these, long, brown, metal, Egyptian, cold, eloquent, black, gigantic, some, broken, horrible, silk, spotted, little, Irish, that, old, South American, young, Turkish, his, square, beautiful, marble, tartan, wet, an, expensive*.
- Ask the children to decide which category the adjectives belong to and add them to their list.
- They could also make up some noun phrases using the adjectives on their activity page.

Rounding Off
- Go over the activity page with the children, discussing their answers.
- If they have done the extension activity, ask some of the children to read out their noun phrases.

GRAMMAR 5 PUPIL BOOK: PAGE 71 & 72

Spelling: ‹-ify›

Spelling Test
- The children turn to the backs of their books and find the column labelled *Spelling Test 23*.
- Call out the spelling words learnt last week.

Revision
- Write these words on the board and identify the verb endings taught on page 64 of the *Pupil Book*: hiber**nate**, hor**rify**, cap**size**, vacci**nate**, sim**plify**, surp**rise**.
- Ask the class to suggest other words with these suffixes, add them to the board and discuss their meanings.

Spelling Point
- Revise the suffix ‹-ify›, which can be added to nouns and adjectives to make verbs.
- Look at the words on the board and ask what the root words are for *horrify* (horror) and *simplify* (simple).
- Go through some of the other spelling words, identify the root word for each one, and discuss how the suffix has been added to the root each time.
- Remind the children that 'toughy ‹y›' appears at the end of such verbs because it is replacing 'shy ‹i›'.
- When the past participle is formed by adding ‹-ed›, 'toughy ‹y›' is no longer needed and so 'shy ‹i›' returns, as in *horrified* and *simplified*.
- This is also true when adding ‹s› to make the third person singular, as in *horrifies* and *simplifies*.
- However, to avoid having two ‹i›s next to each other, the ‹y› is kept when adding ‹-ing› to make the present participle, as in *horrifying* and *simplifying*.

Spelling List
- Go through the list, identify the syllables in each word, find the root words and discuss the meaning of any unfamiliar words. Ask the class to find and highlight each ‹ify› spelling.
- Point out the schwa in *solidify*, the ‹al› spelling in *falsify*, the ‹i› saying its long vowel sound in *identify* and *diversify*, the ‹y› saying /i/ in *typify* and *mystify* and the soft ‹c› in *specify*.
- Point out too that the ‹gn› in *signify* and *magnify* and the ‹ar› in *clarify* are not digraphs, but say both sounds.
- It is a good idea to blend and sound out the spelling words quickly every day with the children, using the 'say it as it sounds' strategy where appropriate, or you could break down the words into root (word) and suffix.

classify
terrify
horrify
glorify
solidify
personify
falsify
identify
typify
simplify
signify
magnify
intensify
mystify
diversify
specify
justify
clarify

Activity Page 1
- The children split each spelling word into syllables (*clas/si/fy, ter/ri/fy, hor/ri/fy, glo/ri/fy, so/lid/i/fy, per/son/i/fy, fal/si/fy, i/den/ti/fy, typ/i/fy,* *sim/pli/fy, sig/ni/fy, mag/ni/fy, in/ten/si/fy, mys/ti/fy, di/ver/si/fy, spec/i/fy, jus/ti/fy, clar/i/fy*).
- They then write the root words for twelve verbs and match six verbs to words in the same word family (nouns: *person, sign, class, horror, type, glory*; adjectives: *simple, intense, false, solid, diverse, specific*; word families: *terrify, clarify, justify, mystify, identify, magnify*).

Activity Page 2
- The children conjugate the verb *to qualify*, starting with: (simple tense) *I qualified, qualify, shall qualify*; (continuous tense) *I was qualifying, am qualifying, shall be qualifying*; (perfect tense) *I had qualified, have qualified, shall have qualified*.
- Remind them that *shall* is only used in the first person singular and plural, but *will* can be used with all the pronouns.
- Then they parse the sentence and complete the wall.
- *My* is a possessive adjective and should be underlined in blue. *At bedtime* is a prepositional phrase acting as an adverb, so orange brackets can be put around it.
The scary story terrified my brother and sister (at bedtime).
Top: *story - terrified - brother/sister*
Bottom: *The scary - at bedtime - my*
Verb: *transitive*

Dictation
- Dictate the following sentences:

1. Please specify which mushrooms are edible.
2. Pam hopes to qualify as a beautician in the future.
3. "We magnify microbes with a microscope," explained the technician.

- Remind the children to use speech marks with the correct punctuation in sentence 3. *Pam* is a proper noun and needs a capital letter.

Grammar: The Order of Adjectives (2)

Aim
- Reinforce the children's understanding of adjectives and develop their ability to write a sequence of adjectives in the correct order.

Introduction
- Remind the children that when we describe something using more than one adjective, we tend to put them in a certain order:
  1. Determiners (*a, an, one, two, some, many, any, this, that*, etc)
  2. Opinion (*lazy, good, nasty, expensive, bad*, etc)
  3. Size and shape (*fat, thin, small, broad, rectangular, oval*, etc)
  4. Condition and age (*broken, battered, hungry, full, ancient, recent*, etc)
  5. Colour and pattern (*black, brown, white, tartan, zigzag*, etc)
  6. Origin (*Welsh, Polish, African, Japanese, Australian*, etc)
  7. Material, including nouns acting as adjectives (*leather, iron, diamond*, etc)
- Revise the different categories, asking the children to give a few examples for each one and write them on the board.
- Now see if the class can make a noun phrase, using an adjective from every category: for example, *two beautiful, old, large, green jade Chinese dragons.*
- Remind the class that the order given is only a general guide and adjectives can sometimes be put in a different order.
- For example, in this sentence both shape and age are mentioned and so the order has been swapped. Also, origin would normally come before material, but here the adjective *Chinese* is part of the compound word *Chinese dragon* and so it comes afterwards.

Main Point
- Explain that we do not normally use so many adjectives in a sentence; usually we use no more than three at a time, but using more than that helps us understand the different categories and the order they are written in.
- Write *an antique pearl black expensive necklace* on the board and ask the class if it sounds correct.
- Ask the class how it should be written and rewrite it on the board for the class to see: *an expensive antique black pearl necklace.*
- Write some nouns on the board (perhaps using some related to a topic the children are studying) and ask the class to think of two, three or four adjectives to describe them.
- Then put them into noun phrases and write them on the board, making sure the adjectives are put in the right order.

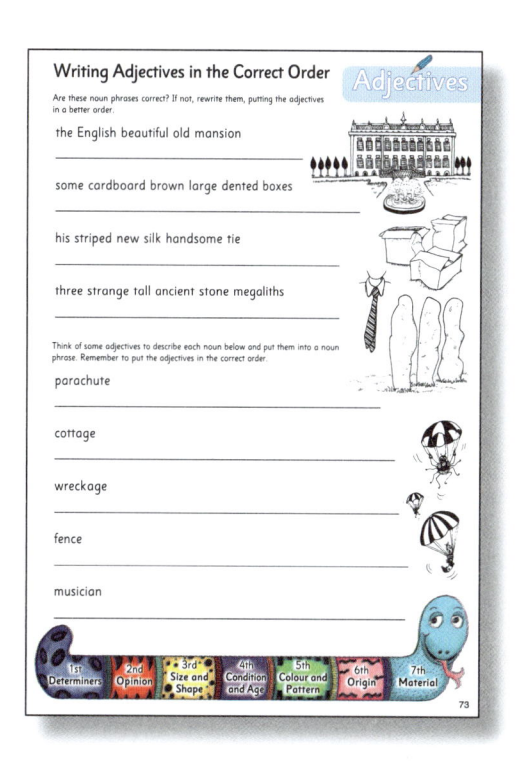

Activity Page
- The children write inside the outlined word *Adjectives*, using a blue pencil.
- They then look at the four noun phrases and decide whether the adjectives are written in the right order (they can use the adjective snake at the bottom of the activity page to help them).
- If not they should rewrite them, putting them in a better order (*the beautiful old English mansion, some large dented brown cardboard boxes, his handsome new striped silk tie, three strange tall ancient stone megaliths*).
- They then think of some adjectives to describe each of the nouns and put them into five noun phrases, writing the adjectives in the correct order.

Extension Activity
- The children write a noun phrase or sentence, but deliberately put the adjectives in an unusual order.
- They then swap their work with a partner and try rewriting the adjectives in a better order.

Rounding Off
- Go over the activity page with the children, discussing their answers.
- If they have done the extension activity, ask some of the children to read out their noun phrases.

GRAMMAR 5 PUPIL BOOK: PAGE 74 & 75

Spelling: ‹-ous›

Spelling Test
- The children turn to the backs of their books and find the column labelled *Spelling Test 24*.
- Call out the spelling words learnt last week.

Revision
- Write these words on the board and identify the different verb endings: *complic**ate***, *horr**ify***, *pr**ize***, *apprec**iate***, *simpl**ify***, *adv**ise***.
- Ask the class to suggest other words with these suffixes, add them to the board and discuss their meanings.

Spelling Point
- Introduce the suffix ‹-ous›, which is found in adjectives that describe something as having the quality of the root word (so a *dangerous* situation is full of *danger*, and if berries are *poisonous*, they contain *poison*).
- Write some of the spelling words on the board and ask the children what each ‹ous› adjective is *full of* or *contains* (*numerous/number*, *nervous/nerve*, *vigorous/vigour*, *fabulous/fable*, for example).
- Most are obvious, but others are less so because of their Latin origins.
- Underline ‹ous› and point out that the unstressed vowel is swallowed and becomes a schwa, and so it sounds more like /us/.

Spelling List
- Go through the list, identify the syllables in each word and discuss the meaning of any unfamiliar words.
- Ask the class to find and highlight each ‹ous› spelling.
- Point out other spelling features, such as the letters saying their long vowel sound in *f**a**mous*, *n**u**merous*, *d**a**ngerous*, *outr**a**geous*, *spont**a**neous* and *simult**a**neous*, the ‹e› saying /i/ in *enormous*, the schwas (as in *num**e**rous*, *gen**e**rous* and *vig**o**rous*), the soft ‹g› in *gen**e**rous*, *dang**e**rous* and *outrag**e**ous*, the ‹ea› saying /e/ in *jealous*, the ‹s› saying /z/ in *disastrous* and the ‹y› saying /ee/ in the middle of *anonymous*.
- Emphasise *disast**rous*** and point out that it does not contain the letter ‹e›, unlike its root word *disaster*.
- It is a good idea to blend and sound out the spelling words quickly every day with the children, using the 'say it as it sounds' strategy where appropriate, or you could break down the words into root (word) and suffix.

famous
nervous
enormous
numerous
generous
vigorous
dangerous
continuous
ridiculous
poisonous
jealous
fabulous
outrageous
hazardous
disastrous
spontaneous
simultaneous
anonymous

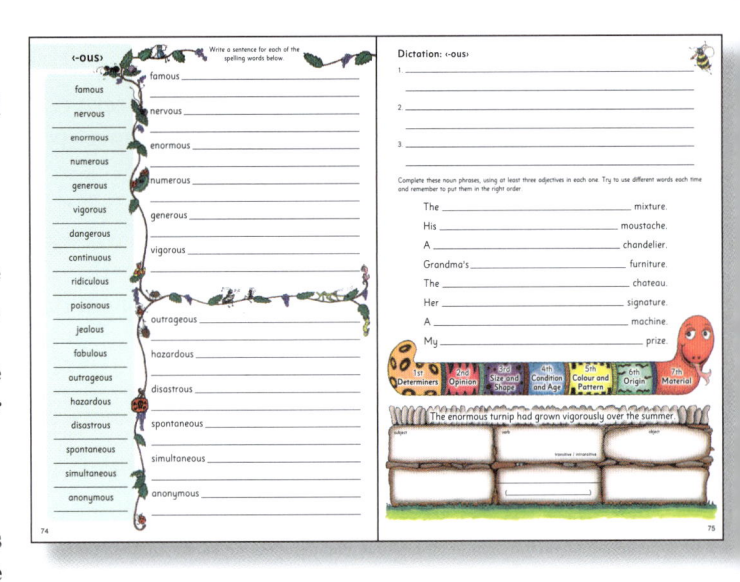

Activity Page 1
- The children split each spelling word into syllables (*fam/ous, nerv/ous, e/nor/mous, nu/mer/ous, gen/er/ous, vig/or/ous, dan/ger/ous, con/tin/u/ous, ri/dic/u/lous, poi/son/ous, jea/lous, fab/u/lous, out/ra/geous, haz/ard/ous, di/sas/trous, spon/ta/ne/ous, si/mul/ta/ne/ous, a/non/y/mous*).
- They then write a sentence for each of the numbered spelling words. Encourage the children to use a dictionary if they are unsure of any words.

Activity Page 2
- The children complete the noun phrases, using different adjectives each time and putting them in the right order.
- Then they parse the sentence and complete the wall.
- *Over the summer* is a prepositional phrase acting as an adverb, so orange brackets can be put around it.
The enormous turnip had grown vigorously (over the summer).
Top: *turnip - had grown - (blank)*
Bottom: *The enormous - vigorously/over the summer - (blank)*
Verb: intransitive

Dictation
- Dictate the following sentences:

1. The multimillionaire gave a generous gift to the local hospital.
2. "Everything will be fine," he reassured the nervous passenger.
3. The explorers made a hazardous journey in freezing temperatures.

- In sentence 2, remind them to think about which part of the sentence is being spoken and then use speech marks with the correct punctuation.

Grammar: Adverbs of Manner

Aim
- Develop the children's understanding of adverbs, which are words that tell us more about how, where, when, how much or how often something happens.
- Introduce the term *adverbs of manner*, which can be used for words that describe how the verb is done.

Introduction
- Revise adverbs with the class. So far the children know that adverbs describe verbs, telling us more about where, how, when, how often or how much something happens.
- Many adverbs are made by adding the suffix ‹-ly› to an adjective, as in *brightly*, *gladly* and *neatly*, or by adding ‹-ally› if the adjective ends in ‹-ic› (as in *scientifically* or *majestically*).
- However, it is important that the children remember that some adverbs – such as *not*, *well* and *always*, for example – do not end in ‹-ly› and that some words, like *lonely*, *hilly* and *friendly*, are not adverbs but adjectives.
- Remind the children that prepositional phrases like *with my friends* (how), *up the hill* (where) and *at the moment* (when) can also act as adverbs. Think of a verb and ask the children to suggest adverbs that could describe it.
- Make a list on the board and make sure the class understands what each one means.

Main Point
- The children know that adverbs can tell us different things about a verb, such as where or when it took place, but so far they have mostly looked at those that describe how the verb is done.
- These adverbs are called adverbs of manner and they are the largest group, usually consisting of words ending in ‹-ly›.
- Check that the adverbs on the board are adverbs of manner and remove any that are not.
- Then explain that if you do something in a certain manner, it means you do it in that particular way.
- Play the 'adverbs game' with the children: ask a child to come up and choose an adverb from the board, without telling anyone what it is. The class then thinks of a verb for the child to act out in the manner of the adverb; so, for example, the child could pretend to brush his or her teeth *happily* or jump up and down *lazily*. The rest of the class has to guess what the adverb is and, if they cannot, the child continues to use the same adverb with a different action chosen by the class.
- Examples of adverbs of manner are: *accidentally, angrily, badly, beautifully, bravely, busily, carefully, carelessly, cleverly, clumsily, correctly, dangerously, deliberately, eagerly, easily, excitedly, foolishly, furiously, gently, gracefully, greedily, happily, hastily, hungrily, hurriedly, kindly, lazily, loudly, mysteriously, nervously, noisily, patiently, perfectly, politely, quickly, quietly, rapidly, sadly, safely, secretly, sensibly, silently, sleepily, slowly, softly, suddenly, unhappily, well, wickedly, willingly, wisely.*

Activity Page
- The children write inside the outlined word *Adverbs*, using an orange pencil.
- They then use one of the adverbs in bold to complete each sentence, writing it on the lines below.
- Any of the adverbs can be used (there is no right or wrong answer, as long as each sentence makes sense) and the children should be encouraged to include some extra information to make each sentence more interesting.

Extension Activity
- The children use some of the other adverbs on the activity page to write new sentences on a separate sheet of paper.

Rounding Off
- Go over the children's work, checking their answers.
- If they have done the extension activity, ask some children to read out their sentences.

GRAMMAR 5 PUPIL BOOK: PAGE 77 & 78

Spelling: ‹-ious›

Spelling Test
- The children turn to the backs of their books and find the column labelled *Spelling Test 25*.
- Call out the spelling words learnt last week.

Revision
- Write these words on the board and identify the different verb endings: frust**rate**, magn**ify**, caps**ize**, activ**ate**, just**ify**, exerc**ise**.
- Ask the class to suggest other words with these suffixes, add them to the board and discuss their meanings.

Spelling Point
- Write the words *mysterious*, *furious* and *spacious* on the board. The children should recognise that these are ‹ous› adjectives, meaning *full of (the root word)*.
- Underline the ‹i› before each ‹ous› and explain that adjectives with this spelling come from Latin, where the original root word contained an ‹i›.
- Also point out that some of these adjectives have root words ending in 'toughy' ‹y›, and so 'shy ‹i›' returns when the ‹ous› is added (as in *mystery/mysterious* and *fury/furious*).
- Words with a soft ‹c› or ‹g› will end in ‹ious› too (as in *space/spacious*).
- When it comes after a consonant, as in *serious*, the ‹i› is usually spoken; the main exceptions are ‹gi› (saying /j/, as in *contagious*) and ‹ci› and ‹xi› (saying /sh/, as in *gracious* and *anxious*).

Spelling List
- Go through the list, identify the syllables in each word and discuss the meaning of any unfamiliar words.
- Ask the class to find and highlight each ‹ious› spelling.
- Point out the ‹e› saying /ear/ in *serious* and *mysterious*, the ‹a› saying /air/ in *various*, the prefix in *pre*vious, the long vowel sounds in *pre*vious, *fero*cious, *gra*cious, *spa*cious, *du*bious and *conta*gious, the ‹u› saying ‹ure› in *curious* and *furious*, the ‹xi› and ‹ci› saying /sh/ in *anxious*, *delicious*, *ferocious*, *gracious*, *precious*, *spacious*, *suspicious* and *vicious*, the ‹n› saying /ng/ in *anxious*, the ‹e› and ‹y› saying /i/ in *delicious* and *mysterious* and the soft ‹g› in *prestigious* and *contagious*.
- It is a good idea to blend and sound out the spelling words quickly every day with the children, using the 'say it as it sounds' strategy where appropriate, or you could break down the words into root (word) and suffix.

serious
various
previous
obvious
curious
furious
anxious
delicious
ferocious
gracious
precious
spacious
dubious
suspicious
mysterious
prestigious
contagious
vicious

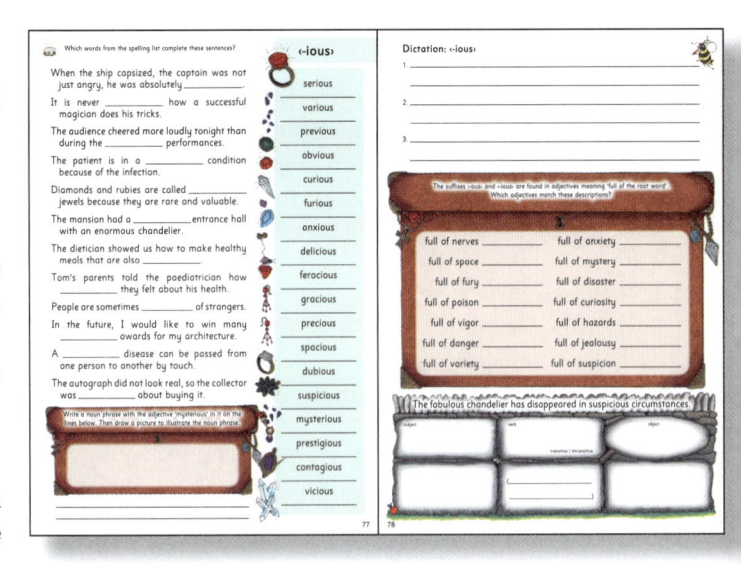

Activity Page 1
- The children split each spelling word into syllables (se/ri/ous, var/i/ous, pre/vi/ous, ob/vi/ous, cu/ri/ous, fu/ri/ous, anx/ious, de/li/cious, fe/ro/cious, gra/cious, pre/cious, spa/cious, du/bi/ous, sus/pi/cious, my/ste/ri/ous, pres/ti/gious, con/ta/gious, vi/cious).
- They then write in the spelling word that completes each sentence (*furious, obvious, previous, serious, precious, spacious, delicious, anxious, suspicious, prestigious, contagious, dubious*).
- Then they write a noun phrase which includes the word *mysterious* and draw a picture in the chest to illustrate it.

Activity Page 2
- The children write the ‹-ous› or ‹-ious› adjective for each description (*nervous, spacious, furious, poisonous, vigorous, dangerous, various, anxious, mysterious, disastrous, curious, hazardous, jealous, suspicious*).
- Then they parse the sentence and complete the wall.
- *In suspicious circumstances* is a prepositional phrase acting as an adverb, so orange brackets can be put around it.
The fabulous chandelier has disappeared (in suspicious circumstances).
Top: *chandelier - has disappeared -* (blank)
Bottom: *The fabulous - in suspicious circumstances -* (blank)
Verb: intransitive

Dictation
- Dictate the following sentences:

1. "There are various disguises I can use," said the spy.
2. They were curious about the mysterious stranger.
3. The supermodel wore a necklace of precious jewels.

- Remind them to use speech marks with the correct punctuation in sentence 1.

Grammar: Adverbs of Degree and Place

Aim
- Develop the children's understanding of adverbs (words that tell us more about how, where, when, how much or how often something happens).
- Introduce the terms *adverbs of degree* and *adverbs of place* for words that describe how much the verb is done or where it takes place.

Introduction
- Remind the children that adverbs which tell us more about how something happens are called adverbs of manner.
- They are the biggest group of adverbs and many of them end in ‹-ly›, but some do not, such as *well* and *fast*.
- Write some short sentences on the board, such as *They have done their homework..., He danced..., We walked..., It blew up..., They called out..., She had cut the picture out..., I dressed..., The clowns juggled..., Sam sung...,* or *The baby gurgled....* Ask the children to think of adverbs of manner to add to each one.

Main Point
- Now write *She had almost finished her book* on the board. Find the verb (*had finished*), subject (*She*) and object (*book*). Ask whether it is transitive or intransitive (transitive verbs have an object).
- Then see if the class can identify the adverb *almost*. It is not obvious as *almost* is not an adverb of manner, nor does it end in ‹-ly›; the class must think more about its role within the sentence.
- Explain that *almost* tells us something more about how much, or to what extent, the person has finished the book: she has nearly finished the book, but not quite.
- Point out that *nearly* and *quite* are also adverbs like *almost* and ask the children if they can think of any more.
- Make a list on the board and explain that these words are adverbs of degree. Unlike adverbs of manner, which can usually be placed in various positions, adverbs of degree tend to go between the subject and verb or between the auxiliary verb and main verb.
- Now write *I went abroad* and ask the children to identify the adverb.
- Again, *abroad* is not an obvious adverb as it does not end in ‹-ly›, nor does it tell us how or to what extent the person *went*.
- However it does tell us more about where the verb happened.
- Ask the children if they can think of other words that could be used instead (such as *away, back, indoors, inside, backwards, downstairs, north, elsewhere, here, in, there* and *upstairs*). Explain that these are called adverbs of place.
- Adverbs of place can be tricky to spot because many of them, like *in, on* and *down* can also be prepositions.
- Remind the children that a preposition relates one noun or pronoun to another, as in *I went in the house* (*in* relates *I* to *house*), whereas adverbs describe the verb, as in *I went in* (*in* describes where the subject *went*).
- Also remind the children that if they were doing sentence walls, they would identify *in the house* as a prepositional phrase acting as an adverb.
  - Some adverbs of degree: *absolutely, almost, barely, completely, deeply, enormously, enough, entirely, fully, greatly, hardly, highly, intensely, just, nearly, quite, rather, really.*
  - Some adverbs of place: *about, abroad, anywhere, around, away, back, backwards, downstairs, everywhere, here, indoors, inside, in, nearby, nowhere, north, there, upstairs.*

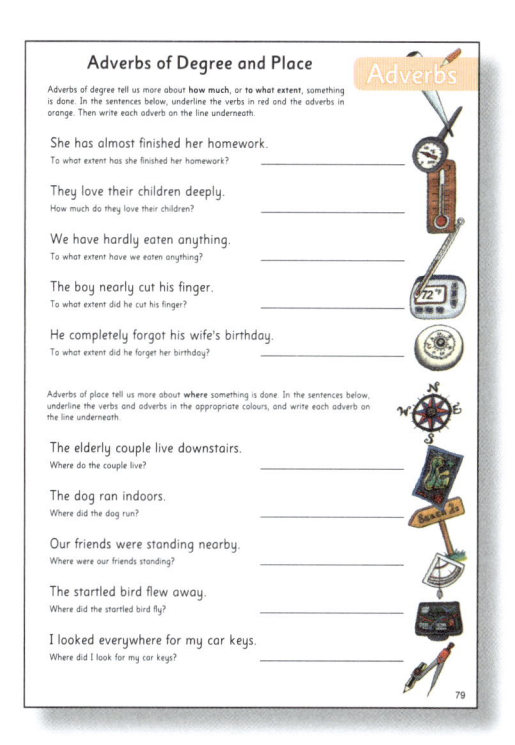

Activity Page
- The children write inside the outlined word *Adverbs*, using an orange pencil.
- They then find the verb and adverb in each sentence and underline them in their respective colours (*has [almost] finished, love [deeply], have [hardly] eaten, cut [nearly], forgot [completely], live [downstairs], ran [indoors], were standing [nearby], flew [away], looked [everywhere]*).
- They then look at the question underneath and answer by writing the adverb on the line provided.

Extension Activity
- The children write some more sentences on a separate sheet of paper, using at least one adverb of manner, degree and place.

Rounding Off
- Go over the children's work, checking their answers.

GRAMMAR 5 PUPIL BOOK: PAGE 80 & 81

Spelling: ‹tious›

Spelling Test
- The children turn to the backs of their books and find the column labelled *Spelling Test 26*.
- Call out the spelling words learnt last week.

Revision
- Write these words on the board and identify the different adjective endings with the children: *famous, dangerous, jealous, anxious, curious, ferocious*.
- Remind them that in these spellings ‹ou› is a schwa and ‹xi› and ‹ci› say /sh/.
- Ask the class to suggest other words with these spellings, add them to the board and discuss their meanings.

Spelling Point
- Write the word *spacious* on the board. The children should recognise that it is an ‹ious› adjective, meaning *containing space*.
- Now add *ambitious* and *infectious* and underline ‹tious› each time.
- Explain that some ‹-ious› adjectives have a ‹t› before the suffix because the original Latin root word has ‹ti› in it.
- In many of these adjectives, the English root word ends in ‹-tion›, so *ambitious* means *full of ambition* and *infectious* means *containing infection*.
- Go through the other spelling words and identify those with a ‹-tion› root word.
- Point out that words with ‹tious›, ‹cious› and ‹xious› spellings all end in the same /shus/ sound and need to be learnt.

Spelling List
- Go through the list, identify the syllables in each word and discuss the meaning of any unfamiliar words. Ask the class to find and highlight each ‹tious› spelling.
- Point out other spelling features, such as the ‹au› spelling in *cautious* and *incautious*, the prefix ‹in-› meaning *not* in *incautious*, the schwas in *contentious, propitious, surreptitious, superstitious* and *facetious*, the long vowel sounds in *nutritious, vexatious, ostentatious* and *facetious*, the double ‹r› in *surreptitious*, the ‹sci› saying /shi/ in *conscientious* and the soft ‹c› in *facetious*.
- It is a good idea to blend and sound out the spelling words quickly every day with the children, using the 'say it as it sounds' strategy where appropriate, or you could break down the words into root (word) and suffix.

ambitious
cautious
incautious
infectious
bumptious
contentious
nutritious
fictitious
propitious
fractious
surreptitious
scrumptious
conscientious
pretentious
superstitious
vexatious
ostentatious
facetious

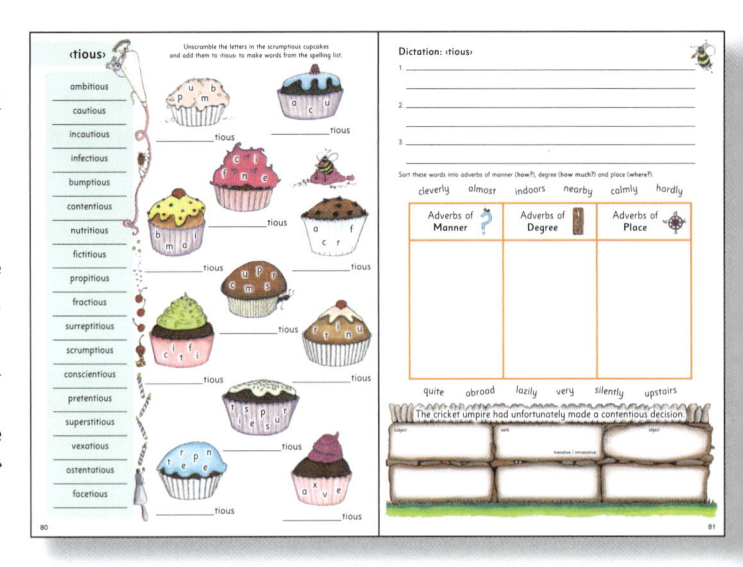

Activity Page 1
- The children split each spelling word into syllables (*am/bi/tious, cau/tious, in/cau/tious, in/fec/tious, bump/tious, con/ten/tious, nu/tri/tious, fic/ti/tious, pro/pi/tious, frac/tious, sur/rep/ti/tious, scrump/tious, con/sci/en/tious, pre/ten/tious, su/per/sti/tious, vex/a/tious, os/ten/ta/tious, fa/ce/tious*).
- They then unscramble the letters in the cupcakes and add them to ‹tious› to make some of the spelling words (*bumptious, cautious, infectious, ambitious, fractious, scrumptious, fictitious, nutritious, superstitious, pretentious, vexatious*).

Activity Page 2
- The children sort the words into adverbs of manner (*cleverly, calmly, lazily, silently*), degree (*almost, hardly, quite, very*) and place (*indoors, nearby, abroad, upstairs*).
- Then they parse the sentence and complete the wall.
- All parts of the verb (*had made*) should be underlined in red. *Cricket* is a noun acting as an adjective and should be underlined in blue.

The cricket umpire had unfortunately made a contentious decision.
Top: *umpire - had made - decision*
Bottom: *The cricket - unfortunately - a contentious*
Verb: transitive

Dictation
- Dictate the following sentences:

1. We enjoyed a nutritious and delicious meal.
2. She was a ferociously ambitious politician.
3. "The illness is infectious but not dangerous," said the nurse.

- Remind them to use speech marks with the correct punctuation in sentence 3.

Grammar: Adverbs of Time and Frequency

Aim
- Further develop the children's knowledge of adverbs (which tell us more about how, where, when, how much or how often something happens).
- Introduce the terms *adverbs of time* and *adverbs of frequency* for words that describe when the verb is done or how often it takes place.

Introduction
- Revise the different types of adverb that the children have learnt so far: adverbs of manner (how), adverbs of degree (how much) and adverbs of place (where).
- Write three sentences on the board and ask the children to suggest appropriate adverbs for them: *He skied...* (manner), *He... won the ski race* (degree), *He skied...* (place).
- The children might say the man skied *quickly, gracefully, powerfully, nervously*; that he *almost/nearly/just/totally/undoubtedly* won the ski race; and that he skied *abroad, away, around, back, everywhere, here* or *there*.
- Some children might also say something like *He skied down the hill*. If they do, remind them that *down* can be an adverb (as in *She sat down*) but that in *He skied down the hill*, *down* is a preposition telling us where *He* is in relation to *hill*.

Main Point
- Now write *He skied today* on the board and discuss the different parts of the sentence.
- Find the verb (*skied*) and subject (*He*) and point out that there is no object.
- Then ask whether it is transitive or intransitive (intransitive verbs have no object).
- See if the children can identify the kind of adverb *today* might be, and explain that it tells us more about when the person skied and so it is called an adverb of time.
- Ask the children if they can think of other adverbs of time and make a list on the board.
- Examples include some specific adverbs like *today, yesterday* and *tomorrow*, but also many more general ones like *already, before, early, eventually, finally, first, last, now, previously, recently, soon, then* and *yet*.
- Point out that if the children were doing sentence walls, they would identify prepositional phrases like *on Monday* or *in the summer* as adverbs of time.
- Also point out that if the adverb is put at the beginning of the sentence it is usually followed by a comma, as in *Yesterday, I went shopping* or *Recently, I learnt to swim*.
- Now write *I never ski* and ask the children what kind of adverb they think *never* might be.
- Explain that adverbs like this tell us more about how often something happens and they are called adverbs of frequency.

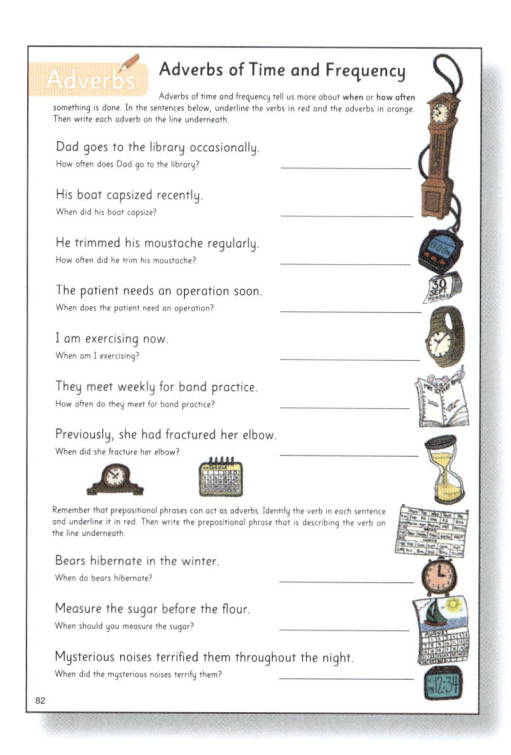

- Make a list of similar words on the board and point out that some adverbs of frequency are quite general (for example, *always, constantly, frequently, occasionally, often, seldom, sometimes, rarely* and *regularly*) while others are more specific (such as *daily, weekly, monthly, yearly*).
- General (or indefinite) adverbs of frequency tend to go between the subject and verb, or between the auxiliary verb and main verb.
- Specific (or definite) adverbs of frequency, however, go at the end.

Activity Page
- The children write inside the outlined word *Adverbs*, using an orange pencil.
- They then find the verb and adverb in each sentence and underline them in their respective colours (*goes [occasionally], capsized [recently], trimmed [regularly], needs [soon], am exercising [now], meet [weekly], had fractured [previously]*).
- In the final sentences they underline the verbs in red and the prepositions in green and put orange brackets around prepositional phrases acting as adverbs (*hibernate [in the winter], measure [before the flour], terrified [throughout the night]*).
- They then answer the question underneath each sentence, writing the adverb or phrase on the line.

Extension Activity
- Write some adverbs of time and frequency on the board. Ask the children to write several sentences, using some of the adverbs, on a separate sheet of paper.

Rounding Off
- Go over the children's work, checking their answers.

GRAMMAR 5 PUPIL BOOK: PAGE 83 & 84

Spelling: ‹cial›

Spelling Test
- The children turn to the backs of their books and find the column labelled *Spelling Test 27*.
- Call out the spelling words learnt last week.

Revision
- Write these words on the board and identify the different adjective endings with the children: *enormous*, *ridiculous*, *gracious*, *dubious*, *cautious*, *fictitious*.
- Remind them that in these spellings, ‹ou› has a schwa sound and ‹ci› and ‹ti› say /sh/.
- Ask the class to suggest other words, add them to the board and discuss their meanings.

Spelling Point
- Revise the suffix ‹-al›, which is found in adjectives that describe something as relating to or having the qualities of the root word, as in *bridal*.
- This suffix can also be spelt ‹-ial›, especially if the root word ends in ‹y› or ‹ce›, (when the vowel is replaced by ‹i›, as in *industrial* or *sacrificial*).
- The suffix ‹-ial› is often preceded by the letter ‹c›, usually when the letter before it is a vowel, as in *glacial*, *special*, *official*, *social* and *crucial*.
- The main exceptions to this are *financial* and *provincial*, which follow the letter ‹n›.
- Discuss how the ‹ci› says /sh/ and the ‹a› is a schwa, so the ‹cial› ending sounds something like /shul/.
- One word in the list, *controversial*, ends in /shul/ but is not spelt ‹cial›. Instead, the /sh/ sound is made by ‹si›.
- Look at some more spelling words and identify the root word where possible.

Spelling List
- Go through the list, identify the syllables in each word and discuss the meaning of any unfamiliar words. Ask the class to find and highlight each ‹cial› spelling.
- Point out other spelling features, such as the letters saying their long vowel sound in *social*, *racial*, *facial*, *glacial*, *financial* and *antisocial*, the ‹u› saying /oo/ in *crucial*, *superficial* and *judicial*, the schwas in *official*, *commercial*, *unofficial*, *superficial*, *provincial* and *controversial*, the double consonants in *official*, *unofficial* and *commercial*, the ‹e› saying /i/ in *beneficial*, the prefixes in *antisocial* and *unofficial* and the ‹sial› spelling in *controversial*.
- It is a good idea to blend and sound out the spelling words quickly every day with the children, using the 'say it as it sounds'

special
social
crucial
racial
facial
glacial
official
artificial
beneficial
financial
antisocial
commercial
unofficial
superficial
sacrificial
judicial
provincial
controversial

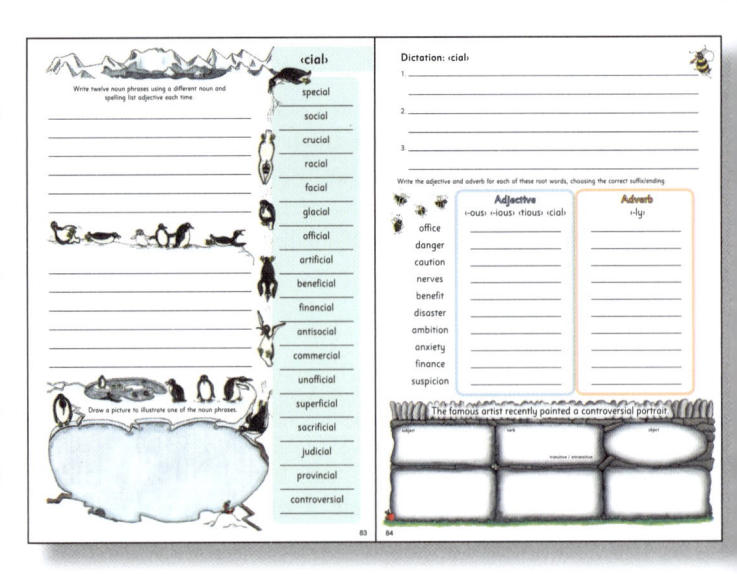

strategy where appropriate, or you could break down the words into root (word) and suffix.

Activity Page 1
- The children split each spelling word into syllables (*spe/cial, so/cial, cru/cial, ra/cial, fa/cial, gla/cial, of/fi/cial, ar/ti/fi/cial, ben/e/fi/cial, fi/nan/cial, an/ti/so/cial, com/mer/cial, un/of/fi/cial, su/per/fi/cial, sac/ri/fi/cial, ju/di/cial, pro/vin/cial, con/tro/ver/sial*).
- They then choose twelve adjectives from the spelling list and write a noun phrase for each one. They then draw a picture to illustrate one of the noun phrases.

Activity Page 2
- The children write the adjective and adverb for each root word (*official/ly, dangerous/ly, cautious/ly, nervous/ly, beneficial/ly, disastrous/ly, ambitious/ly, anxious/ly, financial/ly, suspicious/ly*).
- Then they parse the sentence and complete the wall.
- *Recently* is an adverb made by adding ‹-ly› to the adjective *recent*.
The famous artist recently painted a controversial portrait.
Top: *artist - painted - portrait*
Bottom: *The famous - recently - a controversial*
Verb: transitive

Dictation
- Dictate the following sentences:

1. The artificial flowers were obviously not real.
2. I will bake a scrumptious cake for this special occasion.
3. "The expression on his face was glacial!" exclaimed Jim.

- Remind them to use speech marks with the correct punctuation in sentence 3. Jim is a proper noun and needs a capital letter.

Grammar: Adverbs Describing Other Adverbs

Aim
- Extend the children's understanding of adverbs by introducing the idea that as well as describing verbs, some adverbs can also describe other adverbs.

Introduction
- Revise the different types of adverb learnt so far: manner (how), degree (how much), place (where), time (when) and frequency (how often).
- Write some sentences on the board and ask the children to suggest other adverbs for each one: *She grinned cheekily* (how did she grin?), *We have just arrived* (to what extent have we arrived?), *They ran outside* (where did they run?), *He is always laughing* (how often is he laughing?), *Yesterday, I was working* (when was I working?).
- Remind the children that when the adverb comes at the beginning of the sentence, it is usually followed by a comma, as in the last example.

Main Point
- Write *She really enjoyed the book* on the board. Discuss how *really* is an adverb of degree because it tells us more about how much the person enjoyed the book.
- Now write *She grinned really cheekily* and ask what *really* is doing here.
- Explain that it is not telling us how much the person grinned; then we would say *She really grinned*.
- Instead *really* is telling us how cheekily she grinned; it is describing the adverb, not the verb.
- Write *He is nearly always laughing* and ask the class what *nearly* is describing here. The person is not *nearly* laughing, but *nearly always* laughing and so *nearly* is describing the adverb too.
- Explain that some adverbs (often adverbs of degree) not only describe verbs, but they can also describe adverbs.
- Now draw a couple of sentence walls on the board and put the last two sentences into the boxes. Show the children how to put both adverbs in the box under the verb, with the main adverb going first and the adverb describing it going underneath; then join them with a diagonal line.

Activity Page
- The children write inside the outlined word *Adverbs*, using an orange pencil.
- The children then parse the sentences, underlining each word in the appropriate colour, and complete the wall.

1. The jam jar opened fairly easily.
Top: *jar - opened - (blank) / Bottom: The jam - easily/fairly - (blank) / Verb: intransitive*
2. The cleaner polished the furniture extremely vigorously.
Top: *cleaner - polished - furniture / Bottom: The - vigorously/extremely - the / Verb: transitive*
3. The children were playing perfectly happily.
Top: *children - were playing - (blank) / Bottom: The - happily/perfectly - (blank) / Verb: intransitive*
4. The pastry chef decorated the cake absolutely beautifully.
Top: *chef - decorated - cake / Bottom: The pastry - beautifully/absolutely - the / Verb: transitive*

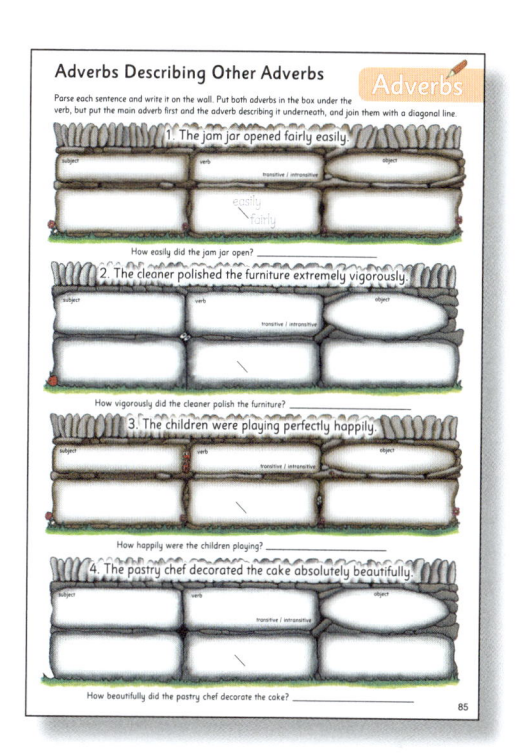

- They then answer the question underneath each sentence, writing the adverb that is describing the main adverb on the line (1. *fairly*, 2. *extremely*, 3. *perfectly*, 4. *absolutely*).

Extension Activity
- Give each child a sheet of paper and ask them to draw some sentence walls.
- Write these sentences on the board: 1. *She did her homework quite quickly*; 2. *The little old lady walked rather slowly*; 3. *The actor was speaking really clearly*; 4. *The nurse removed the splinter incredibly carefully*.
- The children then parse the sentences and complete the walls.

1. She did her homework quite quickly.
Top: *she - did - homework / Bottom: (blank) - quickly/quite - her / Verb: transitive*
2. The little old lady walked rather slowly.
Top: *lady - walked - (blank) / Bottom: The little old - slowly/rather - (blank) / Verb: intransitive*
3. The actor was speaking really clearly.
Top: *actor - was speaking - (blank) / Bottom: The - clearly/really - (blank) / Verb: intransitive*
4. The nurse removed the splinter incredibly carefully.
Top: *nurse - removed - splinter / Bottom: The - carefully/incredibly - the / Verb: transitive*

- Then, underneath, the children write the adverb that is describing the main adverb (1. *quite*, 2. *rather*, 3. *really*, 4. *incredibly*).

Rounding Off
- Go over the children's work, checking their answers.

GRAMMAR 5 PUPIL BOOK: PAGE 86 & 87

Spelling: ‹tial›

Spelling Test
- The children turn to the backs of their books and find the column labelled *Spelling Test 28*.
- Call out the spelling words learnt last week.

Revision
- Write these words on the board and identify the ‹cial› or ‹sial› spelling of /shul/ in each one: *special*, *crucial*, *official*, *artificial*, *beneficial*, *controversial*.
- Ask the class to suggest other words with these spellings, add them to the board and discuss their meanings.

Spelling Point
- Revise the suffix ‹-ial›, which is found in adjectives and is often preceded by the letter ‹c›, usually when the letter before it is a vowel (as in *social*).
- Another letter that often precedes this suffix is ‹t› (as in *essential* and *torrential*) and the ‹tial› spelling usually occurs when the letter before it is a consonant.
- The main exceptions to this are *initial*, *palatial* and *spatial*, which all appear in the spelling list.
- Like ‹cial›, the ‹tial› spelling sounds something like /shul/, only this time it is the letters ‹ti› making the /sh/ sound.
- It appears in adjectives that describe something as relating to or having the qualities of the root (word) (so an *influential* person has a lot of *influence* and a *president* is chosen in a *presidential* election).
- Look at some more spelling words and identify the root word where possible.

Spelling List
- Go through the list, identify the syllables in each word and discuss the meaning of any unfamiliar words.
- Ask the class to find and highlight each ‹tial› spelling.
- Point out other spelling features, such as the double consonants in *essential* and *torrential*, the ‹e› saying /i/ in *essential*, *sequential* and *inconsequential*, the schwas in *potential*, *substantial*, *palatial*, *torrential*, *preferential*, and *insubstantial*, the prefixes ‹im-› and ‹in-› meaning *not* in *impartial*, *influential*, *insubstantial* and *inconsequential*, the ‹s› saying /z/ in *presidential* and *residential* and the ‹a› saying its long vowel sound in *palatial* and *spatial*.
- It is a good idea to blend and sound out the spelling words quickly every day with the children, using the 'say it as it sounds' strategy where appropriate, or you could break down the words into root (word) and suffix.

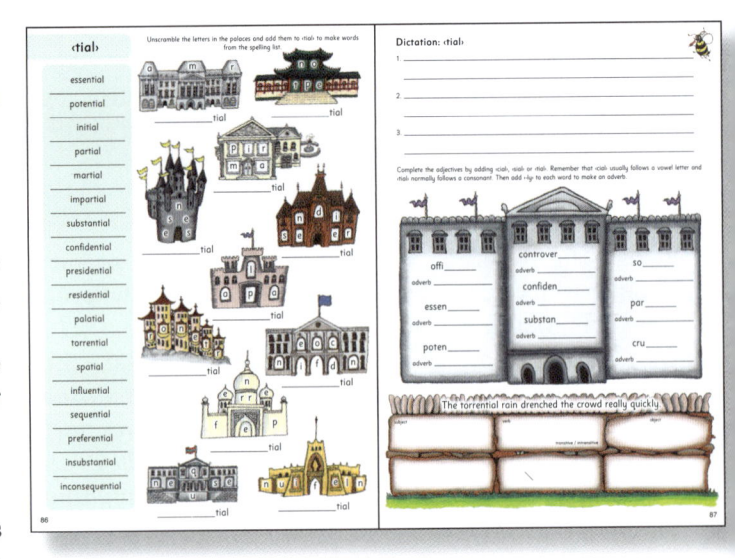

essential
potential
initial
partial
martial
impartial
substantial
confidential
presidential
residential
palatial
torrential
spatial
influential
sequential
preferential
insubstantial
inconsequential

Activity Page 1
- The children split each spelling word into syllables (*es/sen/tial*, *po/ten/tial*, *i/ni/tial*, *par/tial*, *mar/tial*, *im/par/tial*, *sub/stan/tial*, *con/fi/den/tial*, *pres/i/den/tial*, *res/i/den/tial*, *pa/la/tial*, *tor/ren/tial*, *spa/tial*, *in/flu/en/tial*, *se/quen/tial*, *pref/er/en/tial*, *in/sub/stan/tial*, *in/con/se/quen/tial*).
- They then unscramble the letters in the palaces and add them to ‹tial› to make some of the spelling words (*martial*, *potential*, *impartial*, *essential*, *residential*, *palatial*, *torrential*, *confidential*, *preferential*, *sequential*, *influential*).

Activity Page 2
- The children add ‹cial›, ‹sial› or ‹tial› to each word root.
- They then write the adverb for each one (*officially*, *essentially*, *potentially*, *controversially*, *confidentially*, *substantially*, *socially*, *partially*, *crucially*).
- Then they parse the sentence and complete the wall.
- *Quickly* is an adverb made by adding ‹-ly› to an adjective and it is modified by the adverb *really*.
The torrential rain drenched the crowd really quickly.
Top: *rain - drenched - crowd*
Bottom: *The torrential - quickly/really - the*
Verb: transitive

Dictation
- Dictate the following sentences:

1. The crucial documents were strictly confidential.
2. There will be a residential summer school at the college.
3. The dietician declared, "A balanced diet is essential for everyone."

- Remind them to use speech marks with the correct punctuation in sentence 3.

GRAMMAR 5 PUPIL BOOK: PAGE 88

Grammar: Adverbs Describing Adjectives

Aim
- Extend the children's understanding of adverbs by introducing the idea that as well as describing verbs and other adverbs, some adverbs can also describe adjectives.

Introduction
- Remind the children that when we describe something using more than one adjective, we tend to put them in a certain order: 1. Determiners, 2. Opinion, 3. Size and shape, 4. Condition and age, 5. Colour and pattern, 6. Origin, 7. Material.
- Revise the different categories, asking the children to give a few examples for each one and write them on the board.
- Now see if the class can make a noun phrase, using an adjective from every category.
- Remind the class that we would not normally use so many adjectives and that the order given is only a general guide.

Main Point
- Point out that although adjectives always describe nouns or pronouns, we now know that adverbs can describe more than just verbs; they can also describe other adverbs.
- Write *She sang absolutely beautifully* on the board and discuss how the adverb *absolutely* is telling us how beautifully the person is singing; it is describing another adverb rather than the verb.
- Now write this sentence on the board and parse it with the children: She sang with a beautifully clear voice.
- Ask the children what the adverb *beautifully* is describing this time. Discuss how it is describing the adjective by telling us more about how clear her voice is.
- Explain that as well as describing verbs and other adverbs, some adverbs can also describe adjectives.
- Write the sentence *The sun is hot* on the board. Ask the children to suggest adverbs that could describe how hot the sun is. Some possible answers include: *unbearably, surprisingly, intensely, really, always, often, sometimes, very*.
- Point out that some adverbs, like *very* can, in fact, only describe adverbs and adjectives and never describe verbs.

Activity Page
- The children parse the sentences, underlining each word in the appropriate colour.
  The chairs were uncomfortably hard.
  I am quite curious about the surprise.
  The cheese had an unusually strong smell.
  The cakes from the bakery are always delicious.
  Her grandmother's ring was really expensive.
  The prize for the winner is rather unusual.
  She has become an extremely beautiful woman.
  The way through the mountains will be very dangerous.
  The powerfully fragrant flowers had grown exceedingly tall.
- They then rewrite each one, so that the adverb(s) in bold describe the adjective(s).
- Remind the class to change *a* to *an* if an adverb beginning with a vowel is added after it.

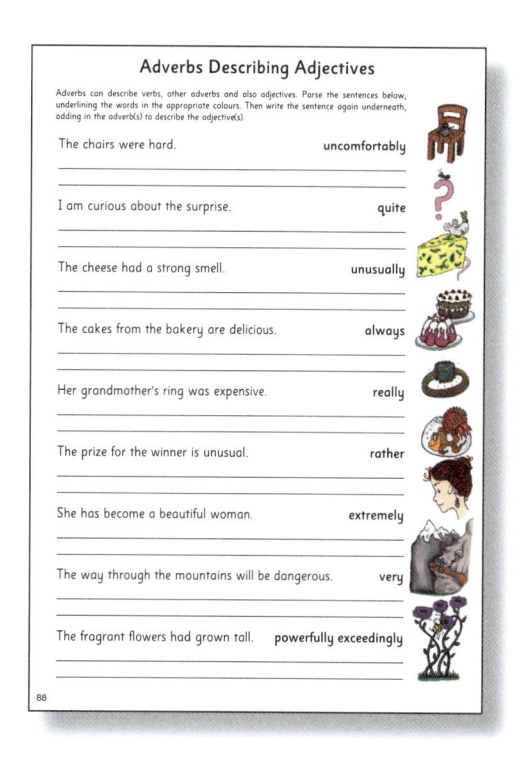

Extension Activity
- Write these sentences on the board: 1. *They have bought a suprisingly big boat*, 2. *She had written enormously successful books*, 3. *The incredibly rare painting has disappeared*.
- Ask the children to draw sentence walls on a separate sheet of paper and put the sentences into the boxes.
  1. Top: *They - have bought - boat* / Bottom: (blank) - (blank) - *a big/surprisingly* / Verb: transitive
  2. Top: *She - had written - books* / Bottom: (blank) - (blank) - *successful/enormously* / Verb: transitive
  3. Top: *painting - has disappeared* - (blank) / Bottom: *the rare/incredibly* - (blank) - (blank) / Verb: intransitive
- Explain that the adverb describing an adjective should go below it in the box, joined by a diagonal line.

Rounding Off
- Go over the activity page with the children, discussing their answers.
- If they have done the extension activity, check that the children have filled in the boxes correctly.

93

GRAMMAR 5 PUPIL BOOK: PAGE 89 & 90

Spelling: ‹-i›

Spelling Test
- The children turn to the backs of their books and find the column labelled *Spelling Test 29*.
- Call out the spelling words learnt last week.

Revision
- Write these words on the board and identify the ‹cial› or ‹tial› spelling of /shul/ in each one: gla**cial**, fa**cial**, finan**cial**, essen**tial**, ini**tial**, poten**tial**.
- Ask the class to suggest other words with these spellings, add them to the board and discuss their meanings.

Spelling Point
- Write the word *ski* on the board and ask the class what is unusual about this spelling.
- In English, the letter usually found at the end of a word like this is ‹y› because 'toughy ‹y›' replaces 'shy ‹i›' on the end of words (see page 29, rule f).
- Ask the children to call out some more examples, write them on the board and discuss what they have in common, apart from the spelling. Explain that these words have usually been borrowed from other languages and absorbed into English.
- *Ski* comes from Norwegian, for example, and many words are Italian, particularly for food (such as *broccoli*, *spaghetti*, *salami* and *pepperoni*).
- Other words, like *bonsai*, *origami*, *tsunami* and *koi* are Japanese, while others are from Arabic (*safari*), Tibetan (*yeti*), Maori (*kiwi*) and Latin (*alibi*). The word *bikini* is named after a Pacific island, *deli* is short for *delicatessen* (from German or Dutch) and *mini* and *semi* are Latin prefixes that are now used as words in their own right.

Spelling List
- Go through the list, identify the syllables in each word and discuss the meaning of any unfamiliar words.
- Ask the class to find and highlight each ‹-i› spelling.
- Point out the ‹i› saying /ee/ in *ki**w**i*, *bik**i**ni* and *graff**i**ti*, the ‹k› in *koi* and *bikini*, the ‹a› saying /ar/ in *s**a**lami*, *origami* and *tsun**a**mi*, the schwas (as in *salami* and *graffiti*), the double consonants in *graffiti*, *spaghetti*, *broccoli*, *pepperoni* and *paparazzi*, the silent letters in *spaghetti* and *tsunami* (and the ‹u› saying /oo/) and the long vowel sound in *pepperoni*.
- Point out that the final ‹i› does not always say its sound; in *koi* and *bonsai* it is part of a digraph making the /oi/ and /ie/ sounds, respectively, and in *alibi* it makes the /ie/ sound.

taxi
kiwi
ski
deli
yeti
koi
bikini
salami
alibi
bonsai
graffiti
safari
spaghetti
broccoli
origami
tsunami
pepperoni
paparazzi

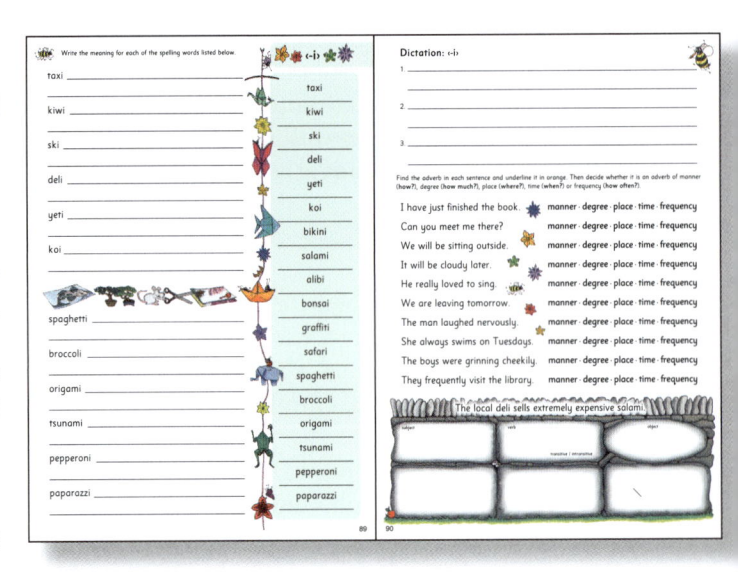

- It is a good idea to blend and sound out the spelling words quickly every day with the children, using the 'say it as it sounds' strategy where appropriate.

Activity Page 1
- The children split each spelling word into syllables (tax/i, kiw/i, ski, del/i, yet/i, koi, bi/ki/ni, sa/la/mi, a/li/bi, bon/sai, graf/fi/ti, sa/fa/ri, spa/ghet/ti, broc/co/li, o/ri/ga/mi, tsu/na/mi, pep/per/o/ni, pa/pa/raz/zi).
- They then write the meaning for each of the numbered spelling words, using a dictionary if they are unsure of any words.

Activity Page 2
- The children identify the adverbs and decide what type they are (*just* [degree], *there* [place], *outside* [place], *later* [time], *really* [degree], *tomorrow* [time], *nervously* [manner], *always* [frequency], *cheekily* [manner], *frequently* [frequency]).
- Then they parse the sentence and complete the wall.
- *Extremely* is an adverb describing the adjective *expensive* and should be written below it on the wall.
The local deli sells extremely expensive salami.
Top: *deli - sells - salami*
Bottom: *The local* - (blank) - *expensive/extremely*
Verb: transitive.

Dictation
- Dictate the following sentences:

1. The film star took a taxi to avoid the paparazzi.
2. The visitors were captivated by the Japanese bonsa trees.
3. "Would you like pepperoni pizza or spaghetti tonight?" asked Dad.

- Remind the class to use speech marks with the correct punctuation in sentence 3. *Japanese* and *Dad* are proper nouns and need capital letters.

Grammar: Irregular Plurals

Aim
- Develop the children's knowledge of irregular plurals.
- Introduce the idea that some singular words make their plural by removing the final letters ‹us› before adding ‹i›. These words have a Latin origin.

Introduction
- Remind the children that most plurals are regular because they can be made by following a few simple rules.
- Write some words on the board and ask the children to say the plurals:
  - *Flowers, pencils, cats, books, cars*: most regular plurals are made by adding ‹s›.
  - *Stitches, ashes, kisses, quizzes, taxes*: nouns ending in ‹ch›, ‹sh›, ‹s›, ‹z› or ‹x› are made by adding ‹es›.
  - *Tomatoes, potatoes, torpedoes, volcanoes/hippos, pianos, photos, studios*: nouns ending in ‹o› are usually made by adding ‹es›, except when the word is foreign, abbreviated or has a vowel before the ‹o›, when ‹s› is added.
  - *Berries, spies, cries, cities, copies, ponies*: nouns ending in a consonant plus ‹y› replace ‹y› with ‹i› before adding ‹es›.
  - *Toys, ways, guys, monkeys*: nouns ending in a vowel plus ‹y› simply add ‹s›.

Main Point
- Remind the children that some plurals are irregular or tricky because they do not follow these rules and have to be learnt.
- Many change the vowel sound in the root word rather than adding a suffix (*feet, mice, women*), some replace ‹f› or ‹fe› with ‹ves› (*wolves, leaves, wives*) and others have the same form for both singular and plural (*sheep, fish, deer*).
- Write the word *fungus* on the board and ask if anyone knows what this word means (*a simple form of plant life such as mushrooms and toadstools*).
- Ask the children if they know what its plural is. They may say *funguses*, following the rule for regular plurals of words ending in ‹s›. They may know that it can also be *fungi*, where the ‹us› is replaced by ‹i› (which usually says /ie/, although some words like *fungi* and *stimuli*, can be either /ie/ or /ee/).
- Remind the children that many words in English have been borrowed from other languages, and this form of plural comes from Latin.
- A small number of words always use this plural; they tend to be scientific or academic words like *stimuli, nuclei* and *alumni*.
- Others, like *hippopotamus, cactus, crocus* and *fungus* can take either the ‹i› plural or the regular ‹es› plural.
- However, most Latin words that have been absorbed into English have regular plurals, such as *viruses*, so the children need to look up words in a dictionary to be sure.
- Furthermore, some words like *octopus* and *platypus* are not Latin but Greek and so their plurals should be formed in the regular way, although because they look similar to Latin words, the incorrect ‹i› plural is sometimes used instead.

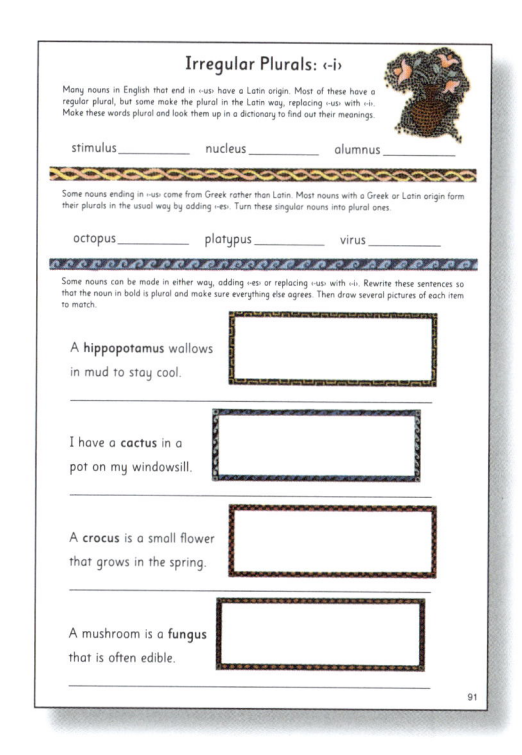

Activity Page
- The children write plurals for Latin words that always use ‹-i› (*stimuli, nuclei, alumni*) and for some words from Greek or Latin that always add ‹-es› (*octopuses, platypuses, viruses*).
- They then rewrite the sentences so that the words in bold are plural and everything still agrees (for example: *The hippopotamuses/hippopotami wallow in mud to stay cool; I have some cactuses/cacti in some pots on my windowsill; Crocuses/Croci are small flowers that grow in the spring; Mushrooms are funguses/fungi that are often edible*).
- The children can choose to use one form or the other and then draw pictures for them.

Extension Activity
- The children put some words ending in ‹us› into sentences. They then use a dictionary to find the plurals. Working with a partner, they swap sentences and rewrite them in the plural.
- Possible words are: *abacus, apparatus, bonus, campus, chorus, circus* (for ‹es›); *radius, rhombus, thesaurus, syllabus, terminus* (for both ‹es› and ‹i›).

Rounding Off
- Go over the children's work, discussing their answers.
- If they have done the extension activity, ask some children to read out their sentences.

GRAMMAR 5 PUPIL BOOK: PAGE 92 & 93

Spelling: ‹graph›

Spelling Test
- The children turn to the backs of their books and find the column labelled *Spelling Test 30*.
- Call out the spelling words learnt last week.

Revision
- Write these words on the board and revise the ‹age› and ‹ege› spellings from page 2 of the *Pupil Book*: man**age**, dam**age**, mess**age**, coll**ege**, privil**ege**, all**ege**.
- Remind the children that both endings say /ij/ and that ‹age› is the more common spelling pattern.
- Ask them to suggest other words with these spellings and discuss their meanings.

Spelling Point
- Remind the class that knowing a prefix, suffix or word root can often help in working out the meaning of an unfamiliar word.
- For example, the root word *graph* comes from the Greek word *graphos*, meaning *written* or *writing*. (When the /f/ sound is written ‹ph› in an English word, it is usually because it has a Greek origin.)
- A graph is information recorded in a visual way and, as a root, ‹graph› appears in words relating to writing, drawing or recorded information, such as *digraph* (two letters written together to make one sound), *cartographer* (a maker of maps, another form of visual record) and *calligraphy* (the art of writing in a beautiful and decorative way).
- Look at some further spelling words with the class and discuss their meanings.

Spelling List
- Go through the list, identify the syllables in each word and discuss the meaning of any unfamiliar words. Ask the class to find and highlight each ‹graph› spelling.
- Point out the suffixes in *graph**ic*** and *graph**ically***, the prefixes in *di**graph*** (meaning *two*), *tele**graph*** (meaning *far off*) and *auto**graph*** (meaning *self*), the long vowel sounds in *di**graph***, *photo**graph*** and *bio**graphy***, the ‹e› saying /i/ in *tele**graph***, *ge**ography*** and *chor**eography***, the schwas (as in *par**a**graph* and *cartograph**er***), the ‹y› saying /i/ in *pol**y**graph*, the ‹au› spelling in *autograph* and *autobiography*, the ‹ph› in *photograph* and the soft ‹g› in *geography*.
- It is a good idea to blend and sound out the spelling words quickly every day with the children, using the 'say it as it sounds' strategy where appropriate.

graph
graphic
digraph
telegraph
paragraph
polygraph
autograph
photograph
biography
geography
calligraphy
cartographer
homograph
graphically
bibliography
lexicography
choreography
autobiography

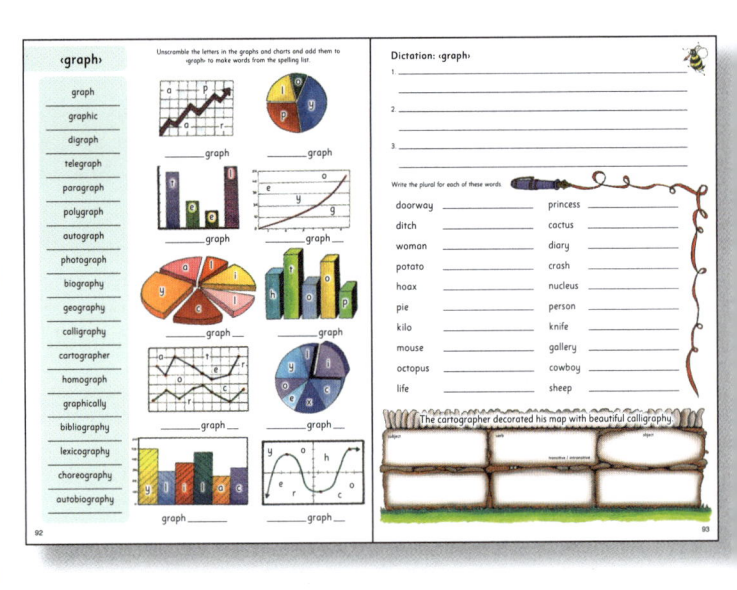

Activity Page 1
- The children split each spelling word into syllables (*graph*, *graph/ic*, *di/graph*, *tel/e/graph*, *par/a/graph*, *pol/y/graph*, *au/to/graph*, *pho/to/graph*, *bi/og/ra/phy*, *ge/og/ra/phy*, *cal/lig/ra/phy*, *car/tog/ra/pher*, *hom/o/graph*, *graph/i/cal/ly*, *bib/li/og/ra/phy*, *lex/i/cog/ra/phy*, *chor/e/og/ra/phy*, *au/to/bi/og/ra/phy*).
- They then unscramble the letters in the graphs and charts and add them to ‹graph› to make some of the spelling words (*paragraph*, *polygraph*, *telegraph*, *geography*, *calligraphy*, *photograph*, *cartographer*, *lexicography*, *graphically*, *choreography*).

Activity Page 2
- The children write the plural for each word (*doorways*, *ditches*, *women*, *potatoes*, *hoaxes*, *pies*, *kilos*, *mice*, *octopuses*, *lives*, *princesses*, *cacti/cactuses*, *diaries*, *crashes*, *nuclei*, *people*, *knives*, *galleries*, *cowboys*, *sheep*).
- Then they parse the sentence and complete the wall.
- *With beautiful calligraphy* is a prepositional phrase acting as an adverb, so orange brackets can be put around it. The cartographer decorated his map (with beautiful calligraphy).
- Top: *cartographer - decorated - map*
- Bottom: *The - with beautiful calligraphy - his*
- Verb: transitive

Dictation
- Dictate the following sentences:

1. "Can this photograph of a yeti be real?" asked the editor.
2. Mathematicians often use graphs and charts in their work.
3. The geography book had several paragraphs on glacial valleys.

- Remind them to use speech marks with the correct punctuation in sentence 1.

Grammar: Using a Colon and Bullet Points in a List

Aim
- Extend the children's knowledge of punctuation.
- Introduce them to colons and bullet points and demonstrate how they can be used in lists.

Introduction
- Remind the class that punctuation helps us make sense of the words we use.
- Briefly revise the punctuation the children should know and discuss when they might use it: full stops, question marks, exclamation marks, speech marks, commas, apostrophes and hyphens.
- Point out that speech marks and apostrophes appear above the line and that hyphens also sit above the line, but not so far up.
- Write some lists on the board (they could be lists of colours, animals, food or perhaps words relating to a topic they are studying). Remind the class that commas are used to separate the items, although between the last two items *and* or *or* is added instead of a comma. The commas indicate a short pause to help the reader separate one idea from another.

Main Point
- Explain that another way of making lists is to write them vertically down the page rather than horizontally along a line.
- This can help emphasise the individual items and make the whole list easier to read at a glance.
- For this reason vertical lists are often used in presentations and reports, or for practical reasons, like making a shopping list.
- Write some vertical lists on the board and discuss them with the children:

My favourite animals are: *My favourite hobbies are:*
- *aardvarks* - *Playing the piano.*
- *cats* - *Swimming.*
- *wombats* - *Walking my dog.*

- Point out that a list always needs an introduction. In normal writing it should be able to stand alone as a simple sentence, but in vertical lists this is not so important.
- A vertical list's introduction ends in a punctuation mark called a colon, which is written as two small dots, one above the other.
- Like full stops and commas, a colon marks the place where we should pause in speaking: it is a longer pause than a comma, but not as long as a full stop. Also point out that instead of using commas, each item starts on a new, slightly indented, line with a bullet symbol in front. Both the symbol itself and the items in the list can be called bullet points, although not all vertical lists use them; the items could be numbered *1, 2, 3*, or *A, B, C*, for example.
- The list item can be a word, phrase or clause and it can either have an open punctuation style (with a lower-case initial letter, except when writing proper nouns, and no full stop) or be more formally punctuated; either way is acceptable as long as the style is consistent (although it is more common for clauses to be punctuated as sentences).
- Also point out that, unlike a traditional list, *and* and *or* do not usually appear.

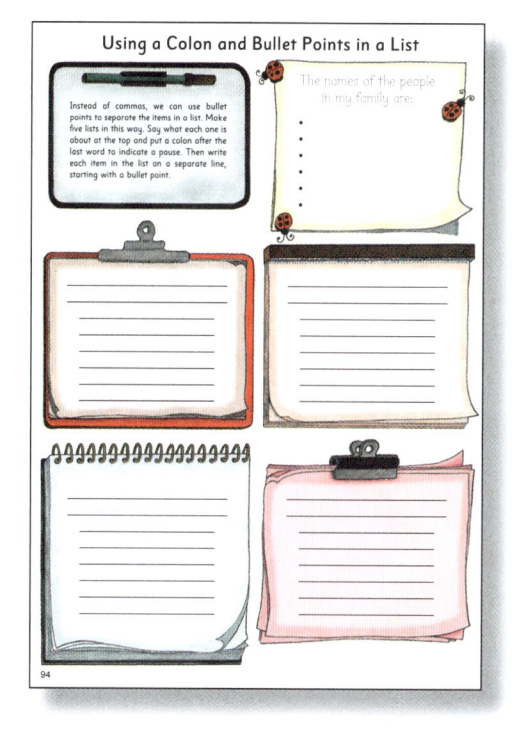

Activity Page
- The children write five vertical lists, starting each one with an introduction.
- They should punctuate each list correctly, putting a colon at the end of the introduction and starting each new line with the bullet symbol.
- Remind them to be consistent, choosing either to use a starting capital letter and closing full stop, or to use a lower-case letter without any punctuation.
- Possible subjects include *My favourite animals*, *The people in my family*, *Things I need to pack for... the beach/school/a weekend away*, *My favourite sports* and *Things I would like to do... on holiday/in my life/this evening*.

Extension Activity
- On a separate sheet of paper, the children write a vertical list of things they think are good or important about school.
- Alternatively, they could write an agenda for a class meeting, using numbered items instead of bullet points.

Rounding Off
- Go over the activity page with the children, asking some to read out their sentences.

GRAMMAR 5 PUPIL BOOK: PAGE 95 & 96

Spelling: ‹-ology›

Spelling Test
- The children turn to the backs of their books and find the column labelled *Spelling Test 31*.
- Call out the spelling words learnt last week.

Revision
- Write these words on the board and revise the noun endings from the lessons on pages 8, 11, 14 and 17 of the *Pupil Book*: ch**ance**, entr**ance**, vac**ancy**, aud**ience**, sent**ence**, emerg**ency**.
- The vowel is often a schwa, which makes it difficult to know whether to write ‹a› or ‹e›, so the spellings have to be learnt. Ask the class to suggest other words and discuss their meanings.

Spelling Point
- Remind the class that knowing a prefix, suffix or word root can often help in working out the meaning of an unfamiliar word.
- For example, the suffix ‹-ology› comes from the Greek word *logos*, meaning *word*, and is used in words to indicate a subject of interest or study, especially something scientific.
- For example, a biologist works in *biology*, the study of plants and animals, and an etymologist is interested in *etymology*, the study of words and their origins.
- Look at some further spelling words with the class and discuss their meanings.

Spelling List
- Go through the list, identify the syllables in each word and discuss the meaning of any unfamiliar words.
- Ask the class to find and highlight each ‹ology› spelling. Point out that it has a schwa, a 'toughy ‹y›' that says its sound and a soft ‹g›.
- Point out the long vowel sounds in b**i**ology, **i**deology, **E**gyptology, s**o**ciology and m**e**teorology, the soft ‹g› and ‹c› in geology, Egyptology and sociology, the ‹e› saying /i/ in g**e**ology, **e**cology, **i**deology and m**e**teorology, the second ‹o› being part of the /oo/ sound, but also saying /o/ in z**oo**logy, the ‹ch› saying /k/ in te**ch**nology, **ch**ronology and ar**ch**aeology, the ‹y› saying /i/ in m**y**thology, Eg**y**ptology and et**y**mology, the ‹s› saying /z/ in co**s**mology, the schwa in chron**o**logy, meteor**o**logy and anthrop**o**logy, the capital letter in **E**gyptology and the ‹ae› saying /i/ in arch**ae**ology.
- Also compare the meaning of *geology* with that of *geography* from the last lesson.

biology
geology
ecology
zoology
technology
terminology
ideology
mythology
cosmology
anthology
chronology
ornithology
Egyptology
sociology
etymology
meteorology
anthropology
archaeology

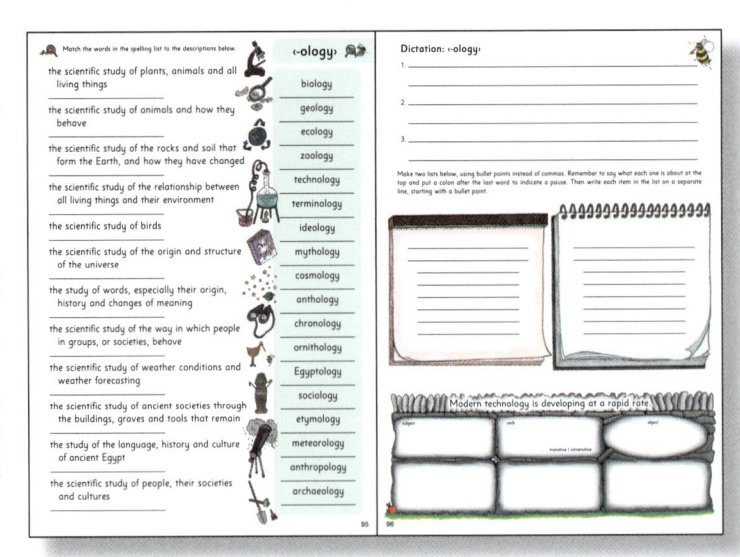

- It is a good idea to blend and sound out the spelling words quickly every day with the children, using the 'say it as it sounds' strategy where appropriate, or you could break down the words into root (word) and suffix.

Activity Page 1
- The children split each spelling word into syllables (*bi/ol/o/gy, ge/ol/o/gy, e/col/o/gy, zo/ol/o/gy, tech/nol/o/gy, ter/mi/nol/o/gy, i/de/ol/o/gy, my/thol/o/gy, cos/mol/o/gy, an/thol/o/gy, chro/nol/o/gy, or/ni/thol/o/gy, E/gyp/tol/o/gy, so/ci/ol/o/gy, et/y/mol/o/gy, me/te/o/rol/o/gy, an/thro/pol/o/gy, ar/chae/ol/o/gy*).
- They then match the spelling words to their descriptions (*biology, zoology, geology, ecology, ornithology, cosmology, etymology, sociology, meteorology, archaeology, Egyptology, anthropology*).

Activity Page 2
- The children use bullet points to write two lists of their choosing.
- Then they parse the sentence and complete the wall.
- *At a rapid rate* is a prepositional phrase acting as an adverb, so orange brackets can be put around it.
Modern technology is developing (at a rapid rate).
Top: *technology - is developing - (blank)*
Bottom: *Modern - at a rapid rate - (blank)*
Verb: intransitive

Dictation
- Dictate the following sentences:

1. "Shall I study geography or geology?" mused the student.
2. The flying horse from Greek mythology is called Pegasus.
3. The anthology has a superb collection of interesting stories.

- Remind them to use speech marks with the correct punctuation in sentence 3.

GRAMMAR 5 PUPIL BOOK: PAGE 97

Grammar: Parentheses

Aim
- Introduce parentheses, which are round brackets that are used to enclose information that is interesting or helpful but not essential to the meaning of a sentence.

Introduction
- Revise how to write vertical lists, which are used in presentations, reports and notes.
- A vertical list always has an introduction followed by a colon, to indicate a pause.
- The list items go below, each one starting on a new, slightly indented, line with a bullet symbol in front.
- Write the following list on the board and correct it with the children:

In the winter we: ✗
- go skiing.
- wrap up warm
- Feeding the birds
- I do not walk to school.

In the winter we: ✓
- Go skiing.
- Wrap up warm.
- Feed the birds.
- Do not walk to school.

In the winter we: ✓
- go skiing
- wrap up warm
- feed the birds
- do not walk to school

- Remind the children that each item can start with a capital and end in a full stop, or it can be lower-case, without any punctuation, but it cannot be both.
- The wording also has to be consistent, so that you can read it aloud as a list.
- The example on the board does not make sense because the last two items do not follow the same pattern as the first two.

Main Point
- These lists provide essential information that can be read quickly and easily.
- Sometimes, however, we want to give the reader an extra piece of information, which is interesting but not essential.
- The main way to do this is to put the information in parentheses, which are round brackets that come in pairs, rather like speech marks; an opening bracket goes at the beginning and a closing bracket goes at the end.
- Then, when we see something is in parentheses, we know the sentence would still be complete, even without that information.
- The extra information provided can be quite varied, but often includes such things as dates, prices, page numbers, explanations and alternative names; it can even be a whole sentence, starting with a capital letter and ending in a full stop, and when this happens, the full stop goes inside the parentheses.

- Parentheses can also be used in a list of options: for example, *The desserts available are (a) carrot cake, (b) strawberry ice cream and (c) fruit salad.*
- Write some examples on the board and discuss them with the class, showing the children where to put the parentheses.
- Then remove the extra information and check that what is left is still a proper sentence.

Activity Page
- The children read the information inside the parentheses (options *a*, *b*, *c* and *d*) and decide which one goes with which sentence (*a, c, d, b*).
- Then they turn each long sentence into two shorter sentences (*He is the author of many books on zoology. Zoology is the scientific study of animals and how they behave; They are going on an African safari to see the lions, giraffes and hippopotamuses. Safari means 'journey'; This biography is about Samuel Morse, who helped invent the telegraph and Morse code. He was born in April 1791*).
- Finally, the children put parentheses around the extra information in the paragraph (*[Young Ornithologists Club], [that's the traditional Japanese art of paper folding], [she's my younger sister], [my favourite!], [a], [b], [c]*).

Extension Activity
- The children rewrite the bottom paragraph on a separate sheet of paper, removing the extra information in parentheses. They then read it again, checking that it still makes sense.

Rounding Off
- Go over the children's work, discussing their answers.

GRAMMAR 5 PUPIL BOOK: PAGE 98 & 99

Spelling: ‹-ment›

Spelling Test
- The children turn to the backs of their books and find the column labelled *Spelling Test 32*.
- Call out the spelling words learnt last week.

Revision
- Write these words on the board, identify the prefixes and discuss how they modify the meaning: ***multi**tude* (many), ***auto**matic* (self), ***mega**phone* (great), ***micro**chip* (small), ***super**ior* (above), ***centi**pede* (hundred), ***milli**pede* (thousand), ***post**pone* (after).
- Ask the class to suggest other words using these prefixes.

Spelling Point
- Revise the suffix ‹-ent›, which is found in nouns and adjectives of Latin origin.
- Nouns with this suffix usually do the action of the root word, as in *student* and *president*.
- However, when the suffix is ‹-ment›, the nouns give the result of the root word, as in *payment* and *disappointment* (if you *pay* for something, you make a *payment* and if someone *disappoints* you, you feel *disappointed*).
- Look at some more spelling words and identify the root word where possible.
- Point out that the vowel in ‹ment› has lost its pure sound and has become a schwa.

Spelling List
- Go through the list, identify the syllables in each word and discuss the meaning of any unfamiliar words.
- Ask the class to find and highlight each ‹ment› spelling.
- Point out the ‹ea› spelling of /ee/ in *tr**ea**tment*, the ‹e› saying /i/ in *el**e**ment*, *emb**a**rrassment* and *enc**ou**ragement*, the double consonants in *co**mm**ent*, *a**ss**ortment*, *emba**rr**assment* and *disa**pp**ointment*, the ‹ay› and ‹oy› in the middle of *p**ay**ment* and *enj**oy**ment*, the schwas (as in *ass**o**rtment*, *agr**ee**ment* and *gov**e**rnment*), the ‹o› saying /u/ in *g**o**vernment*, the ‹u› saying /yoo/ without an ‹e› in *arg**u**ment*, the ‹ia› in *parl**ia**ment* and the ‹ow› saying /u/ and ‹age› saying /ij/ in the antonyms *encouragement* and *discouragement*.
- It is a good idea to blend and sound out the spelling words quickly every day with the children, using the 'say it as it sounds' strategy where appropriate, or you could break down the words into root (word) and suffix.

ailment
treatment
element
comment
payment
assortment
agreement
government
argument
astonishment
statement
enjoyment
parliament
entertainment
embarrassment
encouragement
disappointment
discouragement

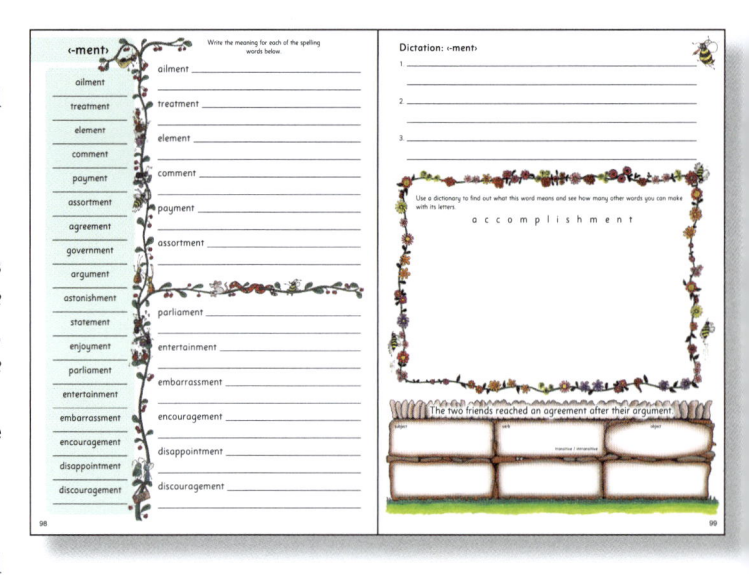

Activity Page 1
- The children split each spelling word into syllables (*ail/ment, treat/ment, el/e/ment, com/ment, pay/ment, as/sort/ment, a/gree/ment, gov/ern/ment, ar/gu/ment, as/ton/ish/ment, state/ment, en/joy/ment, par/lia/ment, en/ter/tain/ment, em/bar/rass/ment, en/cour/age/ment, dis/ap/point/ment, dis/cour/age/ment*).
- They then write the meaning for each of the numbered spelling words. Encourage the children to use a dictionary if they are unsure of any words.

Activity Page 2
- The children look up *accomplishment* in the dictionary to find out its meaning and make as many words as they can with its letters.
- Then they parse the sentence and complete the wall.
- *After the argument* is a prepositional phrase acting as an adverb, so orange brackets can be put around it.
  The two friends reached an agreement (after the argument).
  Top: *friends - reached - agreement*
  Bottom: *The two - after the argument - an*
  Verb: transitive

Dictation
- Dictate the following sentences:

1. The entertainment was a terrible disappointment.
2. The patient had an assortment of treatments to cure his ailment.
3. "Can you comment on the failure of the government?" she was asked.

- Remind them to use speech marks with the correct punctuation in sentence 3.

Grammar: Homophone Mix-Ups

Aim
- Reinforce the children's understanding of homophones and develop their ability to choose between similar-sounding words in their writing.

Introduction
- Ask the children to call out some of the homophones that they have learnt so far.
- These include *our* and *are*; *their*, *there* and *they're*; *your* and *you're*; *its* and *it's*; *to*, *two* and *too*; *where*, *wear* and *were*; *practice* and *practise*; *licence* and *license*.
- Make sure the children know which spellings take which meanings.
- *Our* is more properly pronounced /ou-r/ but in practice it is often pronounced /ar/ and can be confused with *are*.
- *Were* is not strictly a homophone of *where*, but their spellings are often confused so it helps to look at them together.
- Point out that some of these words are parts of the verb *to be* (*are*, *were*) and some are possessive adjectives (*our*, *your*, *their*, *its*), while others are contractions (*they're*, *you're*, *it's*).
- Others are words that use the ‹c› spelling for the noun (*practice* and *licence*) and the ‹s› spelling for the verb (*practise* and *license*).
- Children often find *its* and *it's* particularly difficult because apostrophe ‹s› can also be used to show possession. However, it is only used in this way to make possessive nouns and not possessive adjectives like *its*.
- If the children have particular problems with other homophones, write them on the board and revise them with the class.

Main Point
- Remind the children that it is important to use the correct spelling when writing homophones, otherwise their writing will not make sense.
- Ask the children if they can think of any other homophones and write them on the board, discussing their spelling and meaning.
- Add the words from the activity page, look at their spellings and check that the children know what they mean: *alter/altar*, *sail/sale*, *piece/peace*, *week/weak*, *hire/higher*, *medal/meddle*, *profit/prophet*.
- If the children are unsure of the meanings of any of the homophones, ask them to look the the words up in the dictionary and see who can find them first.
- Remind the children that they need to stop and think before writing a homophone, decide which meaning is needed, and think how the word with that meaning is spelt.
- Using the information they already know can sometimes help the children remember the different spellings and meanings. For example, *higher* is a comparative adjective (or adverb) made by adding the suffix ‹-er› to the adjective (or adverb) *high*, whereas *hire* means to employ someone.
- If the sentence requires the adjective (or adverb), the children should remember to write *higher*.
- Ask the children to think of sentences for some of the homophones and discuss which spelling they would use.

Activity Page
- The children write the meaning for each homophone, looking them up in a dictionary if they are unsure of the meaning.

Extension Activity
- On a separate sheet of paper, the children write sentences for some of the homophones on the activity page.
- They could then work in pairs, taking it in turns to dictate a sentence, and then decide together whether the correct spelling has been used.

Rounding Off
- Go over the activity page with the children, discussing their answers.
- If they have done the extension activity, ask some of the children to read out their sentences before checking which spelling they have used.

GRAMMAR 5 PUPIL BOOK: PAGE 101 & 102

Spelling: ‹-ship›

Spelling Test
- The children turn to the backs of their books and find the column labelled *Spelling Test 33*.
- Call out the spelling words learnt last week.

Revision
- Write these words on the board and revise the spellings for /shun/: posi**tion**, ten**sion**, impre**ssion**, politi**cian**, oper**ation**.
- Remind the children that ‹-tion› can also say /chun/ and ‹-sion› can say /zhun/.
- Ask them to suggest other words with these endings, identify how they are said and discuss their meanings.

Spelling Point
- Remind the class that knowing a prefix, suffix or word root can often help in working out the meaning of an unfamiliar word.
- For example, the suffix ‹-ship› comes from the Old English word *scipe*, meaning *a condition or something with a certain quality*.
- It is used to make nouns having the quality, condition, position, relationship or skill of the root word, as in *leadership*, *hardship*, *lordship*, *friendship* and *craftsmanship*. It can also describe the collective members of a group, as in *membership*.
- Look at some further spelling words with the class and discuss their meanings.

Spelling List
- Go through the list, identify the syllables in each word and discuss the meaning of any unfamiliar words.
- Ask the class to find and highlight each ‹ship› spelling.
- Point out other spelling features, such as the ‹k› spelling in *kinship*, the ‹or› saying /er/ after ‹w› in *worship*, the ‹ow› spelling of /oa/ in *ownership* and *fellowship*, the schwas (as in *own**e**rship*, *spons**o**rship* and *citiz**e**nship*), the silent ‹i› in *friendship*, the soft ‹c› in *citizenship*, *apprenticeship* and *censorship*, the double consonants in *fellowship* and *apprenticeship*, the ‹e› saying /i/ and ‹ation› saying /ai-shun/ in *relationship*, the ‹ea› spelling of /ee/ in *leadership* and the ‹ion› spelling in *championship* and *companionship*.
- It is a good idea to blend and sound out the spelling words quickly every day with the children, using the 'say it as it sounds' strategy where appropriate, or you could break down the words into root (word) and suffix.

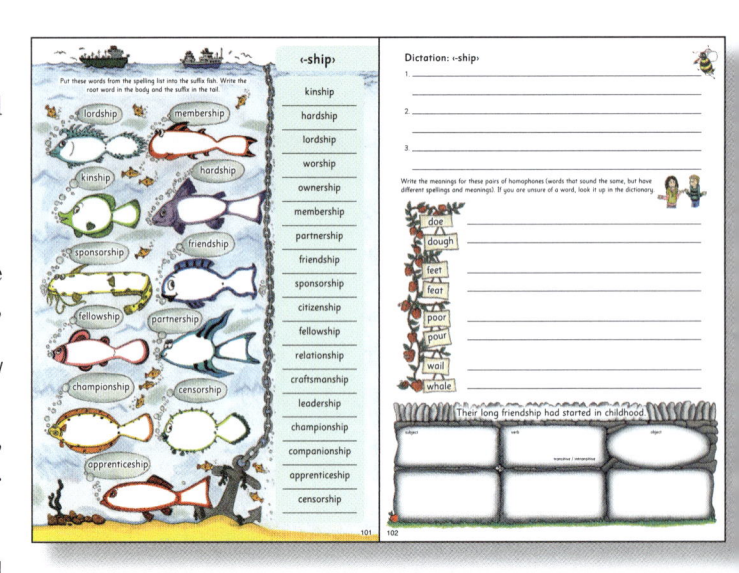

kinship
hardship
lordship
worship
ownership
membership
partnership
friendship
sponsorship
citizenship
fellowship
relationship
craftsmanship
leadership
championship
companionship
apprenticeship
censorship

Activity Page 1
- The children split each spelling word into syllables (*kin/ship, hard/ship, lord/ship, wor/ship, own/er/ship, mem/ber/ship, part/ner/ship, friend/ship, spon/sor/ship, cit/i/zen/ship, fel/low/ship, re/la/tion/ship, crafts/man/ship, lead/er/ship, cham/pi/on/ship, com/pan/ion/ship, ap/pren/tice/ship, cen/sor/ship*).
- They then write out some of the spelling words in the suffix fish, putting the root words in the fish's bodies and the suffixes in the fish's tails.

Activity Page 2
- The children write the meanings for each pair of homophones, using a dictionary if they are unsure of any words.
- Then they parse the sentence and complete the wall.
- *In childhood* is a prepositional phrase acting as an adverb, so orange brackets can be put around it.
  Their long friendship had started (in childhood).
  Top: *friendship - had started - (blank)*
  Bottom: *Their long - in childhood - (blank)*
  Verb: intransitive

Dictation
- Dictate the following sentences:

1. The tennis player was furious when he lost the championship.
2. The ownership of the priceless painting is in question.
3. The art expert exclaimed, "What fabulous craftsmanship!"

- Remind them to use speech marks with the correct punctuation in sentence 3.

Grammar: Homographs and Homonyms

Aim
- Introduce homographs, which are words that share the same spelling, but have a different meaning.
- Homographs that look and sound the same are called homonyms.

Introduction
- Write some homophones on the board and discuss the spellings and meanings of each pair: *air/heir, ate/eight, be/bee, brake/break, clause/claws, days/daze, ewe/yew/you, for/four, groan/grown, knight/night, mail/male, muscle/mussel, pair/pear, right/write, sea/see, waist/waste, wood/would.*
- If the children are having problems with certain homophones, add them to the board and discuss them with the class.
- Point out that the word *homophone* comes from the Greek words *homos* (meaning *same*) and *phone* (meaning *sound* or *voice*).

Main Point
- Explain that as well as homophones, there are also words called homographs.
- The children now know that *homos* means *same* and that *graphos* means *writing*. They learnt the word *homograph* on page 92 of the *Pupil Book*, so they may be able to say what homographs are: words that share the same spelling but have different meanings.
- Write *fly* on the board and discuss some of its different meanings, such as *fly* the insect (as in *the spider caught a fly*) and *fly* the verb (as in *the birds fly high in the sky*).
- Point out that these two words not only look the same, but they also sound the same.
- Homographs like this are called *homonyms*, from the Greek words *homos* and *onoma*, meaning *name*.
- Ask the children if they can think of any more examples of homonyms and write them on the board.
- Possible words include: *jam (the food/to block), bank (the river's edge/where we keep money), lean (slim/to tilt), date (the time/the fruit), rock (a boulder/to sway), change (coins/to alter)* and *bear (the animal/to carry).*
- Point out that many of these words not only have different meanings, they are also different parts of speech.

Activity Page
- The children draw a picture for each meaning of the word *bat (the small animal with wings/a long wooden stick)* and *wave (moving water/to salute).*
- They then read each pair of descriptions, think of a word that can mean both things and write it in the big leaf (*bark, ball, navy, left, swallow, pupil, duck*).

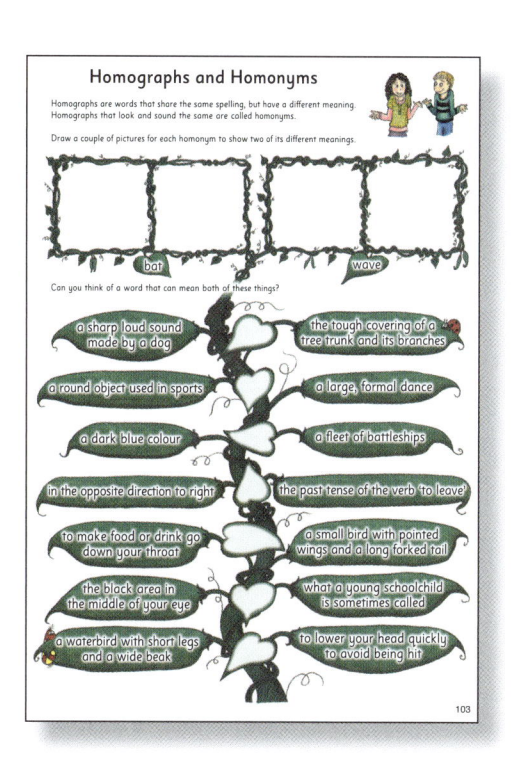

Extension Activity
- Write some homonyms on the board and ask the children to write two different meanings for each one on a separate sheet of paper.
- If they cannot think of more than one meaning, they can look up the word in the dictionary.
- Possible words include: *lap (knee/circuit), roll (bread/to spin), pen (writing tool/small animal enclosure), palm (hand/tree), light (lamp/pale), fair (carnival/just), lie (untruth/to recline), hide (animal skin/to conceal), book (novel/to reserve), break (rest/to smash), nail (spike/finger), train (vehicle/to teach), trunk (tree/elephant).*

Rounding Off
- Go over the activity page with the children, discussing their answers.
- If they have done the extension activity, ask a few children to read out a pair of meanings and see if the class can guess the word.

GRAMMAR 5 PUPIL BOOK: PAGE 104 & 105

Spelling: ‹-ward›

Spelling Test
- The children turn to the backs of their books and find the column labelled *Spelling Test 34*.
- Call out the spelling words learnt last week.

Revision
- Write these words on the board and revise the different spellings: fis**sure**, litera**ture**, poss**ible**, **ch**ute, **ch**alet, cli**che**.
- Remind the children that ‹sure› usually says /zher/, /sher/ or /shor/, ‹ture› usually says /cher/, and ‹ch› and ‹che› say /sh/ in words that have a French origin.
- Ask them to suggest other words with these endings, identify how they are said and discuss their meanings.

Spelling Point
- Remind the class that knowing a prefix, suffix or word root can often help in working out the meaning of an unfamiliar word.
- For example, the suffix ‹-ward› comes from the Old English word *weard*, meaning *turn*.
- It is used to make adjectives and adverbs meaning *being or moving in the direction of (the root word)* (so we can take a *backward* step, and a bird can fly *skywards*).
- Most of the words in the spelling list can be used either as adjectives or adverbs, although the adverbs are more usually written ‹-ward**s**›.
- However, some are only adjectives (*wayward*, *untoward*, *awkward* and *straightforward*), others are only adverbs (*afterwards* and *henceforward*) and *towards* is a preposition.
- Look at the final two spelling words and make sure the children know the points of a compass.

Spelling List
- Go through the list, identify the syllables in each word and discuss the meaning of any unfamiliar words.
- Ask the class to find and highlight each ‹-ward(s)› spelling.
- Explain that when ‹ar› follows ‹w›, it says /or/ (as in *towards* and *untoward*), although the vowel sound is swallowed and becomes a schwa in most of the spelling words.
- Point out the different spellings of /c/ in *backward*, *skyward* and *awkward*, the ‹y› and ‹ay› in the middle of *skyward* and *wayward*, the ‹aw› spelling in *awkward*, the ‹aigh› saying /ai/ in *straightforward* and the soft ‹c› in *henceforward*.
- It is a good idea to blend and sound

onward
forward
outward
towards
backward
skyward
homeward
downward
wayward
untoward
awkward
afterwards
leeward
straightforward
henceforward
windward
southeastward
northwestward

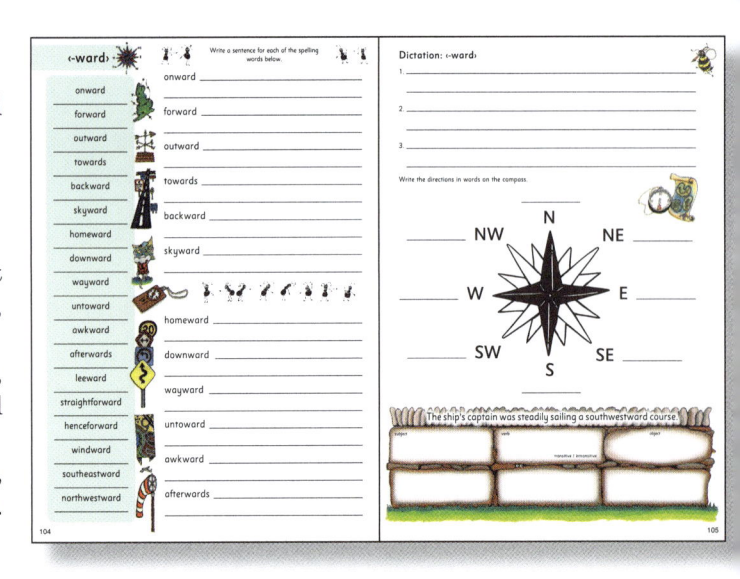

out the spelling words quickly every day with the children, using the 'say it as it sounds' strategy where appropriate, or you could break down the words into root (word) and suffix.

Activity Page 1
- The children split each spelling word into syllables (*on/ward, for/ward, out/ward, to/wards, back/ward, sky/ward, home/ward, down/ward, way/ward, un/to/ward, awk/ward, af/ter/wards, lee/ward, straight/for/ward, hence/for/ward, wind/ward, south/east/ward, north/west/ward*).
- They then write a sentence for each of the listed spelling words.
- Encourage the children to use a dictionary if they are unsure of any words.

Activity Page 2
- The children write the directions on the compass (clockwise from top: *north, northeast, east, southeast, south, southwest, west, northwest*).
- Then they parse the sentence and complete the wall.
- Possessive nouns always act as adjectives, so *ship's* should be underlined in blue.
  The ship's captain was steadily sailing a southwestward course.
  Top: *captain - was sailing - course*
  Bottom: *The ship's - steadily - a southwestward*
  Verb: transitive

Dictation
1. Dad always looked awkward when he tried to dance.
2. Afterwards, the taxi left and drove towards the airport.
3. She said, "I'm looking forward to going home now."

- Dictate the following sentences:
- Remind them to use speech marks with the correct punctuation in sentence 3.

Grammar: Homographs and Heteronyms

Aim
- Develop the children's understanding of homographs, which are words that share the same spelling, but have a different meaning.
- Homographs that look the same but sound different are called heteronyms.

Introduction
- Remind the children that a word that is spelt the same as another word but has a different meaning is called a homograph.
- *Homograph* comes from the Greek words *homos* (meaning *same*) and *graphos* (meaning *writing*).
- Ask the children what kind of homograph they looked at in the last lesson and see if they can remember that homographs that look and sound the same are called homonyms.
- Ask the children to call out some homonyms and write them on the board.
- Then put some of them into sentences with the class, showing their different meanings.

Main Point
- Explain that as well as homonyms, which look and sound the same, there are homographs that look the same but sound different.
- This kind of homograph is called a heteronym (*hetero* in Greek meaning *other* or *different*).
- Write *tear* on the board and ask the children how they would say this word.
- It can be pronounced in one of two ways, depending on which word is being used: /teer/, as in *tears of joy*, and /tair/, as in *to rip* or *to grab*.
- Write these pronunciations on the board and remind the children that when they see the sounds written inside slashes in this way, it is demonstrating how the word is said and not how it is spelt (like the pronunciation guide in the *Jolly Dictionary*).
- Ask the children if they can think of any more examples of heteronyms and write them on the board.
- Possible words include *row*: /roa/ and /rou/; *lead*: /led/ and /leed/; *read*: /red/ and /reed/; *live*: /liv/ and /liev/; *use*: /ues/ and /uez/; *wound*: /woond/ and /wound/; *does*: /duz/ and /doaz/; and *polish*/*Polish*: /polish/ and /poalish/.
- Point out that many of these words not only sound different, they are also different parts of speech.
- Now write *record* on the board and ask what this word means.
- Again, the meaning depends on how the word is said. If it is /**re**cord/, with the stress on the first syllable, it is a noun meaning *best achievement*, *album* or *written evidence*, whereas if the stress is on the second syllable, /re**cord**/, it is a verb meaning *to write down* or *tape*.

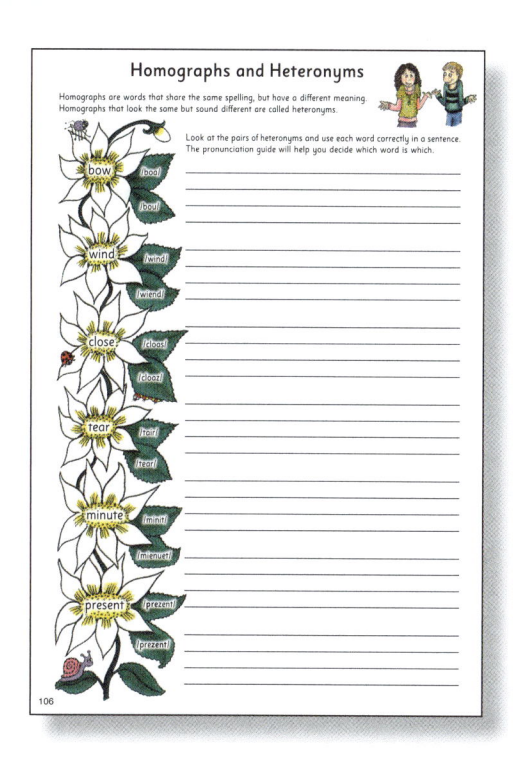

- Other examples include **ob**ject and ob**ject**, **in**valid and in**valid**, **con**duct and con**duct**, **per**mit and per**mit**, **con**vict and con**vict**, **reb**el and reb**el**, **con**sole and con**sole**, **re**fund and re**fund**, **con**tent and con**tent**, **im**port and im**port**, **sus**pect and sus**pect**, **up**date and up**date**.
- Point out that in nouns the stress tends to be in the first syllable, whereas in adjectives and verbs it tends to be in the last or penultimate syllable.

Activity Page
- The children use each heteronym in a sentence to show its meaning.
- The pronunciation guide in each pair of leaves will tell them which word to use.
- If they want to check the meaning before they write the sentence, they can look up the word in a dictionary.

Extension Activity
- The children write some more sentences, using the heteronyms written on the board earlier in the lesson.

Rounding Off
- Go over the activity page with the children, discussing their answers.
- If they have done the extension activity, ask a few children to read out their sentences.

GRAMMAR 5 PUPIL BOOK: PAGE 107 & 108

Spelling: ‹sch›

Spelling Test
- The children turn to the backs of their books and find the column labelled *Spelling Test 35*.
- Call out the spelling words learnt last week.

Revision
- Write these words on the board and revise the different spellings: *hazardous, mysterious, scrumptious, social, palatial, influential*.
- Remind the children that these are adjectives that describe something as relating to or having the qualities of the root (word).
- Also, point out that ‹ti› says /sh/ in ‹tious› and ‹tial›, and *initial* is an exception to the rule that ‹tial› usually follows a consonant.
- Ask the children to suggest similar words, identify how they are said and discuss their meanings.

Spelling Point
- Write the words *school* and *schwa* on the board. Discuss how the letters ‹sch› say /sk/ in *school* and /sh/ in *schwa*.
- Remind the children that the ‹ch› spelling of /k/, found in words like *school*, usually come from Greek, although it is also found in the word *scherzo*, meaning a playful piece of music, borrowed from Italian.
- Words with ‹sch› saying /sh/, however, are usually words borrowed from Yiddish (a language used by older Jewish people, which is related to German) or which have a German (*schnitzel*) or Hebrew (*schwa*) origin.
- This explains why some of the spellings are not usual in English.

Spelling List
- Go through the list, identify the syllables in each word and discuss the meaning of any unfamiliar words.
- Ask the class to find and highlight each ‹sch› spelling.
- Point out other spelling features, such as the schwas (as in *scholar, scholarship, schooner, schemer* and *schoolteacher*), the ‹a› saying /ar/ in *schwa*, the ‹ch› saying /ch/ in *eschew*, the silent ‹e› in *schmooze*, the ‹el› spelling of /ool/ in *schnitzel*, the ‹ea› spelling in *schoolteacher*, the ‹k› spelling in *kitsch*, the ‹a› saying /o/ and single ‹z› ending in *schmaltz*, the ‹er› saying /air/ and ‹o› saying /oa/ in *scherzo*, the ‹s› saying /z/ in *schism*, the ‹e› saying /ee/ in *schematic* and the ‹ph› saying /f/ in *schizophrenic*.
- It is a good idea to blend and sound out the spelling words quickly every day with the children, using the 'say it as it sounds' strategy where appropriate.

school
scholar
schedule
schwa
scheme
scholarship
schooner
eschew
schmooze
schemer
schnitzel
schoolteacher
kitsch
schmaltz
scherzo
schism
schematic
schizophrenic

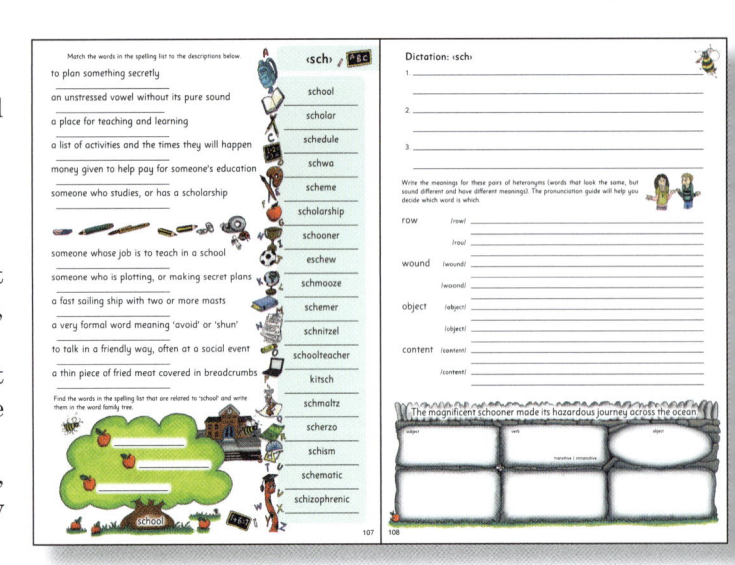

Activity Page 1
- The children split each spelling word into syllables (*school, schol/ar, sched/ule, schwa, scheme, schol/ar/ship, schoon/er, es/chew, schmooze, schem/er, schnit/zel, school/teach/er, kitsch, schmaltz, scher/zo, schis/m, sche/mat/ic, schiz/o/phren/ic*).
- They then match the phrases and spelling words (*scheme, schwa, school, schedule, scholarship, scholar, schoolteacher, schemer, schooner, eschew, schmooze, schnitzel*).
- They then write the three spelling words that are in the same word family as *school* (*scholar, scholarship, schoolteacher*).

Activity Page 2
- The children write the meanings for each pair of heteronyms, using a dictionary if they are unsure of any words.
- Then they parse the sentence and complete the wall.
- *Across the ocean* is a prepositional phrase acting as an adverb, so orange brackets can be put around it.
- The magnificent schooner made its hazardous journey (across the ocean).
- Top: *schooner - made - journey*
- Bottom: *The magnificent - across the ocean - its hazardous*
- Verb: transitive

Dictation
- Dictate the following sentences:

1. The new schoolmaster will teach geography.
2. "The schnitzel is delicious," declared the chef.
3. It is impossible to fit everything into my busy schedule.

- Remind the children to use speech marks with the correct punctuation in sentence 2.

Grammar: Antonyms and Synonyms

Aim
- Reinforce the children's understanding of antonyms and synonyms and develop their ability to use a wider variety of words in their writing.

Introduction
- Briefly revise homophones and homographs. Homophones are words that sound the same but have different spellings and meanings, and homographs are words that look the same but have different meanings.
- There are two types of homograph: those that look and sound the same are called homonyms, and the ones that look the same but sound different are called heteronyms.
- Draw a column for each type of word on the board and ask the children to suggest examples for each.
- Go over the meaning and pronunciation of each word and use some of them in sentences.

Main Point
- Using a varied vocabulary can help children avoid overusing particular words and makes their writing more interesting.
- Remind them that they can use a thesaurus to find synonyms and antonyms for a particular word.
- Like the words *homophone*, *homograph*, *homonym* and *heteronym*, *synonym* and *antonym* also have a Greek origin. *Synonym* means *with name* and is used for words with the same or similar meaning. *Antonym* means *opposite name* and is used for words with an opposite meaning.
- Remind the children that many prefixes and some suffixes can be used to make antonyms.
- Call out some words and ask the class to suggest an antonym for each one: *large* (*small*), *heavy* (*light*), *right* (*left*), *worse* (*better*), *legal* (*illegal*), *painful* (*painless*).
- Then write some word pairs on the board and ask whether they are antonyms or synonyms: *giant/huge* (synonyms), *awake/asleep* (antonyms), *broad/narrow* (antonyms), *journal/diary* (synonyms), *dry/wet* (antonyms), *answer/reply* (synonyms), *love/hate* (antonyms), *hall/corridor* (synonyms), *last/final* (synonyms), *friend/enemy* (antonyms).
- Finally, write the sentence *His noisy neighbours made him furious* on the board. Ask the children to think of synonyms for *noisy* (*loud, rowdy, boisterous, talkative*) and *furious* (*angry, irate, enraged, infuriated*), writing them on the board in word webs.

Activity Page
- The children write an antonym for each word in the mirrors. Possible answers include: *forward/backward, agreement/disagreement, awkward/graceful*.
- They then write a synonym for each word in the spiders' webs. Possible answers include: *illness, sickness, disease, bug, virus* (*ailment*); *fight, quarrel, disagreement, squabble* (*argument*); *later, next, then, after* (*afterwards*).
- Then they write some synonyms and antonyms for each word in the crate. Possible answers include: (*superb*) *great, fantastic, excellent, fabulous, terrific, wonderful/poor, awful, dreadful, terrible, disappointing, inadequate, appalling*; (*brave*) *bold, heroic, fearless, intrepid, daring, courageous/cowardly, timid, fearful*; (*horrible*) *nasty, horrid, unpleasant, disagreeable, horrendous/nice, pleasant, lovely, charming, friendly, agreeable*; (*dangerous*) *risky, unsafe, hazardous, perilous/safe, secure, protected, harmless*; (*miniature*) *tiny, small, little, minute, petite/big, large, huge, enormous, giant*; (*complicated*) *confusing, difficult, involved, elaborate/easy, simple, straightforward, uncomplicated*).
- It does not matter if the children use different words to the ones here, as long as they make sense.
- The children may want to use a thesaurus to help them think of suitable words, or to check that they are correct.

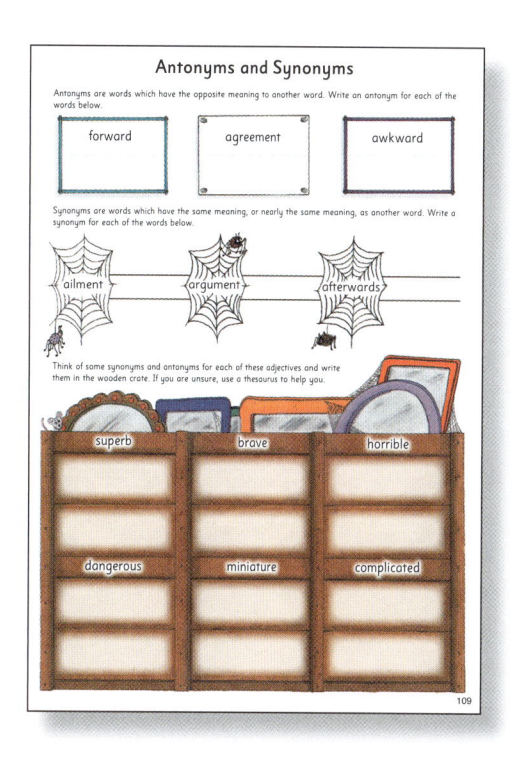

Extension Activity
- The children choose some words from the activity page and write a sentence for each one.
- Then they rewrite the sentences, using a suitable antonym.

Rounding Off
- Go over the activity page with the children, discussing their answers.
- If they have done the extension activity, ask some of the children to read out their sentences.

The Grammar 6 Handbook

The teaching in *The Grammar 6 Handbook* follows on from that in the *Grammar 5 Pupil and Teacher's Books*. Throughout the course of this handbook, the children's understanding of language is further refined.

The children learn new elements of grammar, such as direct and indirect objects, adverbials, the active and passive voice, gerunds, idioms and imperatives. They also learn how to use colons and semicolons in sentences. They further refine their knowledge of the parts of speech, learning about linking verbs, coordinating and subordinating conjunctions and modal verbs and adverbs. The children also build upon their knowledge of sentence structure by learning about simple, compound and complex sentences and relative clauses.

In spelling lessons, the children learn new spelling patterns, including the numerical prefixes for the numbers one to ten, ‹gu› for /g/, ‹cc› for /k/, ‹ci› for /sh/, ‹que› for /k/, various spellings of the /t/ sound, including ‹bt›, ‹te›, ‹tte›, ‹th› and ‹cht›, and various spellings of the /m/ sound, including ‹mb›, ‹mn› and ‹me›. Previously taught spelling patterns are also revised throughout the handbook.

As in the *Grammar 5 Handbook* and *Grammar 5 Pupil Book*, there is one activity page per grammar lesson and two activity pages per spelling lesson.

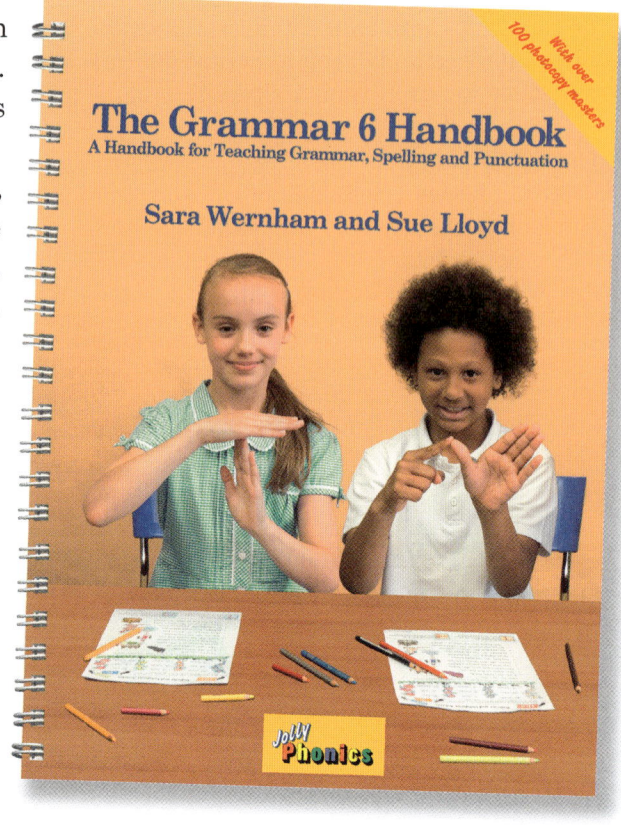

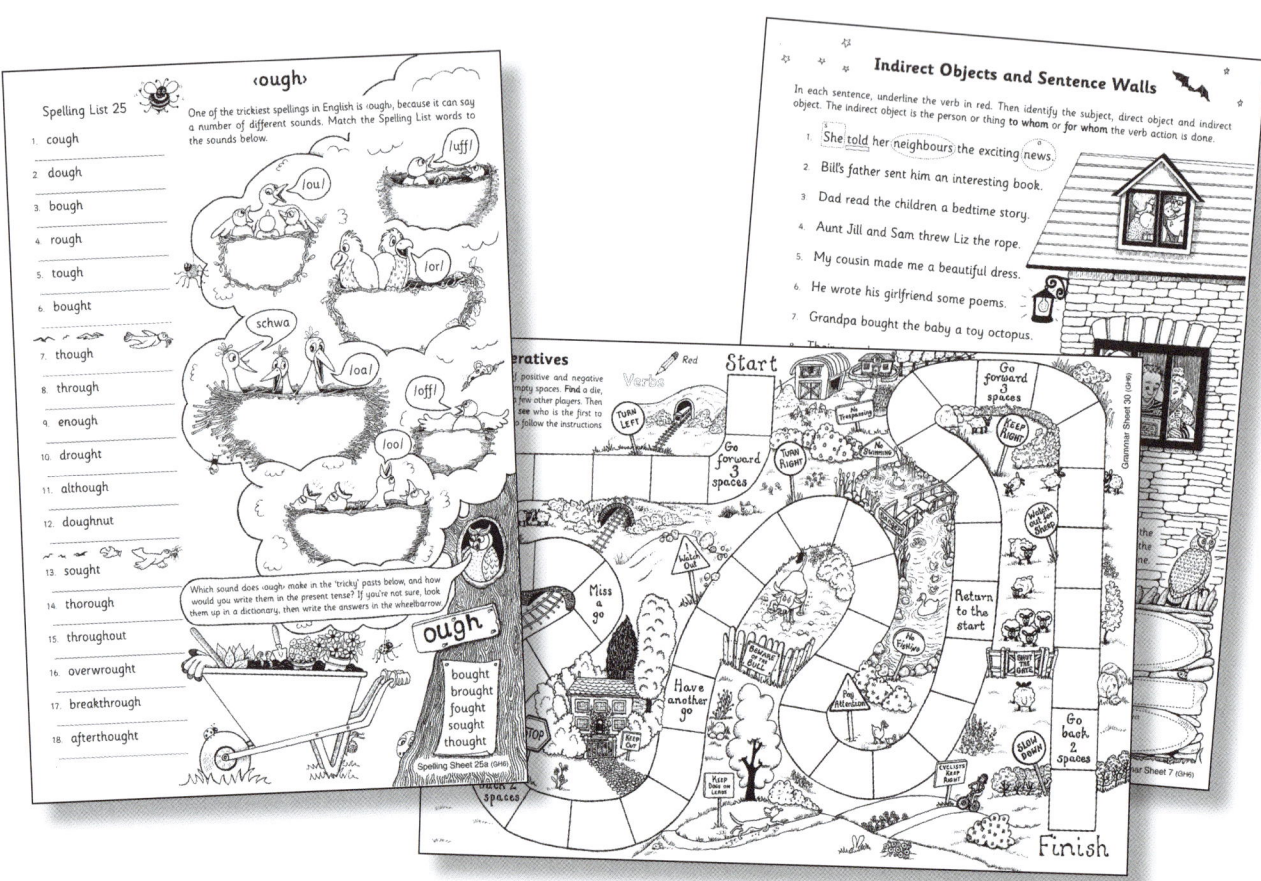